AT SATAN'S THRONE

At Satan's Throne

The Story of Methodism in Bath over 250 years

Edited by Bruce Crofts

CONTRIBUTORS

The Rev E Ralph Bates
Joan Eades
Ian Duffy
Bruce Crofts

ASSISTED BY

Kelvin Thomas
Eve Parfitt
Bill Drinkwater
Katherine Leach
John Dent
Roger Tobin
Stan Roe

Foreword by the Rev A Raymond George MA BD,
President of the Wesley Historical Society,
Ex-President of the Methodist Conference

White Tree Books

First published in 1990 by
WHITE TREE BOOKS
an imprint of REDCLIFFE PRESS LTD.,
49 Park Street, Bristol BS1 5NT

ISBN 0 948265 49 3

Typeset by Blackmore Press &
printed and bound by WBC, Bristol & Maesteg

Contents

Illustrations and Maps

Credits

Avon County Library (Bath Reference Library): **14, 15, 35, 57, 61, 102/103, 105, 107, 214.** Norris Museum, St Ives, Cambs: **22.** Stan Roe: **32, 52, 69, 99, 142, 156, 183, 220.** Bath & West Evening Chronicle: **81, 135, 137, 174.** Graham Moore: **211, 241.** Ken Saunders and the late Leslie Butt: **177, 180.**

Foreword

WHEN John Wesley's heart was strangely warmed on 24th May 1738, he did not immediately begin his great work as an open-air preacher. That happened in a brickyard in Bristol on 2nd April 1739. It led to the building in May of the New Room, and it was in Bristol that many important events in Methodist history occurred. But already in April Wesley had gone to preach to the miners in Kingswood, and to a very different audience in the elegant city of Bath. When a Methodist Society was established there, it was the fourth, for it was preceded only by London, Bristol and Kingswood. Bath, no doubt because of its proximity to Bristol, continued to be the recipient of very frequent visits by Wesley.

I had not fully realised Bath's importance in Methodist history until I read this book published to celebrate 250 years of Methodism in that city. The early part is written by the Rev. E. Ralph Bates, who entered the Methodist ministry in 1922 and is now over 90 years of age. He was one of my predecessors as Warden of the New Room, and I sometimes consult him about its history. I gladly take this opportunity to pay tribute to his extensive knowledge of Methodist history, and to the generosity with which he makes the treasures of his alert mind available to others.

An energetic initiative in compiling this book was taken by Mr (now the Rev.) Ian Duffy, who after holding lay office in the Bath Circuit, entered the Methodist ministry 65 years later than the Rev. E. Ralph Bates.

Further contributions were obtained and written by the Editor, Mr Bruce Crofts, a local preacher in the Circuit, and an expert in the history of Bath who has put much effort into the project. The ready co-operation of people of various generations is a happy symbol of Methodist fellowship, and evidence of the continued witness of Methodism in Bath.

I hope this book will be widely read.

A. Raymond George
The New Room, Bristol

John Wesley on horseback by A G Walker in the forecourt of The New Room, Bristol. The only equestrian statue of Wesley in Britain.

Preface

THE PROBLEM about covering in one volume a historical trail 250 years long is deciding what to leave out. To some extent this has been pre-determined by the degree of availability of material. We depend upon minute-books and documents which at the time they were compiled may have seemed to the custodians to hold no more than passing interest. They never visualised some earnest historian years later poring over their handwritten account with intense interest. Consequently many of those records were not preserved and there are yawning gaps which despite earnest endeavours cannot be filled. And this applies even to recent times.

The really vital aspects of Methodism concern the manner in which ordinary people have reacted to the Gospel message; the way that lives have been revitalised; and the effect of sacrificial love shown towards members of the flock. Sadly, there must also have been times when these influences failed to achieve their objective. However, such matters rarely appear in church records, and cannot therefore be given as much prominence as they deserve.

Church meetings had, and still have, a tendency to record with pride the start of new activities, but rarely mention those which peter out. Appointments of office-bearers are religiously set down, and financial statements show the minutest detail. But it is only on those rare occasions when committees get down to debating "the work of God" that the heart of church life is revealed. Sadly, churches are often treated as being buildings rather than people.

Occasionally, verbatim comments have been quoted at some length because they reveal a whole world of meaning. Every effort has been made to present a balanced picture and not to dwell on success. Perhaps some of the discarded activities and attitudes revealed by this book are, on reflection, worthy of being revived to serve the church of today?

Sums of money mentioned in the text often seem ridiculously small. To take account of the ravages of inflation, we suggest that multiplying 19th century amounts by a factor of at least 30 will provide a reasonable comparison with modern values. Contemporary spellings of names of places and persons have been used in the text, and these sometimes change with the passage of time.

We owe a debt to Ian Duffy for initiating the idea of this book, and for his dogged determination at the outset in persuading a small team of amateur historians to produce their quotas of basic research material. In the stories of the individual churches towards the end of the book, use has very properly been made, and with permission, of some existing church histories. These have been adapted to match the scale of the book. They are listed in the Bibliography. We are indebted to Glenys Hirst for the dramatic design on the dust-cover, to Stan Roe for artistic support and to Joan Crofts for wifely patience and forbearance.

Several of the illustrations have been selected for their historic value rather than their photogenic quality. A magnifying glass may be needed to read some of the details.

And so we offer this book in celebration of 250 years of Methodist activity since John Wesley made the first of his 100 visits to Bath. He wrote of Bath: "Is it possible? Can the Gospel have place where Satan's throne is?" This book is one answer.

Bruce Crofts

1

Venture and Tenacity 1739–1757

The First Year

JOHN WESLEY went to Bath fully 100 times over a span of 51½ years. Only London, Bristol and Kingswood (on the outskirts of Bristol), the scenes of his first Societies, saw more of him. He preached on some 150 occasions in Bath. During that time the city was moving through its spectacular splendour under Beau Nash, the self-styled "King of Bath", to the zenith of its social glory towards the end of the 18th century. Visitors flocked there from far and near. Relatively few showed interest in Wesley's work. Both the Wesley brothers referred to Bath as "Satan's Throne," and Charles characterised it as "That Sodom of our land". A contemporary couplet from an old song, quoted later by Richard Warner, suggests the background for their endeavours in Bath:–

> 'We three Bath deities be
> Humbug, Follee and Vanitee'

Thirty years after his first visit Wesley had written of the enrolled membership of his Society in Bath: "It was very small this autumn, consisting of only 11 or 12 persons". Twenty years later he wrote: "The scene has changed again. Here we have the rich and honourable in abundance". That may reflect the fact that they came specially, though not always in large numbers, to hear him preaching.

As the 1734 view and the 1735 map demonstrate, Bath's mushroom development had then hardly started. Wesley's first visit to the city on Tuesday, 10th April, 1739 was noteworthy for more than one reason. Not only was he to be seen

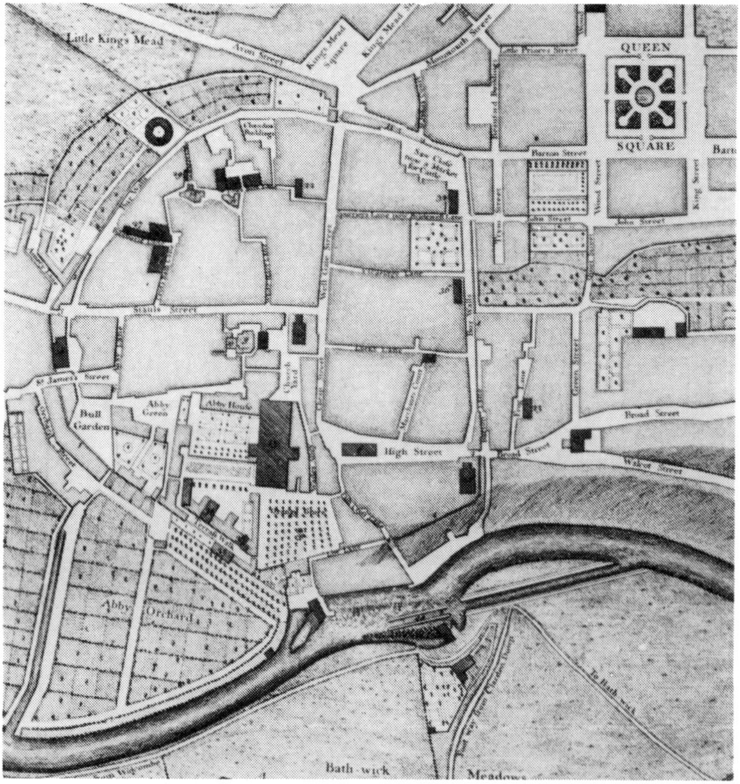

John Wood's Map of Bath in 1735. This shows many of the places mentioned by John Wesley.

in Bath on 13 occasions that year, it also provided the setting for his first open-air preaching beyond the Bristol-Kingswood area. On the 2nd April, in his own words, he had "submitted to be more vile" by preaching in the open air at Bristol. During the following week he continued the witness within the Bristol-Kingswood area. It was in Bath he first widened his sphere of activity. At five o'clock on the 10th he preached in a meadow above, what is today, Queen Square, near the entrance to the present Royal Victoria Park. A crowd, variously estimated to number from 1,000–2,000 gathered. At eight o'clock that same evening he preached "remission of sins to many casual hearers, from some steps at the end of a house in

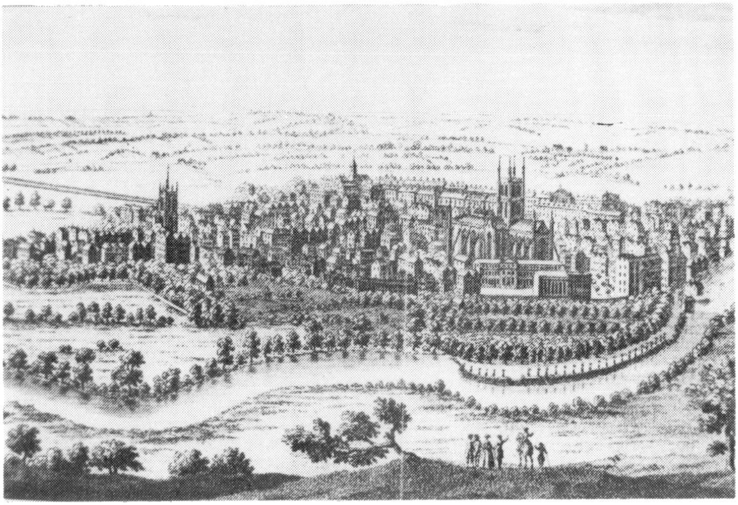

South East Prospect of the City of Bath 1734. "The Ham" is to the left of centre skirting the river.

Gracious Street." Those steps, leading from the forecourt of the YMCA down to Walcot Street, still survive.

After spending the night at the *Three Cups Inn,* which was located in Northgate Street, he preached again in the meadow before returning to Bristol. He estimated the crowd on the Wednesday morning to number even more than the previous evening.

He had demonstrated that a crowd would gather in Bath to listen to him and also that it could be a meeting place with distinguished visitors. He had conversation with Rev. Griffith Jones, whose Welsh Free Schools became an astonishing feature in the life of Wales.

From that date forward Wesley's routine to the end of August included going to Bath on alternate Tuesdays. Only once, when he had to be in London, did he break the sequence. Normally, apart from that first occasion, he did not stay overnight in Bath. Indeed, as the opportunity and response grew in the Bradford-on-Avon locality and elsewhere, the time which he spent in the city lessened.

Difficulties and opposition had to be faced. The first time he preached in Bath the owner of the field in which the crowd was gathered threatened prosecution if Wesley spoke there again. "A good woman" came to the rescue and offered the use of her own field. After two occasions she withdrew her permission, following which a wealthy Quaker, Mr Richard Marchant, who had a field in the Ham (present Manvers Street area), came to Wesley's help.

Five times the crowds gathered there, but Marchant then withdrew his permission on grounds of theft, damage sustained and objections from his neighbours. Possibly no other equally convenient site was found; certainly numbers diminished rapidly, and on one occasion, Wesley noted that he preached to "a small congregation suddenly gathered a little distance from town". His ever-faithful supporter, John Feacham, had made sure Wesley had a site for preaching by offering his own, but this was inconvenient for gathering a crowd.

Wesley's appearance on 5th June at the Ham was the occasion of spectacular opposition and may be recounted in his own words:

> "There was great expectation at Bath of what a noted man was to do to me there, and I was much intreated not to preach because no-one knew what might happen. By this report I also gained a much larger audience, among whom were many of the rich and great. I told them plainly the Scripture had concluded them all under sin — high and low, rich and poor, one with another. Many of them seemed to be a little surprised, and were sinking apace into seriousness, when their champion appeared and coming close to me, asked by what authority I did these things. I replied: 'By the authority of Jesus Christ, conveyed to me by the (now) Archbishop of Canterbury, when he laid his hands upon me and said: 'Take thou authority to preach the Gospel.' He replied: 'This is contrary to Act of Parliament; this is a Conventicle.' I answered: 'Sir, the Conventicles mentioned in that Act (as the preamble shows) are seditious meetings, but this is not such, here is no shadow of sedition, therefore it is not contrary to the Act.' He replied: 'I say it is, and besides, your preaching frightens people out of their wits.' 'Sir, did you ever hear me preach?' 'No'. 'How then can you judge of what you never heard?' 'Sir, by common report.' 'Common report is

> not enough. Give me leave sir, to ask, is not your name Nash?' 'My name is Nash.' 'Sir, I dare not judge of **you** by common report; I think it is not enough to judge by.' Here he paused awhile, and, having recovered himself, said: 'I desire to know what this people comes here for.' Upon which one replied: 'Sir, leave him to me, let an old woman answer him. You, Mr Nash, take care of your body, we take care of our souls, and for the food of our souls we come here.' Nash replied not a word, but walked away."

That was Wesley's fifth visit. On the seventh a great crowd gathered in Marchant's field for the last time. Wesley estimated 2,500 were present. A month later, meeting elsewhere, the figure he noted was 500. In the autumn he paid three visits and preached on two of them, the last being on Sunday, 18th November at nine in the morning. The meeting place is not known. As far as can be discovered, two years elapsed before he came again.

One man, John Feacham, had been faithful from first to last. He met Wesley at the inn on the first visit and repeatedly Wesley accepted hospitality at his home. Others, such as Richard Marchant, and the "grey-haired silversmith" named Dibble, appear for a time. John Feacham, whom Wesley describes

"Sir, leave him to me."

as "a man full of the Holy Ghost", remained the central person locally, and continued to visit Wesley in Bristol after he had deleted Bath from his programme. Wesley was disappointed and puzzled. "Hath God left himself without a witness?" he asked. He concluded that some of the most serious persons he had known were either **solitary** Christians or **prudent** Christians.

The First Society

Before a Methodist Society under John Wesley's direction was established in Bath, his brother Charles came to the city and preached. He had a lively reception. The date was 11th July, 1741. He wrote: "I preached at Bristol, then among the colliers, a third time at Bath, a fourth at Sanford (*sic* Saltford) and yet again in the wood . . . Satan took it ill to be attacked in his own quarters, that Sodom of our land, Bath. While I was explaining . . . he raged horribly in his children. They went out, and came back again and mocked, and at last, roared, as if each man's name was Legion. My power increased with the opposition. The sincere were melted into tears and strong desires of salvation."

Exactly five months later, on 11th December, John Wesley visited the city by invitation. He stayed the night and agreed to return on the 15th to take the names of some who wished to form a religious society under his direction. Up to that date only three Societies — those at London, Bristol and Kingswood — had been enrolled under the Wesley leadership. The difficulties and opportunities relating to those three had not permitted a margin of time or strength for concentration elsewhere.

Wesley noted that on the 15th December 1741 there was a hard frost, so that he walked to Bath from Bristol. He would not trust his horse on the treacherous Keynsham road, said by one critic to be the worst in Europe for the money spent on it! He had "a conversation of several hours" on theological matters with "a famous man" (probably the great Bath specialist for gout, Dr Cheyne, whose brother-in-law was Charles Wesley's physician, and of whose medical books on dieting John Wesley thoroughly approved).

After meeting the group who asked to see him, Wesley wrote: "In the evening I took down the names of some who desired to strengthen each other's hands in God. Thus 'the bread' we have cast upon the waters is found again after many days. I returned to Bristol the next day."

His fourth Society had been established. Spectacular advances would take place in 1742 into new areas as far north as Newcastle-on-Tyne. In setting up his characteristic connexional, that is his country-wide linked organisation, including lay preachers both local and itinerant, Bath's place, almost unbelievably, was that of a pioneer in this dramatic development.

The list of names which Wesley made on that December evening has not survived. Whether the formerly faithful John Feacham still headed it, as he did the nine names of those who agreed to meet in two Bands in April 1739 (but who disappointed Wesley) is not known. Just one name, that of Mrs Mary Naylor, still survives from the 1740s. She was a remarkable person and her presence may explain why Wesley had renewed confidence in Bath. Her social standing and Christian dedication paved the way to intimate association with the home of the Charles Wesley family and others. Her hospitality was available for the Wesley brothers and their helpers.

As already stated, Wesley had stayed at the *Three Cups* on his first visit to Bath in 1739 and he spent the night at the *White Hart* when he brought George Whitefield to preach in Bath later that year; otherwise at night he returned to Bristol. This was not always practicable on winter nights and Mary Naylor's home may have provided both meeting place for the new Society and hospitality for Wesley.

Within a week of listing the names of his Society at Bath, London claimed Wesley until early February. Then, after an uncomfortable journey on horseback, he reached Kingswood at noon to be greeted by "many friends from Bath, Bristol and Wales." The new Society was showing it had members who realised they belonged, not to an isolated community, but to a "Connexion" of Societies. Wesley visited Bath the next day and preached in a room where "some noisy persons" were bent on causing a disturbance. He wrote: "I went and stood in the midst of them, but the greater part slipped away to that end from which I had come and cried aloud again. I paused to give them their full scope and then began a particular application to them. They were very quiet in a short time, and I trust will not forget it as soon as some of them may desire."

When he visited Bath again the following week it is reported that he was not interrupted or disturbed.

It is unlikely that Bath saw him again during 1742. His life of incessant travelling on horseback then began. Wales, London, the Midlands and the far north-east all claimed his attention. Twice he travelled to Newcastle-on-Tyne. The West Country has less than two months of his next ten, and there were special needs at Bristol (with its 700 members), and at Kingswood both in the Society and the School. Charles Wesley may have been able to give some oversight because Sunday preaching, even occasionally, from Wesley's lay helpers had yet to be developed.

John Wesley's record of his visit on 24th January, 1743, shows the 13-month-old society in interesting and pleasing light. Clearly Mary Naylor had won a reputation as a friend of the poor without alienating the more affluent. Wesley wrote: "I preached at Bath. Some of the rich and great were present . . . one, my Lord, stayed very patiently until the middle of the fourth head. (*Sic,* Heading in sermon). Then, starting up he said, 'Tis hot! Tis very hot' and got downstairs as fast as he could". After preaching, Wesley met the enrolled members of the Society, which was his means of personal contact with them and of giving instruction to members as distinct from a mixed congregation. But "some gentry" asked if they might remain and Wesley agreed. He explained "the nature of inward religion". One of them, possibly Dr Oliver, (whom Wesley describes as "a noted infidel"), when he went "left half a guinea with Mary Naylor for the relief of the poor."

Probably the Bath members did not see Wesley again that year. The number of Societies was increasing rapidly. He travelled east as far as Grimsby, and added Cornwall to his itinerary. When in Bristol *even he* took "a week of rest and peace", though it should be recognised that his idea of rest could be little more than a change in the form of his activity! Charles Wesley went to see the Bath Society twice in 1743, preaching in May and October. However, whether the

Wesleys were present or not, Mary Naylor had friendships with the leading members in Bristol. While she lived, the Bath Society would never be an isolated community.

A dramatic episode in October 1745 is best recounted in Charles Wesley's own words: "After preaching in Bath, a woman desired to speak with me. She had been in our Society, and in Christ, but having lost her grace through spirit of offence, left the fellowship and fell little by little into the depths of vice and misery. I called Mrs Naylor to hear her mournful account. She had lived some time at a wicked house in Avon Street, confessed it was hell to see our people pass to the preaching, knew not what to do or how to escape. We bade her fly for her life, and not once look behind her. Mrs Naylor kept her with herself till the morning, and then carried her with us in the coach to London and delivered her to the care of our sister Davey, 'Is not this a brand plucked out of the fire'?" Clearly Mrs Naylor was a forceful, dedicated personality with influence in Methodist circles far beyond Bath.

The Circuit System is Introduced

Meanwhile a pattern was emerging which became characteristic of Wesley's movement. As Societies multiplied throughout England and Wales, on into Ireland, Scotland and the Channel Islands, it became impossible for him to know his members individually as was the case in 1741, or to preach frequently in each place, and to administer discipline and organisation everywhere. Societies had to be grouped into circuits, lay preachers had to be accepted, some to preach locally within the circuit of residence, and some to serve full-time, travelling by annual appointment as Wesley's representatives throughout a particular circuit. These itinerants, as Wesley called them, served as preachers, pastors and administrators on his behalf. They were a vital unifying force within and throughout the "Connexion of Societies".

At first circuits were so large and the number of travelling preachers so small that Societies still had to be satisfied with occasional preaching. Then it would be on a week-day or on a Sunday afternoon or evening. Wesley's people were instructed to attend their parish church on a Sunday morning. Occa-

Selina, Countess Dowager of Huntingdon. Engraving from an original painting by J Russell.

sionally the Bath society had a bonus. During the 1740's Lady Huntingdon gave the Wesleys her generous support and while in the city could entertain a preacher. She was a strange and determined woman, as her portrait suggests. In 1745 Thomas Richards, one of the first three of Wesley's preachers, stayed in Bath as her guest for some time, and preached with much power. Whether Bath received help from local preachers in Bristol, such as John Hall, the Bedminster farmer, is not known. In any case **regular** Sunday preaching was not to become a reality for a long time ahead. The whole of England and Wales was in 1746 divided into a mere seven circuits. Two years later there were nine, one of which was Wales and one other Ireland! Probably there were not more than two dozen itinerants to travel the three countries.

Bristol Circuit, in which Bath had been placed, had 12 Societies of which Taunton was the furthest. It would not be rash, however, to conjecture that the forceful Mary Naylor (by means of her Bristol friendships and personal contacts with the Wesleys) would keep Bath to the fore.

No matter what other claims on their time they had to consider the Wesley brothers did not neglect Bath. Year after year from 1741 onwards and into the 1750s John Wesley fitted Bath into his crowded itinerary. Not until 1755, the year when serious illness prevented travel for much of the time, did Wesley miss the city for more than 12 months. Sometimes this was accomplished only with considerable contriving. In 1746, for example, he travelled to Bath in the evening and preached after presiding over a four-day conference in Bristol. He left, on horseback, at three o'clock the next morning for an appointment at Blewbury in Berkshire.

More than once he travelled to Bath in time to preach at noon and then rode on to preach again elsewhere later in the day. Once, on a February morning, he preached in Bath at eight o'clock, and after attending to business, rode on to Coleford to preach to a crowd of his responsive and beloved miners. He wrote on one occasion that the congregation which gathered was "more than the room would contain". Opposition during services is no longer recorded; on the contrary, the wealthy were interested in meeting the great man. Thus he could write in October 1755: "I dined with some serious persons in a large stately house standing on the brow of a delightful hill. In this paradise they live in ease, in honour and in elegant abundance. And this they call retiring from the world!" Ralph Allen's mansion at Prior Park, Bath, could well be the stately house, although there is not any corroborative evidence. At times Bath disappointed Wesley, yet he was still an encourager in 1758.

Available portions of Charles Wesley's Journal shed light on Mary Naylor's hospitality, her widespread Methodist involvement and her relationship with the Wesley family. Without doubt Bath did sometimes have the services of a preacher because he could stay the night in her home. Thus Charles Wesley wrote in December 1748: "I preached at Bath on my way to London." When he took his betrothed, Sally, with her father, Squire Gwynne, to the Foundery in London, he called at Mary Naylor's house and, after all had stayed the night there, she accompanied them to London, sharing a room with the prospective bride for nearly three weeks.

On another occasion, upon hearing of his brother's very serious illness, Charles set off for London with a companion. They had to spend the night somewhere en route. Mary Naylor again came to the rescue. Apparently his emergency journey to London left his wife in some financial difficulty in Bristol. He wrote to her: "Mary Naylor has, or will send you, six guineas". The Methodists at Bradford-on-Avon and the New Room had contact with Mary Naylor, and she was in Devizes at the time Charles Wesley was involved in the rioting there. John Wesley's sister, Mrs Wright, had correspondence with her and they met in London. Thus Mary Naylor's relationship with the Wesley family is more to the fore in Charles Wesley's writing than the vicissitudes of the Bath Society itself.

One incident, however, was noted by Charles Wesley and has peculiar interest. Under Wednesday, 25th October, 1749, he wrote: "Among my hearers today at Bath was a son of Lord Chief Justice Lee, my old school fellow, Sir Danvers Osborn and Lord Halifax. They behaved decently and were particularly taken with the singing. In the evening God sent forth His awakening power and His fear fell on all who heard the word." In view of a story of Methodist singing in Bath preserved by Robert Southey, the biographer of John Wesley, Charles' note is of special interest, Southey records: "At a meeting in Bath, Mrs Hughes heard Wesley say, when the singing did not please him, 'There are two ways of performing this devotional exercise, singing and screaming — don't scream'." Southey does not give the date.

Travelling Preachers

Names of Wesley's appointed itinerant preachers, each serving the circuit for a year, have been preserved from 1765 onwards, but it is only by chance that appointments can be traced for the earlier period. One name, that of Joseph Cownley, sent in 1746, has particular interest. He was a native of Leominster, but as a young man was travelling as secretary to a Justice of the Peace and heard Wesley preach in his native place. Three years later Wesley accepted him as one of his itinerants and appointed him to Bath. Wesley believed him to be an outstanding preacher. Among others who would share the hospitality of Mary Naylor's home was William Hitchens. He was one of the three sons of the Cornish blacksmith near Gwennap who all left the forge to serve under Wesley; two of them died after only two years of service. Travelling long distances in all weathers by foot or on horseback, sometimes without the refuge of even moderate accommodation at the end of the day, took a heavy toll of Wesley's itinerants.

A colleague of William Hitchens in 1755 was Peter Jaco, the tall, handsome young Cornishman from Newlyn. He wrote of his previous circuit that, after preaching three or four times a day, and riding 30 or 40 miles, sometimes he had finished with no more than a canvas sheet and a little straw for his bed. Another from the list of four on the Bristol circuit in 1755 was John Furz of Wilton. Incredible as it sounds, becoming a Methodist itinerant involved him in leaving his wife and children behind "for the Gospel's sake". Such then were the men who travelled in the Bristol circuit in those years and ministered in Bath.

Yet the visits of such itinerants, the attentions of the Wesleys, and the local presence and service of Mary Naylor met with relatively slender response.

In 1755 Wesley wrote: "Even here a few are joined together and hope they shall be scattered no more." Two years later the enrolled membership of 35 was no more than that in the small agricultural village of Freshford in the nearby countryside.

Two events in 1757 adversely affected the Bath Methodists. First, Mary Naylor died; second, Bath was removed from the Bristol Methodist Circuit. When Mary Naylor died in London, John Wesley was there. He wrote: "On Sunday, 27th March, 1757 I buried Mary Naylor, who for several years was a most eminent pattern of truly Christian courage, plainness of speech and plainness of apparel". He thought she had weakened somewhat in this witness and told her so. Brother Charles believed John was mistaken and after her death wrote two hymns of tribute, and an elegy in six parts. In this elegy he recalled:

When she heard the Gospel sound . . .
With joy she flew her all to sell . . .
Away she cast, with eager strife,
Kindred and friends, and more than life,
She cast her fame away . . .
Where Satan keeps his gaudy throne,
Firm as the righteous Lot, alone,
Against the world she stood . . .
A nursing mother to the poor,
For them she husbanded her store . . .
To feed both friend and foe . . .
Fast as her well-got wealth increased,
She laid it up in heaven . . .
Ye preachers of the joyous word,
Constrained with her to abide;
With Lydia's open house and heart . . .
She all your wants supplied,
I want to love my foes like her . . .
As safe and sudden to depart . . .

The Bath Society did not have anyone else to take her place. There is not any evidence to suggest that Betty Naylor, married woman living in Avon Street, a toymaker and Methodist member, and Sarah Naylor, unmarried, of the same address, were Mary Naylor's kinsfolk.

Within six months of Mary Naylor's death Bath was transferred from the Bristol circuit to the newly-formed, far-flung, "Wiltshire" circuit. There were 25 Societies in this circuit, 13 of them in Somerset, six in Wiltshire, five in Hampshire and one in Dorset. Bath was the northern extremity and the Isle of Wight the southermost. The mining village of Coleford far outstripped all other places in membership with 174 names on the roll. Next came the cathedral city of Salisbury (120 members), the manufacturing town of Bradford-on-Avon (118). Freshford and Bath (joint eighth in the list — 35 members each), were outstripped by Paulton and Deverill (37 apiece). The fact that members of the Bath society soon looked longingly in the direction of Bristol is not surprising.

The name, address, marital status and occupation of each member were recorded on, apparently, two sheets of paper. Sheet one consisted of 16 members, listed under two Class Leaders and 19 were named on the second, seven of them a continuation from sheet one, the remaining 12 constituting the third class. Sheet one has been lost, so that a true picture of the society as a whole cannot be seen. The names of two of the three Class Leaders are unknown. It is also interesting to note that 15 of the 19 members lived in Avon Street. The Leader of the final 12 was a shoemaker named John Peacock who lived in Holloway. The occupations of the seven men on sheet two were joiner, carpenter, filer, carver, husbandman and two shoemakers. The husbandman lived in Avon Street which, in 1757, was near to open countryside; the carver and his wife were from Abbey Green, possibly indicating the skilled nature and social standing of his occupation. The women's occupations, where stated, were a nurse, a toy maker, a shopkeeper and three laundresses. Single man Bennett Sholl, the filer, resided in Kingsmead Street. John Gale, the shoemaker of Avon Street and Hannah his wife, did not share the same class. The name at the top of the page, Michael Hemmings, joiner, of Avon Street, is of particular interest because of the part he was to play in later years. It is likely that Leonard Ball, the husbandman, of Avon Street, was father of Thomas whom Wesley held in high regard and trust in London in the 1770s. The Society, of which Wesley wrote, "Even here a few are joined together", held possibilities.

2

Sadness and Resurgence 1758–1777

Avon Street Preaching House

WESLEY came to Bath in the autumn of 1757 following Mary Naylor's death. He preached at noon and then hurried away to Eastcott, on the edge of Salisbury Plain, where he preached in the evening. With Mary Naylor's hospitality no longer available, he did not linger in Bath.

Nearly a year later he called again and preached, this time on his way to Shepton Mallet where he was due to be heard in the evening. During that brief call he was told one heartening piece of news. It was that the little company had it in mind to build a preaching house. For nearly 17 years they had met in private houses or hired premises. Now at last they planned to have their own building. Wesley was cheered by the size of the congregation he faced on that September day in 1758. He noted: "The room could ill contain the congregation." Also their enterprise pleased him: "I encouraged them in their design of taking a piece of ground and building without delay." The word "encouraged" may be interpreted as a promise of financial help. The profits from the sale of his books were widely distributed in support of the development of his work. How much be promised and how soon the scheme materialised are no longer known. Probably the land was secured and the building erected in 1759.

The site was in Avon Street, not far from Corn Steet where the hired room formerly used was situated. Already the area had associations of ill repute which one day would become pronounced. At least half of the members of his Society lived in the locality and Wesley's own comment years later suggests their wholesome influence. In 1777 he spoke of "the chapel in the midst of sinners where I never heard an immodest word — but prayers and blessings in abundance".

The new room was unpretentious, but it had one advantage over the hired room in Corn Street — it was at road level, whereas the rented premises were upstairs. How humble it was is suggested by the single fact that when it was sold about 20 years later — having been enlarged in the meantime — the price paid was only £50. When Wesley saw it he did not make any comment in his journal. His silence possibly suggests disappointment. On the other hand he would certainly have been critical if he considered that the Society's money had been spent wastefully.

Thus Bath had its first Methodist chapel and called it a "Room" or a "Preaching House" — Wesley was insistent on this. He would not use the word church. That was reserved for the Church of England. He was a clergyman and wanted his movement to revive that Church if its bishops, clergy and members would allow it. The words Meeting House were not permitted either; they were used by dissenters and he claimed that he was not one of their number. Only in his later years did he use the word chapel. Twenty years later he called his more pretentious building in New King Street a chapel.

Hopes raised by the erection of the Avon Street Room were doomed to disappointment. The 1760s were probably the darkest years in Methodism's earlier story in Bath. The number of members listed in 1757, as we have said, was 35. Five years later this figure had fallen to 31. Wesley commented in the autumn of 1769 that numbers had fallen to 11 or 12.

Superficially the decline is surprising because mob opposition had virtually ceased. There are not any records of meetings in Avon Street suffering disturbances, although there were from time to time ridicule and opposition from the printed word. Strange to say that had not been the case when Wesley first came to Bath. On the contrary, two Bath publishers and booksellers had been willing to have their names on the title pages of some of Wesley's works in the early 1740s. Their names were then withdrawn, and in 1749 the *Bath Journal* published an anonymous venomous attack on Wesley and "persons of great eminence among the Methodists". When Wesley saw it he quickly wrote a trenchant reply which silenced his opponent. Anstey's *New Guide to Bath* in 1760 made scurrilous reference to the Methodists of which the following is an example. ("Roger" is a Methodist preacher):

> O how shall we know the right way to pursue!
> Do the ills of mankind from religion accrue?
> Religion, designed to relieve all our care,
> Has brought my poor sister to grief and despair:
> Now she talks of damnation, and screws up her face,
> Then prates about Roger, and spiritual grace;
> Her senses, alas, seem at once gone astray —
> No pen can describe it, no letter convey.
> But the man without sin, that Moravian Rabbi,
> Has perfectly cured the chlorosis of Tabby;
> And, if right I can judge, from her shape and her face,
> She soon may produce him an infant of grace.
> Now they say that all people in our situation
> Are very fine subjects for regeneration;
> But I think, my dear mother, the best we can do
> Is to pack up our all, and return back to you.

As late as 1771 Richard Graves (then rector of Claverton) produced a satire on Methodism under the title of *The Spiritual Quixote*. It is thought unlikely that such attacks seriously affected the real work of Wesley's people in Bath. The decline in the 1760s must be explained along other lines.

Decline and Adversity

A number of minor contributory factors doubtless had their place. As we have said, one may have been the removal of Bath from the Bristol Circuit. From Bristol it would have received more preaching and closer pastoral oversight than was possible from its new geographical perimeter. That, however, was remedied in 1761 when members complained to Charles Wesley, who was then on an extended stay in the city following a severe illness. After Charles had passed on their complaint to his brother, Bath was reinstated in the Bristol Circuit, but that did not work the miracle of stemming the decline.

John Wesley himself tended to call on Bath on his way to other venues, and as he now did not have the availability of hospitality, it is probable that he could give Bath less of his time than previously was the case. Inevitably this can be seen as another contributary cause in the decline. Still further, during 1763–64 a Mrs W__, (which is how Wesley's Journal describes her, her actual identity is still a mystery), then staying at Combe Grove (just outside Bath and still there), sought his company and he stopped overnight in the large house. At first he was impressed with her religious enthusiasm but seems to have questioned her eccentricity. This association would, it seems, detract from involvement at Avon Street. Mary Naylor's influence was sorely missed.

Gradually leadership locally became the responsibility of one man of staunch loyalty but restricted gift. He was Michael Hemmings. No other member spans the whole period from the 1750s into the 19th century, yet there was a need for leadership with qualities which he did not possess. That new leadership did not emerge until near the end of the 1760s. When it did arrive it was allowed scope — Hemmings remained, but others took the lead. Without those others decline became nearly death, and it was to Hemmings' credit that whilst taking a back seat his enthusiasm for the cause never wavered.

The Countess Again

It may be assumed that the opening of the Countess of Huntingdon's chapel in the Vineyards on 6th October, 1765, added to the difficulties of Wesley's little company in Avon Street. The Vineyards chapel in the Paragon (see illustration) was spacious, well planned, and in Walpole's words, "had luxury creeping in". He added: "Very neat, with true Gothic windows." The Countess had her cathedral; Avon Street was the poor relation. That this might operate to the detriment of Avon Street is indicated by an entry in Wesley's Journal. In the week before the official opening in the Vineyards the Countess held a service which coincided with Wesley's preaching in the Avon Street Room. He commented: "I had only the poor to hear me, there being a service at the same time in Lady Huntingdon's chapel. So I was in my element. I have scarcely ever found such liberty in Bath before."

The superiority of the Vineyards building was not the main

The Countess of Huntingdon Chapel, The Vineyards, in 1989. The house stands in front of the chapel. The buildings are occupied by the Bath Preservation Trust and used for secular purposes. Line drawing by Stan Roe.

element in the popular appeal. The services were ordered with a combination of cultural and popular features. Horace Walpole, the prolific letter writer, wrote of "boys and girls with charming voices who sang hymns in parts to Scotch ballad tunes". His criticism was that the hymns were so long that "one would think they were already in eternity". The Rev. John Penrose in his *Letters from Bath* explained "had there been no preaching nor extempore prayer, the whole had been very much to my satisfaction".

The Countess considered that her special mission was to reach "society". Wesley aimed to reach all people, especially the poorer sections of the community. Walpole's description of the service suggests it had elements which would appeal to the poor as well as to the socially privileged. Tickets of admission which were distributed and used by certain visitors most probably would have given access to special places in the chapel rather than being intended as a means of excluding the poor. Probably the poorest would never feel at home in the Countess' chapel, but Wesley's comment already quoted indicates there was a section of the community which turned from him to the Vineyards — at least on occasion.

Against this background it was difficult for the Avon Street members to understand the attitude of John and Charles Wesley. Both were willing to preach in the new chapel. John offered his services and the next time he was in Bath the Countess accepted and he admits that some were surprised. A few weeks later he administered Holy Communion there at eight o'clock one Sunday morning; he also preached at 11am. His people were bewildered and he offered what he called a "healing sermon" in Avon Street. The following year saw him preaching again for the Countess, and in March, 1769, both brothers shared a service at the Vineyards, Charles reading prayers and John preaching the sermon.

On their part it was a gesture of friendship and Christian fellowship. From the time the Countess had been a member of Wesley's chapel in West Street, London, friendship between them had persisted. Theologically the Countess and the brothers had moved apart, but all three were ready to think that which united them was more basic than that which divided.

When Mrs Charles Wesley lay seriously ill with smallpox in Bristol the Countess had visited her every day, disdaining the perils of infection. She and the brothers were more concerned to gloss over theological differences in 1765 than to parade them. Twenty-five years earlier similar differences had existed between the brothers and that great orator George Whitefield. John was not disposed to think that the three were preaching such different messages that they should part company — Whitefield in one camp and the Wesleys in another. The Countess had moved towards Whitefield's Calvinistic thought, but shared Wesley's view that it was a secondary consideration.

During that year the Wesleys and Whitefield might have separated into opposing camps, but the Countess ensured that this did not happen. Wesley told the Countess that her preachers were as welcome at Avon Street chapel as his own. In time gossip and rumour distorted what he had said, and his people were bewildered by a report that he was handing the Avon Street building over to the Countess. Wesley had to tell them he had never hinted at such a course and had no intention of doing any such thing. Nevertheless, for the faithful few in his Society at Avon Street the last year of the Sixties opened with gloom.

Shining brightly in that dark decade is an incident, which happened on a Sunday in 1765. A stranger, wearing the uni-

Captain Thomas Webb from the pastel by L Vaslet.

form of an army officer, joined the little congregation. He had been wounded in battle in North America and had lost his right eye and wore a patch over the socket; his manner was friendly and exuberant. One day he would be a corpulent veteran; that day was yet to come. The congregation were awaiting the preacher who failed to arrive. They asked their visitor if he was a preacher. He had to say he was not, and at 40 years of age, had only been converted that year. But, he added, he could tell them what Jesus had done for him. The offer was accepted and he related the story of his conversion with such power that the story reached Wesley. The visitor became a member at the New Room in Bristol, though only temporarily in that city before returning to America. Wesley gave him preaching credentials on the basis of what he had heard from Bath. Shortly afterwards the Army captain returned to New York and the American States fired with passion to preach within the fellowship of Wesley's people. The work which he did earned him the designation "American

Methodism's Number One Layman". That man was Captain Thomas Webb (see illustration). One day after he returned from America he visited Bath again and preached in obedience to Wesley's specific call.

New Faces, New Life

The sad, tragic 1760s were followed by the exciting, heartening 1770s. Despite writing of only a dozen members in 1769, Wesley was within a year, prompting them to get on with enlarging the Avon Street Room. His senior preacher in the Bristol circuit for 1770–71 was one of his outstanding men, Alexander Mather. He wrote of that year "Good was done in Bristol and in several other places, particularly in Bath, where they were obliged first to enlarge, and then to gallery, the chapel". The interior of the building thus took on the pattern of a chapel and Mather again used the term when he wrote several years later.

One cause of the dramatic change was undoubtedly an accession of new leadership. A letter written by Wesley on 5th November, 1769, gives a clue. In it he mentions a Mr Hodsal. No such name is to be found elsewhere. He was writing from

High Street, Bath in 1856 with the Christopher Hotel on the left opposite the Guildhall.

East Anglia and doubtless, despite a wonderful memory for names, in this case he was mistaken. From other sources it is known that, about this time, the licensee of *The Christopher Inn*, (which is still in High Street today; our illustration shows it in 1856), was converted and he and his wife became loyal members of Avon Street. Their surname was Hadden. In their care the inn became a centre of Christian hospitality and a pattern of conduct above reproach. All staff were freed from duties at the hours of Sunday worship. Mr Hadden died in the 1770s. His wife continued as the licensee both before and after her second marriage (when she became Mrs Grange). On occasion when Wesley was in Bath overnight he stayed at *The Christopher*. Her son, who lived until 1824, continued the loyal association with Bath Methodism.

A second name Wesley mentions in the letter of 5th November, 1769 is "Mr Harries". Wesley collected a few names of persons associated with Avon Street who had not been members of Michael Hemmings' Class. He "divided them into two classes and appointed half of them to meet with Joseph Harris". (Possibly the other half met with Mr Hadden). Joseph Harris was an acquisition from Kingswood. What is known of him portrays a gifted, dedicated, enthusiastic worker, and one with vision. He was not in Bath for many years. On leaving for a place without a Methodist Society, he duly established one.

The third new name is Miss Mary Bishop. During 1769 she was a teacher in Bath with an address in The Vineyards. She had been associated with the Countess of Huntingdon's Chapel but there had been some point of disagreement which alienated her. She had contacts with the Misses Owen of Publow whose school was entrusted with some of the daughters of Wesley's travelling preachers. Also she knew Miss Marsh, "a lady of fortune and piety" and of good education, who sometimes made excursions to Bristol and elsewhere meeting Society classes and in general supporting Wesley's work. Through Miss Marsh, Wesley first wrote to Miss Bishop. He was restrained in his periodic correspondence and did not make any attempt to hasten her acceptance of Methodist membership. She joined the Avon Street Society and became leader of a young women's fellowship. She, together with the

Hadden partnership, must have done much to fill the gap left by the death of Mary Naylor, especially while Joseph Harris was in Bath. Following a period of ill health Miss Bishop left Bath and established a school in Keynsham. Wesley visited it and his comment was: "The whole place was transformed by the spirit and behaviour of the children in her school and Mr Simpson's."

Wesley soon realised that Miss Bishop had much to offer within the revised Society. Exactly a year after his first letter he wrote one in which he entrusted her to convey his message to others. The Avon Street room was being enlarged and he wrote to Miss Bishop: "Let them remember to make the aisles on the side of the room, and to place the forms in the middle crossways with a rail running from the pulpit downwards, to part the men from the women. And I particularly desire no pews and no backs to the forms."

During the early 1770s Wesley observed a "tide of the Spirit" in the West Country. He wrote in 1770: "I preached at many of the towns round Bristol and found the congregation increasing in every place." Two years later he confirmed: "I preached at Bath. Our room, though considerably enlarged, will not yet contain the congregation, which is still continually increasing."

Sadly, the opening years of the 1770s were a time of bitter dispute between the Countess of Huntingdon's Connexion and the Methodist Connexion. Whitefield had died and Wesley had preached his memorial sermon. Those closest to the Countess lacked the personal, affectionate ties which had never allowed theological differences between the Wesleys and Whitefield to become acrimonious. The "new men" in whom the Countess placed her trust were of a contrary spirit, whereas the principle had formerly been "that which was held in common was more vital than that on which they differed." The battle was waged in the 1770s on the difference between the Calvinism preached in the Vineyards Chapel and the Arminianism preached in the Avon Street Room. Attempts to assess responsibility or to relate events in detail do not have a place in this record. Sufficient to say that it must have become increasingly difficult for any who would sing *"For all, for all, my Saviour died"* to remain in the Vineyards Chapel. It is at least possible that Avon Street gained members in the early 1770s because of the controversy.

Wesley knew that his people in Bath were witnessing in the face of antagonism. Even before the controversy had burst on them in full force, and while the Avon Street pulpit was still open to the Countess' preachers, her cousin, the Hon Walter Shirley, had preached controversially in Wesley's pulpit. "You should give Mr Shirley a hint not to contradict me when he preaches in my house," he wrote to Miss Bishop. One of the distinguished visiting preachers at the Vineyards who added fuel to the fire was the Rev. Rowland Hill. At the time, Captain Webb was visiting England from America, and Wesley invited him to preach in Bath. He wrote to Miss Bishop: "Captain Webb is not sent to YOU as to the unawakened world. And perhaps he may do good to Rowland Hill by being abundantly more popular than him." (It is pleasant to think of the Captain back in Avon Street Room as preacher and not as a stop-gap giving his testimony).

In the midst of controversy, Bath Methodism progressed steadily, On Wednesday, 18th September 1776, Wesley preached at Avon Street at noon, and recorded: "I preached . . . as usual, to a crowded audience".

By that time, Mr Hadden had died, Mr Harris had left Bath, Miss Bishop's health had given concern, but others who could give strength to the society had joined. One such was John Fowler, probably the first local preacher in the Avon Street Society. Wesley wrote of him: "God has owned HIS preaching more than that of most local preachers in England."

3

The Vindication of Faith 1778–1799

New King Street Chapel

IN SEVEN years the progress had been so marked that Wesley gave enthusiastic support to a scheme for building a chapel in one of Bath's new streets. A site was secured in New King Street which was in process of completion as a smart residential thoroughfare. The eminent musician and astronomer, William Herschel, had taken up residence at No 19 opposite the plot for the new chapel. He was destined to sight the planet Uranus there in 1781. The setting was in strong contrast to the relative poverty of Avon Street. Wesley's ardent support was evidenced by his determination to be present at the stone-laying of the chapel, designed to accommodate a congregation of 650.

On the Sunday he preached twice in London and then, in the evening, at Brentford. At midnight he "took chaise" and on the Monday "easily reached Bath in the afternoon". On the Tuesday he visited Bristol, where he preached in the evening and again early on the morning of Wednesday 17th December, 1777. He then returned to Bath and at one o'clock laid the foundation stone of the new chapel. He wrote: "The wind was piercing cold, yet scarce any of the congregation went away before the end of the sermon." Tradition lingered that his hands were chapped and bleeding. Despite this he preached in the evening at Avon Street before taking chaise to be back in London the next afternoon. It may be noted that he was in his 74th year. Two winter nights without bed were part of the price which he paid to lay the foundation stone of the building he was willing to call a chapel.

Before the new chapel was ready for use Wesley returned to

Bath twice, staying the night on both occasions. On the first, he preached in the evening. He was travelling from London to Bristol. A somewhat hasty annual appearance had become inadequate.

About this time there occurred an incident at Avon Street, pregnant with future possibility for Bath Methodism, and indeed for Connexional Methodism, but which at the time was seemingly of slender import. A young German, named Frederick Schumm (subsequently Anglicised to Shum), had come to Bath to be with two older brothers and also in search of health. He was lonely and his knowledge of the English language was slender. He confided his loneliness to a young German Jew who replied: "You should come with me to the Methodist preaching house in Avon Street. You wouldn't be lonely there."

He responded to the invitation of Samuel and was caught up in the warmth of the fellowship, although he understood but little of the sermon. Samuel told him that the apex of his delight was in the intimate fellowship of the Society Meeting and promised that he would ask permission for Frederick to be present, though not a member.

The Saturday evening came when the meeting was to be held and that week-end Samuel was away from Bath. Frederick stood at the door hoping against hope that someone would take him in. One of the officials noticed and recognised him and invited him inside. Frederick felt more than he could understand, but understood more of the testimonies than of normal sermons. In elation of spirit, loneliness vanished, and in his own words he resolved: "This people shall be my people and their God shall be my God." In time his brothers joined him and a more challenging family witness in the history of the new chapel in New King Street is not on record.

Among his honoured descendants have been Presidents of Methodist Conferences. The Shum name lingered on the New King Street chapel membership roll for over a century. More of this later.

Just about the time when the foundation stone of the new chapel was being laid, Miss Mary Bosanquet, later the wife of Rev. John Fletcher of Madeley, visited Bath, and stayed the winter in the city and district. Miss Bishop was very unwell at the time, and Wesley believed that Miss Bosanquet arrived just at the moment of special opportunity among women in the Society. At the end of the winter he thought Bath had used her services more advantageously than Bristol would have done! At a Love-feast on the evening of the stone-laying of the new chapel she had spoken very effectively and the Methodists in Bath were ready to welcome her support.

Meanwhile the building proceeded in the names of Michael Hemmings, carpenter, and Moses Potter, poulterer, both named in the deeds as "of Bath". Almost 15 months elapsed between the stone-laying and the opening of the new chapel. At length, on 11th March 1779, New King Street chapel was opened. Thus the Avon Street building was superseded within a month of the 40th aniversary of Wesley's first coming to Bath.

When the new chapel was first opened for worship, Wesley officiated himself, and chose as his text: "We preach Christ crucified; to the Jews a stumbling block and to the Greeks foolishness." He noted: "We concluded the service with the Lord's Supper." He was pleased with the occasion and "believed God had sent His word home to many hearts". Also, he was well satisfied with the premises, and in later directions for the building of chapels, wrote: "Let every square house be built after the model of Bath or Scarborough." That model included: "doors and windows enough, all the window sashes opening downwards . . . no tub pulpit, but a square projection with a seat behind . . . no pews and no backs to seats . . . aisles each side . . . seats parted in the middle, by a rail running all along to divide the men from the women . . . plain and decent, but no more expensive than is absolutely necessary." There was one innovation, Michael Hemmings owned an organ. This he loaned, and subsequently gave, to the chapel. It was the first organ in any of Wesley's buildings. Unfortunately the owner remained possessive and set terms as time passed which helped to create a prejudice against organs in Wesley's premises. There was not likely to be difficulty in finding a competent organist for the opening ceremony. One of the supporters was Benjamin Milgrove, sometimes described as "musician", and formerly organist or precentor at the Vineyards chapel. His compositions still find a place in

Methodist hymn books. He was later a trustee of the chapel.

Possibly Wesley's people had never observed the Lord's Supper in Avon Street chapel, though Wesley had officiated at the service in the Vineyards. The new chapel was to be one of the places where Wesley would administer the Sacraments to his own people in their own building. It was a step from their status as a Society in a Connexion of Societies to the full life of a Church.

Six months passed before Wesley was able to come to Bath again. Almost all his time had been taken up with long journeys throughout England, Scotland and Wales. When, on Monday, 13th September, he did see his model chapel again, the day had to be shared with Bradford-on-Avon. He planned to return to Bath six months later. Sadly, he was required to be with them again in November. He wrote: "The Society was torn in pieces and thrown into the utmost confusion."

Problems and Solutions

The unexpected storm centred on the reaction of Mr Alexander McNab, Wesley's assistant (i.e. superintendent minister at a later time), to an action of Wesley himself. A clergyman who had been on good terms with Wesley, and had been a successful preacher in Ireland, was spending the winter in Bath for the sake of his wife's health. Wesley invited him to preach in the New King Street chapel on Sunday evenings. McNab objected and roused opposition on the grounds that Wesley had intruded on his prerogative. Wesley wrote pointing out that it did not limit McNab's preaching in Bath, because his appointments, from the Bristol circuit, were all on Sunday mornings or afternoons and on week-day evenings. Also he pointed out that his action came within the regulations under which the preachers served. McNab refused to accept the letter of explanation, and therefore Wesley's trip was made to attempt reconciliation in Bath itself. Charles Wesley also came on that occasion. Attempts at reconciliation failed and McNab was suspended from duty. Charles Wesley was pleased that his brother had acted so firmly. He feared that John might have given way through paternal concern for the preacher. However, at the next Conference, John appointed McNab to another circuit. Wesley spent time trying to heal the wound and hoped "brotherly love" was restored. The following July he stayed several days in Bath seeking the renewal of good fellowship, but wrote: "The wound is not yet healed." He could not forget them and returned yet again. He called them "a poor, shattered people". Eight years elapsed before, as we shall see, he was able to claim: "The Society is, at length, at unity in itself."

The bright hopes of March 1779 were further clouded by debt. It is not known how much money had been raised towards building the chapel, or how much the total cost was. Wesley's assistant in the circuit wrote of raising money for the new chapel before it was opened. Doubtless wealthier members in Bristol had contributed and the 150 members in Bath itself had taken part. When all accounts were received it was found that the debt was £1,100. This was utterly beyond anything allowed by connexional regulations, and beyond local resources. The phenomenal increase of membership in the 1770s had not largely been among the wealthy of the city. Doubtless Wesley advised in finding a solution and placed his influence behind a scheme which, as far as is known, had no parallel anywhere else in his Methodism.

The scheme involved finding 11 people who were each able and willing to lend £100 at five per cent interest for an indefinite period. Repayment, in equal proportions, would be made as funds allowed. These 11 would be appointed trustees of the property and would be called to an annual Trustees' Meeting to receive a statement of accounts and transact necessary legal and financial business. On death or withdrawal of a trustee, the survivors were responsible for appointing a successor so as to maintain permanently the number at 11. When all loans had been repaid a Trust of 11 must be continued perpetually.

Safeguards were included to avoid the 11 trustees becoming proprietors of the property in the manner of the owners of Bath's Anglican Proprietory Chapels. Possibly the plan was unique in Wesley's Connexion, in that trusteeship involved ability to provide money. Only four of the 11 appointed belonged to Bath itself, and one of them, Michael Hemmings, had to borrow the £100 which he provided. Wesley and Dr Coke headed the list and John Goodwin, Wesley's assistant in the Circuit when the chapel was erected, also provided £100. The remaining four were from the Bristol Circuit. The list of 11 is as follows:

> The Rev. John Westley, *(sic)* clerk, Master of Arts, of the City Road, London.
> The Rev. Thomas Coke, clerk, Doctor of the Civil Law, late of Jesus College, Oxford.
> Michael Hemmings, the elder of the City of Bath in the County of Somerset, Carpenter.
> Benjamin Milgrove, of Bath, aforesaid, Musician.
> Moses Potter, of Bath, aforesaid, Poulterer.
> William ffry, of the City of Bristol, Gentleman.
> William Green, of the same City, Gentleman.
> William Wait, of Norton Malreward, in the County of Somerset, aforesaid, Gentleman.
> John Goodwin, of Stroud, in the County of Gloucester, Gentleman.
> Thomas Simpson, of the Parish of St George, in the said County of Gloucester, Gentleman.
> William Mandrill, of Bath, aforesaid, Milliner.

Wesley was anxious to get the debt cleared quickly. His Conference in 1780 instructed that a scheme must not proceed until two-thirds of the cost had been raised. Doubtless the New King Street building finance was far wide of such a plan. Wesley suggested a debt clearance scheme by means of small weekly contributions from a large number of members. It was started and quickly dropped because of a foolish and ungracious grievance. Wesley recorded that at Plymouth, with larger debt and smaller membership, the debt was cleared. At Bath it remained. Unhappily there was a readiness among a section of the Bath members both to give and take offence. There were splendid people within the membership, yet it was by no means the happiest of his Societies.

Nevertheless, Wesley's comments indicate increasing harmony and strength as the 1780s proceeded. In 1785 he noted: "This Society . . . is much improved since I was here last. Many stumbling blocks are removed out of the way and brotherly love is increased." Two years later he believed the Society was "in better state than it has been for many years". In February, 1788 he commented: "Here I found a pleasing prospect. The congregations are larger than ever. The Society is at length at unity in itself, and considerably increases both in grace and number." Six months later he "found the Society at Bath in a more flourishing state than it had been for many years, and the congregation . . . unusually large, and as usual, seriously attentive". On one Saturday evening in 1789, despite storms, "the rich and honourable . . . were in abundance" and "seemed as attentive as colliers"! Discord had yielded to devotion, and debt, though burdensome, had diminished.

Strong Leadership

Many factors had contributed to the progress. Visitors to Bath played a part. Among them was Wesley's staunch helper and pioneer in the Channel Islands, Squire Brackenbury of Lincolnshire. His part was in the later stages of the decade. In a letter to him, Wesley confided: "I exceedingly approve of your spending the winter in Bath. I believe God will make you of use to many there." One who helped Wesley in the sacrament in Bath in September 1788 was the Rev. Richard H. Shepherd, for many years minister of Ranelagh Chapel in Chelsea. Wesley's comment was: "it could not have been more seasonable." Still another was the Rev. James Creighton, a Church of England presbyter who assisted at Wesley's Chapel in City Road for more than a quarter of a century. He had taken part in the ordinations for service in American Methodism in 1784. About this time the Rev. Brian Bury Collins, another Church of England presbyter, lived in Corn Street, Bath, and was enthusiastic in his willingness to preach at New King Street. Sometimes he preached there three or four times a week, yet he told Wesley he found "restraint upon his spirit" when preaching in Bath.

None, however, could have carried more inspiration than Captain Thomas Webb who took up residence at 25 Charles Street, Bath, in 1784, only a stone's throw from the chapel. Since his visit in 1773 at Wesley's special request, the gallant Captain and his wife had fallen upon hard times. After that occasion they had spent several years in America, he in his apostolic journeyings and she caring for his home and the family. All had suffered in the War of Independence, and almost as by miracle, after a period of detention, they had managed to escape and return to England. Sources of income had largely failed. Their purpose in coming to Bath was to secure a house where they could take paying guests.

Meanwhile the Captain's gout had become very troublesome and they hoped that the Bath waters could be of service. Nothing daunted, he continued preaching with fiery enthusiasm. It was still true that revival broke out where he preached, and the leaders at New King Street would not be able to ignore his presence. From this point Wesley said that the Bath Society was "much improved". He also noted that he had dinner at "brother Webb's".

Probably the Captain's residence in Bath lasted only three years. He returned to Bristol for his closing years, where his witness as active, benevolent enthusiast and encourager of young and old alike continued to his last day. It may be assumed that the New King Street Society received much inspiration from his dedicated, dynamic personality.

Bath in the 1780s shared the service of some of Wesley's leading itinerants. These included:

John Pawson, twice President of the Conference after Wesley's death.
Thomas Rankin, powerful Scot who had served in America with Captain Webb.
George Shadford from Lincolnshire who also had been in America with Thomas Rankin and the Captain.
Samuel Bradburn, the outstanding orator among Wesley's preachers in that generation.
Benjamin Rhodes, author of the hymn *My Heart and Voice I Raise.*
Adam Clarke, destined to be President of Wesley's Conference three times and one of the greatest linguists of his age.
John Valton and John Murlin, both of whom held honoured places among Wesley's veterans; and
John Broadbent and Thomas Tennant, from the privileged company who shared appointments to the London Circuit with City Road Chapel at its head.

Such men would strengthen a cause in an age when good preaching was an outstanding attraction to a wide community.

John Wesley's Ceaseless Energy

Wesley's personal contribution was astoundingly intimate. In 1783 he celebrated his 80th birthday, and enrolled membership of his Societies in the British Isles reached 46,000. He still travelled from Land's End to Inverness and crossed the sea to Ireland and the Channel Islands. He was no longer able to ride his horse, but travelled in his own little chaise, by post chaise or stage coach, and sometimes, after 1784, in order to save time, by mail coach.

Wesley came to Bath three times in 1783. Normally after that he was in the city every spring and early autumn for about three days at a time. Gone were the hurried calls of the 1750s and 1760s when a few hours' pause on his journey elsewhere included preaching and a meeting with the small society! In the 1780s he preached three times on a Sunday, met Society classes, conferred with bands, visited members (especially poor and sick), talked with leaders and trustees, included the Sacrament of the Lord's Supper on Sunday mornings, once (possibly more than once) held a Watchnight Service, and christened an infant. He also found time to view items of interest such as the new buildings being erected on Lansdown and in the Pulteney Street district, and held himself available to answer personal requests for help.

He showed himself the friend of little children and was known to order his chaise half an hour before he needed it so that it could be filled with children for them to have rides before he set out. He made time to prepare his sermons, write letters, deal with accounts and place all in the context of prayer after rising, probably at 4am, and before retiring towards 10pm. Before the end of the decade week-end visits were usual.

His diary for his March 1783 visit outlined his activity. Sunday evening, 2nd March, after preaching twice at City Road Chapel, London, officiating at Holy communion, writing letters and meeting preachers, leaders and Society in three sessions, he boarded the stage coach at 10pm for Bath. He arrived on Monday evening at 6pm. His diary reads:

> "At brother Sinclair's, tea, within[1]; 6.30 1 Cor xiii 8; at brother Symes', supper, conversed, prayer, 9.30[2].
> *Tuesday, 4th March:* 4 prayed, 1 John ii 12 13; Class visited; 8 tea; conversed, prayers; 9 class; 11 trustees; 1 at brother Sinclair's, dinner; conversed; visited; 2.15 letters; 4.30 tea, conversed, prayer; 5.45 prayed; 6.30 read prayers Phil iii 8; class; 8.30 supper, conversed, prayer; 10[2].
> *Wednesday 5th March:* 4 prayed, Phil iii 9; class; 8 tea, conversed, prayer, visited; 10.15 letters; 1 dinner, prayer; 3 accounts, on business; 4 prayer; 5 tea, conversed, prayed; 6.30 read prayers, Phil iii 15, communion; 8.30 supper, conversed, prayer; 10.15[2].
> *Thursday, 6th March:* 4 prayed, 1 Jn ii 15, writ narrative; 7.30 at Miss Cave's, tea, within[1], visited; 9 coach (Bristol at 12)."

In Bristol each autumn, after meeting the classes, he rewrote the membership list of 1,000 members, giving marital status, address and, where appropriate, occupation. If he did the same for Bath his lists have been lost. Happily, Bristol lists for several years have survived in his own writing.

Such names as have survived for Bath give evidence that the social structure of the Society was widening. Representation of professional occupations increased, side by side with traders, artisans and paid labourers and employees. During his last preaching trip to Bath in the 1780s, John Wesley notes: "At Mr Vaslet's." The one contemporary portrait of Captain Webb which has survived is a pastel by the artist, L. Vaslet. Wesley's reference may suggest that, some years after the Captain had returned to Bristol, the artist had an association with the New King Street Chapel.

Two aristocratic names appear in connection with Dr Coke's arrival in September, 1789. Mr John Valton wrote in his diary of Dr Coke: "performing the church service at Bath

NOTE:

[1] means personal prayer;

[2] represents time at which he withdrew to his bedroom. The Scripture references are the passages from which he preached at the early morning and other services. It would appear that on most mornings there was a service at about 6am.

in the morning" and "making a wonderful sermon in the evening." He noted that Lady Mary Fitzgerald and Lady Douglas were present, and added: "Lady Douglas bespoke a seat in the front of the gallery." When contemporary records became available, both Lady Douglas and Lady Fitzgerald were found to be seat holders "in the front of the gallery". Meanwhile, the Shum family from the Duchy of Franconia had become very prosperous in business and enthusiastic in supporting the chapel. The 1790s would show them fitted for very varied service at New King Street.

That decade opened with John Wesley making his usual journey to Bath both in March and September, although his Journal entry for New Year's Day was: "I am now an old man . . . my eyes are dim, my right hand shakes much, my mouth is hot and dry every morning. I have a lingering fever almost every day, my motion is weak and slow." Nevertheless, he added: "However, blessed be God, I do not slack my labour. I can preach and write still." On the occasion of 2nd to 4th March he demonstrated his indomitable spirit. He rose at 2.30am on 2nd, having preached at Newbury the previous evening. He took chaise at 3am, reached Bath at 1.30pm and preached at 6pm. He retired at 9.30pm and rose the next morning at 5am. He indulged in a walk to see Lansdown Crescent and new building works, preached in the evening and met his Bath members separately.

The next morning he took chaise at 8am for Bristol. His September visit demonstrated the same vigour. He reached Bath on Saturday, 4th, at 3.45pm and preached in the evening. That Sunday morning he preached and administered Holy Communion to "more communicants than ever I saw here before". He spoke again in the evening and afterwards met members separately. Monday evening saw him preach for the fourth time. The congregation was almost as large as on Sunday evening. Again he met members afterwards. It proved to be his last preaching in Bath, and his final comment was: "The power of God was mightily present."

A small company saw him once more. Monday, 27th September, on his way from Bristol to Devizes and Salisbury he paused at 6.45am, drank tea, transacted business, and prayed before leaving at 7.30am to conduct the service at

Devizes at 11am. He died in London on 2nd March, 1791, the anniversary of his last spring visit to Bath, in his 88th year, and just when he had planned another pilgrimage to the west.

It would appear before his final call he had planned a new status for the New King Street Society. Bath was to become head of a circuit. In 1790 it was transferred from Bristol to Bradford-on-Avon Circuit and the senior preacher, Mr George Snowden, was moved into the living accommodation at New King Street. Wesley wrote, on 17th October, to him "at the Preaching House, in Bath". His word was "Be zealous . . . everywhere restore either preaching or prayer meeting in the morning." He also added a word for Mrs Snowden: "Let Sister Snowden also stir up the gift of God that is in her, no preacher's wife should be useless." As so often when writing to his preachers, Wesley concluded: "I am, dear George, your affectionate friend and brother."

The Bath Circuit

At the Conference after Wesley's death, the Bath Circuit was officially formed, with three appointed "ministers". Its exact bounds are no longer known. After two years Bradford reverted to its association with Trowbridge and North Wiltshire. Bath Circuit, for a time, had only two appointed ministers. Those involved included some of the outstanding itinerants in the Connexion. Among them were Henry Moore, Samuel Bradburn again and Walter Griffith, all three future Presidents of the Conference.

During the 1790s, with the city's social status still not far after its peak, New King Street chapel ranked high as a preaching centre in Wesley's Methodism. The time was at hand, however, when the large chapels in industrial centres and other cities would outstrip Bath as its social glory declined, so that New King Street would no longer be a model building to be copied, and Bath Circuit would lose pre-eminence.

In 1767, one man, Michael Hemmings, had been leader of about a dozen members. A list of stewards serving between 1793 and 1800 highlights the phenomenal growth of the society in 25 years. In that period 20 men served a term as society stewards, none holding office for more than three years. At first, continuity with Wesley's lifetime is apparent. As hosts, leaders or correspondents, his own records name them:

John Giles, Joseph Symes, Abraham and Isaac Orchard, John Baker and Edward Hadden all met him in the intimacy of their own homes, or had close association with him.

The appointment during 1796 of William White as a Steward has a particular interest. He came to Bath in 1790, and thus may have met Wesley on his final visits to the city. By profession he was a surgeon. He was 28 years of age on arrival and had nearly 38 years of residence in Bath. His Methodist loyalty never flagged and many members and ministers connected with the chapel had good reason to be grateful for his skill and devotion.

New names appear, including Henry Newton, Henry Pedlar, Charles Dewstow, Elijah Miles, Marmaduke Ashton and Samuel Sims, Isaac Orchard is named for a second term in 1800 as Society steward. One surname occurs with unrivalled frequency. It is the family Shum. Four of the family are named: John as Chapel Steward for many years, and brothers Michael, Frederick and George as Society Stewards. In passing, it may be noted that their younger brother, Yerrick, who was a class leader for many years, had not arrived in Bath when Wesley died.

The oldest of them, and first to arrive, was John. It is believed he came to England in 1774. He combined zealous business ability and success as a baker with intense kindliness and enthusiastic generosity. He outlived all his brothers, and long before he died at 86 years of age was affectionately known in Bath as "Daddy Shum". He joined the Methodists just before Avon Street chapel was closed, became a class leader in the 1780s and was a chapel steward in the 1790s. His three children all died young. So long as his wife lived their home was a centre of hospitality for ministers, visitors to Bath and members of the chapel. The second brother, George, came to Bath in 1775, and joined the Methodists with his brother John. His attachment was not as sustained as that of his brothers. The Moravians, with their Continental association, attracted him. He was, nevertheless, Society steward in 1799.

The third brother, Frederick, for many years was class leader and local preacher, although his native speech limited

Mr Frederick Shum, a line drawing by Stan Roe based on an old portrait.

his mastery of English and his effectiveness as a preacher. Recovery of health followed his arrival in Bath and he prospered in business as a pork butcher. He married a member of the Methodist Society from Keynsham and their five children were all christened at New King Street, between 1797 and 1804, but none settled in Bath. Frederick's name appears as a Society steward in 1796, though his term was cut short by a visit to his parents. His enthusiasm never wavered, and his minister wrote that he prayed with his family in the early morning of the day of his death.

John Michael, the fourth brother, came to England in the early 1780s with his cousin Caspar. At Rotterdam they found they lacked sufficient money for the full journey. Michael wrote to John, who, instead of sending money, went to Rotterdam to meet them and bring them to Bath. Caspar preferred to stay in London, where he joined the Methodists at City Road. Michael joined his brothers at New King Street and served his first term as Society Steward in 1794. Already he was serving the Society as class leader. He married the sister of Frederick's wife, and together they encouraged their son, a second John Michael, in Methodism and music. The boy played for his first service on his seventh birthday, became organist at the chapel when only 12, and served until his death 64 years later. Yerrick, was brought to Bath for health reasons, by Frederick. He alone did not attain the three score years and ten. His part in the family witness within Methodism is less prominent. Their liberality and active support contributed largely to the erection of Walcot chapel.

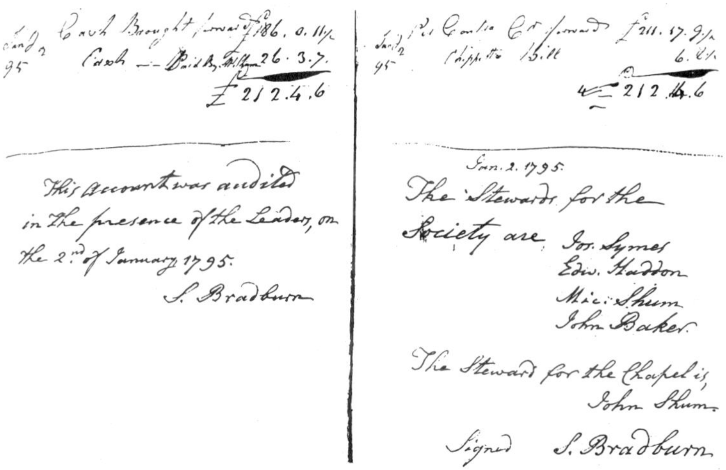
Cash Brought forward £186.0.11½
£212.4.6

This account was audited in the presence of the Leaders, on the 2nd of January 1795.
S. Bradburn

By Contra Cr forward £211.17.9½
212.4.6

Jan. 2. 1795
The Stewards for the Society are Jos. Symes
Edw. Haddon
Mic: Shum
John Baker

The Steward for the Chapel is
John Shum

Signed S. Bradburn

Rev Samuel Bradburn certifies the New King Street Society accounts for 1794.

The list of Society stewards is not the only indication of the chapel's strength as Wesley's people approached the 60th anniversary of his first visit to the city. Our illustration records that the Rev. Samuel Bradburn, the superintendent minister has certified the Society's accounts for 1794 and designated the Stewards for the forthcoming year. In 1797, Mr Bradburn noted in the account book: "Thank God for the Society, being out of debt." That, of course, did not mean the Trust was free from financial burden and the Building Fund cleared. The will of one of the trustees, dated 1807, indicates that there was still money outstanding on the property at that time. The debt was carried forward until 1849 and was then absorbed into the costing of the new chapel which was built in that year. What Samuel Bradburn's note reveals is that there had also been a deficit on the Society Account, dealing with people rather than property, and especially with the maintenance of the ministry. Only occasionally were collections taken at Sunday services. The class and ticket money, with spasmodic collections, had been insufficient to avoid such a reverse in funds. Probably the brilliant oratory of Mr Bradburn's preaching had attracted larger numbers of people and this increased income when collections were taken.

Domestic Details

Meanwhile the Bath Circuit was being established on the normal pattern. Fragmentary accounts make reference to the Quarterly Meeting on 21st July, 1792. Members met in the morning and stayed together — possibly with preaching — for most of the day. The Quarterly Meeting dinner entire cost was £1.4s.5½d. When Dr. Coke preached that year the Sacrament collection raised £1.9s.6d. His expenses came to £1.0s.3d. From 1793 the chapel-keeper, Isaac Challenger, was receiving six guineas per annum, plus accommodation, and five per cent of seat moneys collected by him "as shall not be paid unto Mr John Shum".

Small details can be interesting. In 1794 a chamberpot cost 10d, letters from Bristol and Frome cost 2d each, from London 5d. This is a reminder of the days before adhesive postage stamps were used and when the recipient paid the postage. In 1795 a mysterious entry records the payment of 2s.9d to "the Affrican Friers and Preacher". And "bad silver" cost the account 8s! By 1799 "Dinner at the *Christopher* (Mrs Grange) at the Quarterly Meeting" was costing £3.9s.6d. Shortly afterwards the Society indulged in a bottle of port at 3s.3d. The preacher's horse was another expense. Hence in 1800: "Purchase of a horse £10.14s.9d" towards which £7.17s.6d was contributed by the Society — probably by the preachers who would use it. The horse was sold the following year for £10 to Mr Paul Rose, a collier, who was leader amongst the Methodists at Twerton.

A financial statement, found loose in an old account book, and reproduced describes the funding of a preacher's horse in 1803. A note added in 1807 explains its subsequent disposal. Jonathon Parkin was the minister at the time.

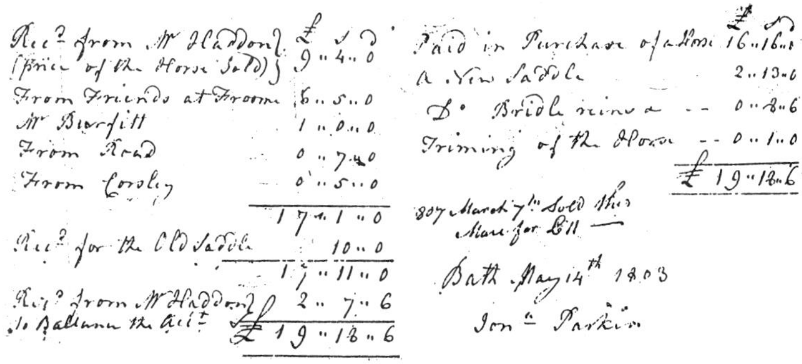

	£ s d		£ s d
Rec^d from Mr Haddon (Price of the Horse Sold)	9..4..0	Paid in Purchase of a Horse	16..16..0
From Friends at Frome	6..5..0	A New Saddle	2..13..0
Mr Burfitt	1..0..0	D^o Bridle [illegible]	0..8..6
From Road	0..7..0	Triming of the Horse	0..1..0
From Corsley	0..5..0		£19..18..6
	17..1..0		
Rec^d for the Old Saddle	10..0		
	17..11..0		
Rec^d from Mr Haddon to Ballance the Acc^t	2..7..6		
	£19..18..6		

1807 March 7th Sold this Mare for £11 —

Bath May 14th 1803

Jon^n Parkin

This loose statement from 1803, and endorsed in 1807, summarises the finances involved in the provision of a horse for preachers' use.

Something which the account book does not reveal is that in the year 1794–95 Bath came to the help of Bristol. The story is involved, but in brief, it is that sadly the congregations at the New Room and Guinea Street, Bristol had been split on the subject of the administration of Holy Communion by their own preachers in their own buildings. Kingswood was also involved. Within Bristol three congregations desired the Sacrament and only one appointed preacher was prepared to meet their wish. Samuel Bradburn was willing to give some occasional assistance. Thus Bristol, which for so long had given strength to Bath, now received a little help in return.

Though a period when Wesley's people had to face considerable dissension following his death, the 1790s decade was one of spectacular Methodist advance. Membership in 1790 passed 57,000 in Great Britain: by 1800 it had exceeded 90,000. Bath Circuit shared in this advance, not only numerically, but in the rise of new Societies. Batheaston sent £1.1s.0d to the circuit funds in July 1797. More than a year earlier a plot of ground had been secured there for the erection of a chapel. A local Circuit, as distinct from a widespread association of Societies, was on the way. The accounts for March 1799 include "Ticket money from Twerton, Conqwell *(sic)* and Hinton". As the 18th century closed Bath Methodism was poised for spectacular advance.

[Editor's note: Don't forget to multiply sums of money by 30!]

4

Early Expansion 1800-1815

Methodical Organisation

THE 18th century had been one of fluctuating fortunes for the Methodists in Bath; the 19th century was to see the pinnacle of Methodist expansion. Undoubtedly it was a time of growth, division and more growth as the various schisms tore mainstream Methodism apart. It was the age when Non-conformity became respectable and Non-Conformists began to take a prominent part in local politics and institutions.

Towards the end of the 19th century Christian beliefs and ethics had permeated City life to such an extent that, not only were the leaders noted for their genuine religious fervour, but for the extent to which they also seriously catered for the moral needs of the people. It became the practice that for every 300 or so new houses built, a new church would also be erected. The different denominations leapt at this opportunity and their places of worship were sometimes to be found within yards of each other.

At the beginning of the century as the 1801 map of Bath shows the city had only one purpose-built Methodist chapel — that at New King Street. It inevitably soon proved to be too small for the needs of the Methodist Society which was using it. All the members could not worship together at one time, and special occasions also presented some insuperable problems. The obvious solution was to build a second chapel to serve the rapidly expanding eastern side. A suitable site was found at Walcot. (See Chapter 2 for the full story of the Walcot Church).

Church registers compiled during the early part of the century reveal a picture of sustained activity at New King Street and in the villages surrounding Bath. There was an intricate

Map of Bath in 1801. Buildings are shaded; most inhabitants still live near the city centre. The lists include 23 churches and chapels of various denominations. Within 70 years this number doubled.

pattern of Society classes with elaborate records of attendances and the payment of class moneys.

Taking at random one annual summary, for the year 1806

for instance, the minister has listed a total membership of 759, and reveals in the following tables a statistical review demonstrating the frenzied activity occurring throughout the entire church life:

Statistics for 1806

Classes at New King Street

Leader	*No in class*		
John Shum	16	Tuesday	7 pm
Joseph Syms	28	Sunday	2 pm
Mary Gerrish	18	Sunday	2 pm
Levi Purnill	17	Sunday	8 am
Fred Shum	25	Sunday	8 am
Fred Shum	20	Thursday	7 pm
Rachel Shum	25	Wednesday	6 pm
John Baker	20	Thursday	7 pm
Michael Shum	20	Sunday	8 am
Paul Rose	10	Sunday	3 pm
Marmaduke Ashton	14	Tuesday	7 pm
William Bowin	24	Wednesday	7 pm
Charles Dewstoe	18	Wednesday	7 pm
James Williams	21	Tuesday	7 pm

Classes in Country Societies

Batheaston	James Rogers	14
Twerton	Jasper Jones	18
Priston	John Syms	4
Camerton	George Savage	14
	William Goold	8
Dunkerton	George Flower	5
Conkwell	William Trimby	5
Hinton	James Tupsill	9

Circuit Membership and Finance

	New Members	*Removals*	*Back-sliders*	*Deaths*	*Decrease*	*Increase*	*Whole Membership*	*Yearly Collection*			*Kingswood Collection*			*Preachers Fund Subscribers*		
								£	s	d	£	s	d	£	s	d
Bath	60	16	19	5		20	277	11.	3.	0	14.	1.	0	9.	4.	6
Batheaston	2	1				1	14		7.	7		17.	4			
Twerton	10	1	3			6	18		5.	0						
Priston							4									
Camerton			3		3		22		5.	0		8.	8			
Dunkerton	1	2			1		5									
Conkwell	1					1	5									
Hinton	3	1				2	9									
Frome	17	8	11	6	8		160	4.	18.	6	6.	5.	0	5.	7.	0
Corsley	2			3	1		23		7.	0		5.	0			
Warminster	9	1	3			5	34		16.	0	1.	3.	0			
Roade	4	2	1	1			38		17.	5	1.	5.	6	1.	11.	6
Crockerton	1	4	2		5		19		5.	0						
Beckington	5					5	18									
Bradley				1	1		9					5.	0	1.	1.	0
W Woodlands	3	11			8		29		17.	0		10.	0	1.	0.	0
Tilsford		1		2	3		9									
Kingston D	9					9	9									
Gair Hill							5									
E Woodlands			5	1	6		10									
Blatchbridge	1	3	1		3		10									
Brewham Ldg	2	1	2		1		16	1.	1.	0						
Longbridge D	5					5	5									
Corston	11					11	11									
Total	146	52	50	19	40	65	759	19.	12.	6	25.	0.	6.	18.	4.	0

Minister's comments on some individual members

Ann Arnold — a woman of sound experience in the things of God. For many years a leader in the Bath Society. After more than 40 years of experience of the vital growth of Godliness she finished her course with joy. 4th October, 1805.

Rebecca Young — 40 years member of the Methodist Society. The former part of her Christian life was not as steady as might have been desired. Her latter days were crowned with the fruits of righteousness. She closed the mortal scene in peace 16th October, 1805.

> **Hanna Bowen** — a mute and lowly follower of the Lord Jesus for 18 years. Her last affliction was long; the constant language of her soul was: Lord now lettest Thou Thy servant depart in peace. The Lord granted her this thing she requested 4th September, 1805.

> **William Barnett** — at an early period of life was brought to a clear and saving knowledge of God. Sometime before his death had many trials arising from affliction and poverty. Finished his course June, 1805.

These records hide stories of struggle and caring by the Church leaders. By using our imagination and our knowledge of the harsh social conditions of the times we gain an insight into the lives of these 759 people and the change which the Methodists must have made to them. Periods of such rapid expansion in membership inevitably led at times to tension and misunderstanding. For instance, at Roade: "I have had much trouble with one, T. Lucas. He is a very dubious character and sundry things led to the breaking up of the society on his account. I then received, after reading the rules of the society, as many as were inclined to be Methodists . . . and have not considered either him or those that meet with him as members of our society . . . I request that you do not do anything by way of receiving him again but in conjunction with the Local Preachers of the present Society at Roade." This note in the register is initialled "G. H." The Rev. G. Highfield was appointed to the Bath Circuit from 1806 to 1808. The problem was inherited by the Rev. Samuel Bradburn. Membership fell from 38 to 12. Rev. Bradburn wrote in August 1810: "To the above request I most religiously attended believing it to be from God. After two years' labour I have reason to be thankful. Roade is in a very prosperous way. A good new chapel and 29 members."

This chapel, built in 1806 is the oldest on the above list to survive from those early days. It finally closed in 1986 having been transferred to a newly formed Frome circuit as long ago as 1811. By this time the numbers were so great that one circuit could not manage efficiently. Frome circuit including all the townships in its vicinity began with 595 members; Bath retained 603.

This map, which dates from about 1800, shows the location and the contemporary spelling of many of the villages which feature in the narrative and on the Circuit Plans.

About this time Conference authorised Dr Thomas Coke to prepare for a mission to Ceylon. He visited Bath and the register records that contributions there totalled £65; at Frome £8. "There may be a little error. Dr Coke took this with him" the account book coyly admits, Mr Bradburn left the Bath Circuit in 1810. Before doing so he added this endorsement to the record: "I intended the account of the numbers in this book to have been perfect; but I dare not affirm that it is, as some of the very small places I never was at . . . before I could get the names I was obliged to leave. . . I doubt not the Superintendent will find to his satisfaction that there has been no intentional fraud practised to make the numbers seem more than they were."

Mr Bradburn's successor was the Rev. William Myles. The latter's somewhat critical contribution to the Record Book is as follows: "I know not the reason why two leaves are pasted together, nor why some of the leaves are cut out of this book. We did not get it from Mr Bradburn of Bristol till the year 1812, Mr Bradburn left a debt as follows:

	£	s	d
To Mr Orchard for his furniture	186	0	0
To Mr Rose for his coals for two years	30	0	0
	216	0	5
Collected towards this:			
From individuals	139	0	5
From Bath Trustees	30	0	0
From Conference 1811	30	0	0
From sale of part furniture	34	7	4
	233	7	9"

In his memoirs Mr Bradburn refers in 1809 to his "sufferings of mind for want of money". Later, "The Lord sent me money". In 1810 he refers to the emptiness of all wordly possessions but repeats his plea for "a little more".

The geographical whereabouts of several of the chapels mentioned in this chapter and elsewhere can be located on the map showing the surroundings of Bath in the early 1800's.

5

Rural Problems
1815-1850

Duty and Discipline

DURING 1817, with Walcot Chapel now open, the Rev. James Buckley decided to improve the control of business in the Bath circuit. Leaders' meetings, attended by all stewards and class leaders would be held monthly, and each leader undertook to bring 1d a week plus a shilling a quarter for each member. Quarterly meetings would be preceded by a plain mid-day dinner, the expense to be met from a collection immediately afterwards. One Leaders' meeting in 1820 expelled Thomas Bush as an improper member for refusing to live with his wife, and running into debt.

By 1825 the circuit membership had risen to 1,290, a number never again to be reached. The vast bulk was in Bath and included the two purpose-built chapels at Batheaston and Twerton. The village causes were struggling to keep going. Their membership varied from two to 19. Many were quite unable to make any contribution to circuit expenses because of the money they had to find for the rent of hired rooms. The Local Preachers were most concerned that Methodism did not appear to be growing in the countryside as quickly as in the town. On 24th November 1826 they called a special meeting to consider the problem. The debate and especially the conclusions became a historic point of reference.

They decided that:

(1) the people generally had never been properly trained in the usages of Methodism;

(2) there was a want of proper persons to act in the important office of Class Leader to watch over the spiritual interests of the people;

> (3) preachers had neglected to meet the country Societies to urge upon the people the great doctrines and precepts of the Gospel.

The sudden expansion in membership, and the setting up of village causes over a wide area, made tremendous demands on the small band of preachers. Occasional disciplinary problems arose. The monthly Preachers' Meeting did its best to vet the ability and sincerity of new applicants, and tried to deal with complaints that were sometimes raised about the efforts of a largely uneducated band of brothers. Here are some of the matters with which they dealt:

> 1827: Many "neglects as to supplying places" had occurred. The Secretary was to keep a list; and names of defaulters were to be read out. Brother Cross was appointed to the full-time ministry for missionary work and was sent to New Zealand (where he served at Tongataboo and later Vavou).
>
> 1828: Brother Harris applied to join but refused to answer questions about experience and doctrine; he later yielded. The brothers felt he had been unnecessarily alarmed and received him as a preacher. Brother Moxley was in debt. His wife "encouraged young people to the house to drink beer etc". As a tailor, Moxley had been unkind to juvenile clients. A deputation of three brethren appointed to investigate put the blame squarely on his wife. A move to put him off the plan was defeated by six votes to five. But three months later he resigned.
>
> 1829: Brother John Rice having been appointed to the West Indies, returned to Bath a year later. In 1837 he went to the United States as a minister in the Methodist Episcopal Church. After working in New York and New England, he moved to Baltimore in 1840 where he died a year later aged 37.
>
> 1830: At this time 29 preachers and two exhorters were serving 28 preaching places in the circuit. It was agreed that horse hire would be paid to cover preachers' winter visits to the more distant villages namely Falkland, Norton St Philip, Marshfield and Box. Money would be raised by

THE BATH WESLEYAN PREACHERS' PLAN, 1835.

" They that be wise shall shine as the brightness of the firmament; and they that turn many to righteousness, as the stars for ever and ever."—*Dan.* xii. 3.

MONTHS ☞	Hours.	JANUARY.					FEBRUARY.				MARCH.			
SUNDAYS ☞		3	10	17	24	31	7	14	21	28	6	13	20	27
MORNING LESSONS ☞		Isaiah 41. Matthew 2.	Isaiah 44. Matthew 8.	Isaiah 51. Matt. 15.	Isaiah 55. Matt. 22.	Isaiah 57. Matt. 28.	Isaiah 59. Mark 7.	Isaiah 65. Mark 14.	Gen. 1. Luke 4.	Gen. 3. Luke 11.	Gen. 7. Luke 17.	Gen. 19-30. Luke 24.	Gen. 24. John 4.	Gen. 39. John 14.
New King Street *Monday* *Friday* *Saturday*	10½ 6 7 7 7	Atherton Lusher Lusher Atherton Lusher	Rogers Q C Atherton QC Atherton Rogers Atherton	Lusher Rogers Rogers Lusher Rogers	Atherton Lusher Lusher Atherton Lusher	Rogers Atherton Atherton Rogers M P Atherton	Lusher S Rogers Rogers Lusher Rogers	Atherton C Lusher C Lusher Atherton Lusher	Rogers Atherton Atherton Rogers Atherton	Lusher Rogers Rogers Lusher M P Rogers	Atherton Lusher Lusher Atherton Lusher	Rogers Atherton Atherton Rogers Atherton	Lusher Rogers Rogers Lusher Rogers	Atherton L Lusher Lusher Atherton M P Lusher
Walcot Chapel *Wednesday*	10½ 6 7	Lusher Atherton Rogers	Atherton QC Rogers Q C Lusher	Rogers Lusher S Atherton	Lusher Atherton Rogers	Atherton Rogers Lusher	Rogers Lusher Atherton	Lusher C Atherton C Rogers	Atherton Rogers S Lusher	Rogers Lusher Atherton	Lusher Atherton Rogers	Atherton Rogers Lusher	Rogers S Lusher Atherton	Lusher Atherton Rogers
Ebenezer Chapel, Widcombe *Tuesday*	11 6 7	Britton Rogers Lusher	Lusher Lewis Atherton	Rice Atherton Rogers	Rogers S Fletcher Lusher	Gregory Lusher Atherton	Atherton C Willcox C Rogers	Rice Rogers Lusher	Lusher Turner Atherton	Luckman Atherton Rogers	Rogers Q C Lewis Lusher	Rice Fletcher Atherton	Atherton James Rogers	Britton Rogers Lusher
Larkhall *Tuesday*	11 6 7	Rogers Luckman Rogers	Gregory Howe Luckman	Atherton QC Turner Atherton	Rice Lewis Millard	Lusher Willcox Lusher	Morris Atherton Rice	Rogers C James C Rogers	Fletcher Harris Luckman	Rice Britton Atherton	Millard T. Pond Harris	Freeman Lewis Lusher	Turner Morris Luckman	Rogers James Rogers
Avon Street *Thursday*	6 7	Dowson Lusher	Hunt Willcox	Morris Atherton	King Luckman	Preece Rogers	Clift Howe	Drake Lusher	King Willcox	Howe Atherton	Dowson Luckman	Kent Rogers	Turner Howe	Drake Lusher
Brass Mills and Bristol Road	3. 6	Kendall	Preece	T. Pond	James	Morris	Kendall	Read	Preece	Kent	Britton	James	Kendal	Gregory
Beacon-Hill	6	T. Pond	James	Gregory	Read	Turner	Preece	Britton	James	Harris	Gregory	Read	Dowson	Preece
Weston *Monday*	6 7	Gregory Luckman	Read	Harris Lusher	Hunt	King Q C Rogers	Fletcher	Freeman C Atherton	Fletcher	Kendall Lusher	James	Morris Rogers	Howe	Turner Atherton
Twerton *Tuesday*	11 6 7	Dowson Fletcher Atherton	Morris Lusher S Rogers	James Luckman Lusher	Turner Rogers QC Atherton	Drake Kendall Rogers	Millard Turner Lusher	Morris C Willcox C Atherton	Rice Freeman Rogers	Atherton Lewis Lusher	King Rogers Atherton	T. Pond Hunt Rogers	Gregory Atherton Lusher	Clift Kent Atherton
Batheaston *Thursday*	10½ 6 7	Harris Millard Rice	Rice Britton Rogers	Willcox Q C Freeman Turner	Drake J. Britton Lusher	Read T. Pond Willcox	Rice James Atherton	Noble C King C Freeman	J. Britton Gregory Rogers	T. Pond Freeman Harris	Preece Turner Lusher	Britton Kendall Rice	Willcox Harris Atherton	Rice Read Willcox
Box *Monday*	3, 6 7	Drake	King	Willcox Q C Atherton	Noble	James	Read	Millard C Rogers	J. Britton	Drake	Noble	Dowson Lusher	Willcox	T. Pond
Bathford *Monday*	6 7	Noble	Freeman	Howe Q C	Harris Rogers	Clift	Noble	Hunt C	Kent Lusher	Howe	Read	Preece	Noble Q C Atherton	King
Midford, Twinney, & Southstoke	10½. 2½. 6	J. Britton	Drake	Millard	T. Pond	Freeman	J. Britton	Howe	Clift	Hunt	Willcox	Harris	Drake	Howe
Midford *Wednesday*	6 7	Turner Atherton	Millard	Lewis	Willcox C	Luckman Rogers	Rossiter	Dowson	Howe	King Lusher	Harris	J Britton QC	W. Pond	Rossiter Atherton
Norton St. Philip *Wednesday*	11. 6 7	Read Lusher	Willcox Q C	Britton	Freeman	Harris Rice	Drake	Turner	Millard	Rossiter Rogers	Clift	Howe C Lusher C	Lewis	Hunt Lusher
Falkland *Wednesday*	11 2 5 6	Freeman Freeman Luckman	Howe Howe	J. Britton J. Britton QC	Rossiter Rossiter	Hunt Hunt Atherton	Lewis Lewis	Clift Clift	Willcox Willcox	Read Read Willcox	Rossiter Rossiter	Lusher C Howe C	Millard Millard	J. Britton J. Britton Freeman
Wellow *Thursday*	10½ 2, 5 7	Willcox	Fletcher Q C Lusher	Hunt	Howe	J. Britton	Harris Atherton	Rossiter C Rossiter C	Dowson Lusher	Preece	Drake Rogers	Millard	Clift	Luckman
Tunley *Wednesday*	3, 6 6	Hunt	T. Pond	Clift Rogers	Millard Q C	Lewis	Dowson	Kent Lusher	Rice C	Willcox	J. Britton	Drake Atherton	King	Harris
Priston *Tuesday*	6 7	Preece	Kent	Dowson	Kendall Q C Rogers	Kent	Freeman	Luckman	Lewis C Lusher	J. Britton	Millard	Willcox	T. Pond Atherton	Freeman
Corston *Wednesday*	6 7	Kent	Kendall Atherton QC	King	Dowson Lusher	Howe	T. Pond Rogers	Lewis C	Drake Atherton	Millard	Kendall Lusher	Gregory	Freeman Rogers	Fletcher
Kelstone and Swineford	3, 6	Howe	Dowson Q C	Kent	Clift	Millard	King	Kendall C	Drake	Dowson	Clift	Turner	Read	Willcox
Combe Down	6	King	Clift	Drake	Kent	Dowson	Gregory	J. Britton C	Britton	Clift	King	Luckman	Preece	Lewis

Preachers.

ATHERTON
ROGERS
LUSHER
WATSON
MORRIS
GREGORY
ROSSITER
POND
TURNER
LUCKMAN
RICE
JAMES
READ
T. POND
HARRIS
BRITTON
FLETCHER
NOBLE
FREEMAN
KING
KENDALL
J. BRITTON
MILLARD
HUNT
CLIFT
WILLCOX
LEWIS
KENT
HOWE

ON TRIAL.
DOWSON.

Hymn-Books, Magazines, Commentaries, and all other Books sold at the Wesleyan Book-Room, to be had of the Rev. W. Atherton, 13, Great Stanhope Street, Bath; the profits of which go towards the support of the work of God.

NB.—S. stands for Sacrament.—L. for Love Feast.—M. P. for Missionary Prayer Meeting.—Q. C. Quarterly Collection.—C. Chapel Fund Collection.—Quarterly Fast Day, April 1st. —Local Preachers' Meeting, March 18.—Quarterly Meeting, March 29.—Every Preacher is expected to supply his own place, *or provide an accredited substitute.*—The Stewards at every place will have the Collections published on the preceding Sunday, and the Preachers will not fail to make them on the days on which they are marked in the Plan.

The Wesleyan Preachers' Plan for the January to March quarter 1835.

subscriptions. Any preachers not subscribing would not participate in the benefits! Brother Edwards denied intoxication but admitted "other improprieties" and resigned.

1831: Brother Howell was suspended at his own request for "scruples of conscience". This arose from his having to light the lamps at the theatre, "which the brethren would not consider consistent with his engagement as a local preacher".

1832: Brother Cook was allowed to take only three appointments per quarter for very special reasons.

1833: Brother Drake resigned "in consequence of worldly embarrassment".

Total Commitment

As the reproduction of the Preaching Plan for January to March 1835 demonstrates many brethren were on the road most Sundays and often took mid-week services too. To summarise a typical example, the June to August Plan for 1839 appointed Brothers Turner and Dunn as follows:-

	Brother Turner	*Brother Dunn*
9th June	Weston 6pm	Batheaston 6pm
16th June	Combe Down 6pm	Tunley 3pm & 6pm
23rd June	Priston 6pm (and Larkhall Tues)	Nothing! (Avon St Thurs)
30th June	Box 3pm & 6pm	Twerton 11am
7th July	Corston 3pm & 6pm	Wellow 2.30pm & 5pm
14th July	Norton St Philip 11am & 6pm	Weston 6pm
21st July	Bathford 6pm (& Avon St Thurs)	Falkland 2pm & 5pm
28th July	Larkhall 6pm	Box 3pm & 6pm
4th August	Nothing!	Widcombe 6pm
11th August	Midford 11am Twinney 2pm South Stoke 6pm (& Widcombe Tues)	Tunley 3pm & 6pm

18th August	Holloway 11am	Hinton 6pm
25th August	Tunley 3pm & 6pm	Norton 11am & 6pm
1st Sept	Falkland 2pm & 5pm	Midford 11am
	South Stoke 6pm	Twinney 2pm
Total Appointments	22	21

The advent of the railways — Bath was connected in 1840 — must have assisted the movement of preachers greatly. In 1846 a collection was to be made "if arrangements can be made with the GWR for the transit of preachers to Conference". That year the Conference was held in Bristol.

6

The Onset of Primitive Methodism 1830–1860

Pioneering Days

THOSE WHO were critical of the ordered ways of official Methodism and sought a more zealous form of outreach had started their camp meetings and revivalist activities under Hugh Bourne and William Clowes in the industrial North and Midlands quite early in the century. Their influence was slow to penetrate the more conservative South. The usual form of expansion involved the "planting" of a missionary in new territory. So it was that the Frome Primitives decided in 1828 to appoint the Rev. N. Towler to live in Bath and "establish a mission there and in the surrounding neighbourhood". Evidence of their activities is found in Wesleyan circles, for inevitably some of their initial supporters were culled from those Methodists attracted by the fiery evangelism of the new movement. "The Ranters have gotten 16 or 18 of our members, beside many of our hearers; yet we seem not to miss them" wrote the Rev. Joseph Sutcliffe in 1829. The *Bath Chronicle* describes a typical local Camp Meeting; it is interesting to read an account by an onlooker who was presumably impartial.

> On Sunday last a numerous body of Methodists had a camp meeting on Combe Down. Two waggons were placed for the preachers including three females. If the goodness of the singing had been in proportion to its loudness, it would have been excellent. After the sermon the Director commanded all to separate lots — Camerton friends to the left, Frome to the right, Coleford to the front, Bath stay near the waggons. Each company then began singing different tunes, then kneeled to pray, swaying and bawling as loud

> as they could until black in the face and suffused with perspiration. This continued until the evening when they separated.

During the next few years a number of local preachers transferred their allegiance, and some small preaching places had to be abandoned due to poor attendance, but generally speaking the losses of members by the Wesleyans were not significant. A few country causes were transferred to nearby circuits for geographical reasons. That tension existed however is revealed by this entry in the New King Street Leaders' minute book: ". . . deeply deploring the present disturbed state of the Society, resulting from the non-observance of the Constitutional principles of Methodism, RESOLVED that in order to prevent the recurrence of such evils . . . we will in future abide by the decisions of the Quarterly Meetings and use our influence to prevent others disturbing the decisions of the same."

This was signed by the minister, supernumaries, and 31 members. The Secretary of the meeting however registered his disassociation from it.

This line drawing by Stan Roe shows the façade of Thomas Street chapel in 1989.

By 1836, The *Primitive Methodist Magazine* was able to claim a membership in Frome of 500 and at Bath 100. "It affords us unspeakable pleasure to be able to state that our circuit is happily rising, and that we are out of debt." But in Bath they were short of property. Accommodation for worship was the big worry. For 17 years the congregation moved from one hired hall to another, visiting in succession Hetling House (today's Abbey Church House). Parsonage Lane and Thomas St Chapel. Today all that remains of the latter is shown in the line drawing. It was built in 1830 on an incredibly steep street in Walcot named after Thomas Cottle, shoemaker. The building has recently been converted to commercial use.

Eventually in 1845 they purchased No 4 Westgate Buildings, a substantial house containing 15 rooms, at a price of £400. The Trust Deed carries the names of: Rev. Robert Tuffin, Messrs William Vaughan, John Coward, Thomas Watson, Giles Goodenough, James Hancock, George Parker and Thomas Gilbert.

The opening services took place on 29th June and 1st July 1845. Interestingly, the visiting preachers were Rev. J. J. Richards (Countess of Huntingdon Connexion) and Rev. J. Carr (a local Wesleyan minister). At this time there was room for 150, but this soon proved inadequate. Under the energetic ministry of the Rev. T. Hobson drastic alterations were made and the seating was increased to 500. At the re-opening in January 1849 the well-wishing visiting preachers included three Wesleyans, two Baptists and one Countess of Huntingdon. The collections amounted to £90, "one third of the cost of the enlargement". During subsequent years attendances increased. The sincerity of this exuberant Movement is reflected in reports appearing in the denominational magazine.

For instance, in 1856:

> On 1st November a penitents' meeting was attended by a goodly number of sincere seekers of salvation . . . all who were determined to strive to obtain mercy there and then were invited to kneel at the penitents' form. Five persons hearkened to the invitation, cried to God for mercy, and four obtained forgiveness.

During December three services were being held on each of six days of the week, at 6am, 1pm and 7pm. The minister, the

Rev. R. Tuffin, who had returned for a second spell, claimed to be "an advocate for the use of extraordinary means" in order to revive the church.

A Turbulent Period

The discipline over Local Preachers was quite severe. Those who neglected an appointment were "to sink one figure on the plan" for each offence, or pay a fine of not less than 6d. In 1849, three preachers suffered loss of position on the plan. Around this time, William Walters "having through sin caught the venereal disease" was taken off the plan. And Geo Freeman's name came off "due to his wife's immorality".

The kind of questions asked of local preacher candidates, and one individual's answers to some questions are shown in our illustration.

The year 1854, Moses Harvey, a young travelling preacher was appointed to the circuit. Soon after being granted permission to marry he found himself in financial difficulties and private subscriptions were needed to help him out. Then his work was unsatisfactory and the Rev. Tuffin, the Superintendent, told the Quarterly Meeting that he had warned Harvey that he faced dismissal from the circuit. The meeting rejoined by reminding the Rev. Tuffin that lay members and not the minister were responsible for decisions of that kind! Later the unfortunate young man was admonished for "being generally late at the preaching services".

A study of the baptismal registers reveals an interesting assortment of occupations amongst members of the congregation, and provides evidence of industrial and other activity prevalent in Bath in the middle of the 19th century: Coachman, butcher, cooper, umbrella maker, policeman, taylor *(sic)*, gas stoker, clothdresser, carpenter, weaver, porter, painter, shoemaker, presser, gasman, potter, farmer, cordwainer, hat-maker, railroad clerk, minister, springsmith, hawker, chairman, woolwasher, drysalter, coachmaker, wireworker, watchmaker, engine driver, gentleman, professor of music, letter deliverer, dealer in china, and dyer.

Country preaching places appeared and disappeared again with alarming frequency. For the early years records are not

PRIMITIVE METHODIST CONNEXION.

Questions to be answered by the Candidates for the Preachers' Plan.

1. How long have you been converted?
2. What means have you used to cultivate your religious life?
3. What books have you read since your conversion?
4. How long have you been a member of the Primitive Methodist Connexion?
5. Have you read the Rules of our Society? If so, what are your views of our form of Church Government?
6. To what extent have you met in class, and what is your idea of the class as a means of grace?
7. If you knew a friend or neighbour to be under conviction of sin, what steps would you take towards leading him to Christ?
8. Give your views on the following doctrines and supply Scriptural references:
   - *a.* The Being of God, including the Holy Trinity.
   - *b.* The Deity of our Lord Jesus Christ.
   - *c.* The innocence of our first parents when they were created.
   - *d.* Their fall, and that of their offspring.
   - *e.* General redemption by the Lord Jesus Christ.
   - *f.* Repentance, including godly sorrow for sin and corresponding reformation.
   - *g.* The justification of the ungodly by faith on their turning to God.
   - *h.* The witness of the Holy Spirit to our adoption into the family of God.
   - *i.* Sanctification by the Holy Spirit, producing inward and outward holiness.
   - *j.* The resurrection of the dead, both of the just and unjust.
   - *k.* The general judgment and eternal rewards and punishments.

NOTE.—The Candidate, in answering the above questions, must commence by giving the number or letter prefixed to the question to which his answer relates.

1. 26. years.
2. Read Good books. private devotion. attended the means of Grace.
3. Read the Bible some of. Rev. Jays works. Pilgrims Progress: some of Mark Guy. Pearces writings etc.
4. 26. years.
5. yes: I consider the form of our Church governme very good.
6. I. meet in class when I have opportunity: My idea of Class meetings. as a means of grace are one of the most helpful. instructive. and a stimulous to the christian life.

Questions asked about 1860 of Candidates as Preachers under the Primitive Methodist Discipline. Some of the answers of one applicant are shown in this reproduction.

available of membership or attendances. The preachers met before the circuit Quarterly Meetings and consequently their business tended to be hurried. From reference to the proceedings which are contained in the minute book of 1850, it seems that Primitive Methodist services were then being held at the

PRIMITIVE METHODIST PREACHERS' PLAN OF THE BATH CIRCUIT.

"Thou crownest the year with thy goodness."—PSALM lxv. 11.

1857-8. PLACES.	TIME.	OCT. 18	OCT. 25	NOV. 1	NOV. 8	NOV. 15	NOV. 22	NOV. 29	DEC. 6	DEC. 13	DEC. 20	DEC. 25	DEC. 27	JAN. 3	JAN. 10
BATH	11	2	1B	2	1C	2B	1	1A	2B	2	1		2B	1C	2
	6	2	1S	2	1C	2L	1S	1A	3	2	1S	2	2	1C	2S
Wednesday	7*	2	2	1E	1‡	1	2	1E	1‡	2	2		1	1E	1‡
TWERTON	2½	1V	19	16	12	10	20	2C	22	5	7		15	2	1C
	6	1S	19	14L	26	24	21	2C	20	25	14	1S	11	18	1C
Thursday	7*	2	2	1	1T	2	2	1	11	2	2		1	1	2
BRADFORD	2½	24	2V	26	25	1C	11	31	19F	21	2		6	22	20G
	6	24	2L	26	25	1C	11	31	19F	21	2S	23	6	22	20G
Tuesday	7¼	1	2	2T	23	2	1	2	P	1	2		2	2	2
CHEWTON	2½	10	21C	28	18		5	16	6	28	12	28	18	16	10
	6	10	16C	28	18	11	12	28	6L	28	5		18	16	10
Tuesday	7		1T		28		28		2		28		28		28
KEYNSHAM	2½	18	16	6	2C	20	12	28	26	1	5		10	29R	6
	6	18	21	6	2C	19L	5	16	26	1S	12	28	10	29R	6
Thursday	7	30	1	30	2T	30	28	30	2	30	1		30	2	30
SALTFORD	6*	5	12	20	19C	6	18	10	1L	24	16	5	28	2S	11
Thursday	7	1		2		1T		2		1			2		1
STANTON	6	16	20	1L	12	28	26	19C	2S	11	21	10	22	5	24
Wednesday	7		1		2T		10		2		1			2	
FRESHFORD	2½	6	23	24	11	22	2C	5	16	20	26		21	25	19R
	6*	6L	23	24	11	22	2C	5	16	20	26	19	21	25	19R
Wednesday	7	1		2		2T		2		1			2		2
BURNETT	6	28	10	22	5	16	6C	21	24	18	10	16	1L	12	26
Tuesday	7				2T						1				
LOWER BRISTOL RD. P.M.	2½	7		7		26		4		15			8		9
FERRY LANE P.M.	2½		7		4		24		7		19			7	
BATH, *Sunday Morning* P.M.	7	1	21	22	19	20	26	21	1	24	25	1	1	20	1
,, *S. School Address*	2½			11					20					1	
,, *Prayer Meeting*	3	4	25	20	7	7	7	7	4	7	4		7	4	7
,, *Prayer M. & class, M.*	7*8	1	1	1†	1	1†	1	1†	1	1†	1		1†	1	1†
,, *Class, School R..M.*	8	2P	14	2P	2	2P	14	2P	2	2P	14		2P	2	2P
,, *Prayer Meeting ..F.*	7	1	1	1	1	1	1	1	1	1	1		1	1	1
TWERTON, *P.M...Su.Morn.*	7	13	13	11	13	13	6	13	13	11	13	13	13	6	13
,, *PrayerM.......Tu.*	7*	2	6	1	1	1	1	1	6	2	11		1	1	1
BRADFORD, *PrayerM...Fr.*	7¼	2	P	2	P	2	2	P	2	2	P		2	P	2

	Preachers.	Residences.
1	BEST	22, Twerton Hayes
2	HARVEY	Bradford Leigh
3	POPE	6, Walcot Parade
4	FEAR	4, Nelson Place
5	COLLYER	Saltford
6	GILBERT	Twerton
7	COWARD	8, Claverton Place
8	PONSFORD	Bathwick Street
9	RICHARDS	11, Kingsmead Street
10	HOLBOROW	Stanton
11	HUMPHRIES	Twerton
12	TANNER	Stanton
13	STROUD	Twerton
14	HUNT	22, Market Place
15	SALISBURY	33, Walcot Street
16	JANES	Burnett
17	YOUNG	2, Grove Street
18	HUMPHRIES	Stanton
19	REVELL	2, Avon Street
20	BRASS	Stall Street
21	THORLEY	James's Street
22	KNIGHT	Stall Street
23	BOX	Bradford
24	BUTLER	Lower Bristol Road
25	HACKER	Ferry Lane

Exhorter.

26 COWARD, H. 8, Claverton Place

Prayer Leaders.

27 G. J.
28 W. B. T. G.

Supplies.

29 Mr. LAMBERT
30 At Keynsham
31 At Bradford

References.—A. chapel anniversary, B. baptism, C. collection, E. teachers meeting, F. fund collection, G. gas collection, H. school superintendent, L. lovefeast, P. prayer meeting, R. rent collection. S. sacrament. S.A. school anniversary, T. tickets, V. visit to schools, * preachers to lead the class, † leaders' meeting, ‡ circuit committee meeting.

Renewal of Tickets to Bath Classes.

F. W. HUNT'S S... Nov 1st by No. 2
C. CRITCHETT'S... ,, 1st ,, ,, 2
H. POPE'S........ ,, 1st ,, ,, 3
PREACHER'S W. .. ,, 4th ,, ,, 1
F. W. HUNT'S F... ,, 6th ,, ,, 1
PREACHER'S S..... ,, 8th ,, ,, 1
SABBATH EV., VESTRY 8th ,, ,, 1
J. BEST'S........ ,, 9th ,, ,, 1
J. YOUNG'S....... ,, 13th ,, ,, 1
M. HARVEY'S..... ,, 16th ,, ,, 2
Juvenile.......... ,, 18th ,, ,, 1

Notices.

1. The next QUARTERLY MEETING will be held at Bath, December 7th, at one o'clock.
2. Bath CHAPEL ANNIVERSARY.—November 29th, by the Rev. T. Hobson of Hereford.
3. REVIVAL MEETINGS.—Freshford, October 18th, by 6, 21, 22. Stanton, November 1st, by 1, 21. Twerton, November 1st, by 14, 11, 16. Keynsham, November 15th, by 19, 11, 20. Chewton, December 6th, by 6, 12. Saltford, December 6th, by 1, 5, 10. Burnett, December 27th, by 1, 19.
4. TEA MEETING, at Bath November 30th, at Five o'clock p.m.
5. PROTRACTED MEETING at Bradford, fourth week in November, to be Addressed on the Sabbath by 11, 23. Monday, by 2. Tuesday, 2. Wednesday, 1. Thursday, 1. Friday, 2.
6. WATCH-NIGHT Services will be held December 31st, to commence at Ten o'clock p.m.: Bath, by 1, 6, 11, 20. Twerton, by 2, 19, 21, 22. The other places must arrange their own.
7. Persons wishing to become subscribers for the Primitive Methodist large or Juvenile Magazines for 1858, are respectfully requested to give their names to one of the Ministers on or before December 10th, current.
8. The Primitive Methodist Almanack for 1858 will be published at 1d.; bound in leather with diary, 6d.; with diary, cash accounts, and sundry tables, neat pocket book, tucked and gilt, 1s. 6d. Order early of the Ministers.
9. The Circuit Committees are composed of the local preachers and Mr. Horner, to meet when planned. J. Reynolds, circuit steward; J. Best, treasurer; W. Vaughan, secretary.
10. Hymn-Books, and other connexional publications can be obtained of the Ministers.

Regulations.

1. No unauthorized person must occupy our pulpits.
2. Personal offences and trespasses must be adjusted by the law of Christ, in Matthew xviii, 15, 17.
3. Preachers must be punctual to time, attend to rule in reference to the length of preaching services, avoid neglects and unnecessary exchanges of appointments, publish and make collections, and lead class according to plan; and if unable to supply their appointments, must themselves provide an accredited substitute.
4. Any Preacher who shall neglect his appointments, shall, for the first offence be admonished, for the second be left without appointments, and for the third be put off the plan.

The Conqueror from Bozrah—By J. BEST.

"*Glorious in his Apparel.*"—Isaiah lxiii, 1. (*Tune*—"MARY.")

Behold he comes the mighty Lord,
With garments dipped in blood!
His foes are conquered by his sword,
Though long they him withstood.

His aspect is most dignified!
As decked in glory bright;
His name by all is magnified
Who in his cause delight.

His royal brow, majestic, frowns
Destruction on his foes;
He onwards, as his zeal abounds,
To further conquest goes.

With strength invincible his arm
Alone salvation brought,
His thunders spread abroad alarm,
When he for Zion wrought.

Millions redeemed have felt his power,
And yielded to his love,
Who now extol him, and adore
His name in songs above.

His glorious banner soon shall wave,
O'er every land and sea;
The lost shall know his might to save,
The captive shall be free.

"The year of my redeemed is come,"
The long predicted time:
Messiah's will, be gladly done,
By men of every clime.

Hast happy day! expected long,
When at his Sovereign feet,
The *universe* in gladsome song,
His wonders shall repeat.

J. COGSWELL, Printer, 38 Kingsmead Street, Bath. [PRICE 2d.

The Primitive Methodist Preachers' Plan from October 1857 to January 1858. The "Regulations" are interesting.

following places: Chewton, Keynsham (to Bristol 1883), Pipehouse, Corston, Larkhall, Lower Westwood, Winsley, Dover Street, Burnett, Steppes Hill, Saltford, Bradford Wine Street and Farleigh.

In addition, the following places were served before 1850 but survived for only a short time: Combe Down, Kelston, Marksbury, Hinton, Dolemead, Tunley, Bathford, Ashton Hill, Tyning Lane, Oak Street, Philips Norton, Bristol Road, Stoke, Newton, Wilmington, Claverton, Park Corner, Woolard, Compton, Mount Pleasant, Charlton, Batheaston, Swainswick and Stanton Prior.

The extent of the Bath Primitive Methodist Circuit a little later is shown on the facsimile Preaching Plan covering 18th October 1857 to 10th January 1858.

7

Meanwhile at New King Street 1829–1847

Space at a Premium

NEW KING STREET chapel, despite the availability of Walcot, was proving to be inadequate. A chapel south of the river was now needed. At Widcombe, about 1822, a "neat and commodious place of worship" had been erected by "some gentlemen of the Independent denomination". The minister for whom it was intended had "disappointed the hopes of his friends", and it fell into "other hands". It became vacant again and was offered for rent to the Wesleyans who seized the chance to gain a 700 seat chapel just when their need was greatest.

The opening services were held on 28th November 1834, the preachers being the Revs. A. E. Farrar from London, and William Jay from Argyle Street Independents. Why and when the premises were forsaken by the Methodists we do not know; it was before 1851. Ebenezer chapel was eventually taken over by the Baptists, (see the photograph) and its text-covered roofs are a familiar sight in Bath today. By 1851 Methodists were using the Widcombe Temperance Hall, today's Church of the Nazarene, as our photograph shows it (building dated 1847).

In 1829 the 50th anniversary of New King Street's opening by John Wesley was celebrated by special services addressed by the Rev James Wood, who had been present 50 years earlier. "The chapel was crowded to excess and many hundreds could not gain admission." Three surviving Shum brothers, John, George and Michael were present.

For over 40 years John Jacob Shum, the eldest of the family, rose at 4am for prayer and reading. He conducted the Sunday prayer meetings at 5am. When past the age of 80 he walked

Once known as the Widcombe Temperance Hall, the Church of the Nazarene stands in 1989 on a busy Ring Road.

Ebenezer Chapel, Widcombe in 1989, now in Baptist hands. It was occupied by the Wesleyans in the 1830s and 1840s.

several miles each day visiting the sick and poor. In that way he spent his last day. The next morning at 3am he woke his neice explaining: "I'm going home". And so, on 13th January, 1832 he died before a doctor could be summoned. He was the oldest and last of the five. His brother Michael had died three months earlier.

A large sum was spent in 1832 on repairing and cleaning the chapel. Ten years later complaints about the ventilation were still rife. It was widely known as "the Bakehouse" or "the Oven". The pulpit was placed on pillars presumably to enable the preacher to be seen and heard by all present. By this time the debt on the chapel had risen to £1,480, and on the house it was £400. The premises, which were supposed to accommodate 650, were not only overcrowded on Sundays. There were also an incredible number of class meetings every week, no less than 52 in all between New King Street and Walcot, and of these 26 met at the former and eight at the latter. The others met in private premises. The numbers on the classbooks averaged 20, some as high as 29. What proportion attended we cannot tell, but the pressure on some homes must have been quite embarrassing.

A Venture of Faith

It soon became clear that there was only one thing to be done. A new chapel was required to replace the old one. The new project was pursued with speed and efficiency. It would be interesting to estimate how long the process would take in modern days. A "Committee for Enlarging New King Street Chapel" was set up on 9th October 1846. The new chapel was destined to open for worship only 14 months later.

Mr James Wilson, the well-known local church architect, was invited to submit plans for a building seating 1,200 and costing about £1,600. The Committee undertook to raise £700 before any financial commitment was undertaken. Within a week the Committee had obtained promises of £475 mainly out of their own pockets. By the middle of November the architect produced his plans, and these were outlined to a meeting of 600 members and seat-holders. By January 1847 the full £700 had been promised. It was decided to purchase extra adjoining land for £550 which included an inn called *The Heart Encompassed.* All the details having been examined and settled, in May, 1847 the decision was taken to proceed and the building contract was signed. The "Bazaar Room" in Quiet Street was hired for temporary use by the congregation, also a house for class meetings and chapel keeper's residence.

In November the pew prices were settled: Trustees and the Committee would have first choice, those subscribing over £10 would come next. Prices per quarter would be: The body of the church, 12 front pews — 3s; Others — 2s.6d; The rows next to free sittings — 2s; (free pews were without doors); Gallery, front — 3s, then 2s.6d; and the back 2s. The sides — 1s.6d; next to Sunday School 1s.

The new church was opened on 10th December 1847, the preachers being the Rev. Samuel Jackson, President of the Conference, Rev. W. Chalmers, Rev. J. McLean, Rev. J. Rattenbury, Rev. J. Lomas, and of course the Superintendent at Bath, Rev. John Rigg. Mr Jackson was substituting for Dr Bunting who was suffering from influenza. The amount collected at the opening services reached an incredible £285. At the conclusion the financial position was as follows:

Cost of building church, buying land, architect's fee, organ, temporary hiring etc	£4,037
Debt on former chapel and house	£1,830
Total	£5,867
Subscriptions and donations	£832
Mrs Clement's legacy	£500
Collections at opening services	£285
Total	£1,617

This left a deficiency of £4,250 which was raised by securing 26 investments of varying amounts on which interest was payable at 4½ per cent per annum.

The photograph shows the church in the 1930's hemmed in by what were fashionable terrace houses.

New King Street Wesleyan Chapel in the 1930s. Compare this with the photograph in Chapter 15 after the bomb damage (Page 135).

8

Breakaway Movements 1837-1881

The Wesleyan Methodist Association

WE HAVE already described the establishment of the Primitive Methodists in Bath. Another group which had set up independently was the "Wesleyan Methodist Association", started in 1835 as a protest against the over-riding power of Jabez Bunting at the centre of Methodist administration. This organisation had a branch in Bath. They registered "a certain building" in September 1837; in November 1841 they moved to "Wesley Chapel" in Bridewell Lane. The expansion of the General Hospital — today's Royal National Hospital for the Treatment of Rheumatic Diseases — caused them to vacate their premises. They moved first to the Corridor Rooms (capacity 350) in about 1856. Due to a national link-up with the Wesleyan Reformers they became known thenceforward as the United Methodist Free Church. As we shall see, the Wesleyan Reformers in Bath remained aloof from any such union until 1869.

In 1859 the UMFC moved into larger premises in York Street which seated 450; there they remained for seven years. They purchased, at a cost of £650 in 1866 a building in Lower Borough Walls of great religious significance. It was here that the Roman Catholics' new chapel was burned down in the Gordon Riots in 1780 — two days before it was due to open. Since then it had been re-built and occupied by various sects, and eventually by the Quakers. The UMFC re-named it Hope Chapel and remained in occupation until 1913. It subsequently became a printing works as our photograph of 1964 shows.

The United Methodists established Societies at Box, Box

In 1964 Hope Chapel in Lower Borough Walls was still recognisable though converted to commercial purposes.

Hill, Kingsdown, Wadswick and Twerton. As the 1888 Circuit Plan shows, at that time the Twerton Society was independent of the others in the Bath area.

The Wesleyan Reformers

In 1851 a serious breach occurred which divided Wesleyan Methodists in Bath into two roughly equal camps. This was the "Fly Sheets" controversy. A number of anonymous leaflets had been published in London in 1846 and 1848 which were bitterly critical of the manner in which cliques and self-interest were said to predominate in the central organisations of the Wesleyans.

To find out who was responsible for the leaflets the Conference required all ministers to sign a document dissociating themselves from the sentiments expressed in the Flysheets in the following terms: "We the undersigned, agree to declare that we regard with indignation and abhorrence the anonymous attacks on the motives and character of our Brethren that have recently appeared in certain clandestine publications; that we have never intentionally communicated with the authors of those publications with a view to affording informa-

UNITED METHODIST FREE CHURCHES.

PLAN FOR THE PREACHERS IN THE BATH CIRCUIT, 1888.

NAMES OF PLACES. "Take heed therefore how ye hear."—Luke viii. 15.	JULY. 1	8	15	22	29	AUGUST. 5	12	19	26	SEPTEMBER. 2	9	16	23	30
HOPE CHAPEL .... 11 .... 6.30 Tuesday 7	Williams Williams s Fisher	French French Spurway	Anniver- sary CA Nowell	King Hacker Dorey	Isaacs Isaacs Brass	Perry Perry Dorey	Meredith Meredith Spurway	Park Dunston Fisher	Caple Caple Hacker	Isaacs Isaacs Dorey	Nowell King Nowell	Dorey Park Fisher	French French Spurway	Holbrook Holbrook Brass
P.M., Friday Evening............ 7	J. Blake Davis	Meredith Dorey	Nowell J. Blake	West Harding	Dudfield Fisher	E. Blake Baggs	Dorey Nowell	Cottle E. Blake	Harding Davis	Fisher Dudfield	Baggs Harding	Dudfield Dorey	J. Blake Nowell	Martin Perry
BOX .... 11 6 Wednesday 7	Dorey Dorey s Street	Fisher Fisher Hunt	Dancey Dancey Dancey	George George Hobbs	French French Stowers	Hobbs s Hobbs Street	Spurway Spurway W. Dancey	King King Hobbs	Hunt Hunt W. Dancey	Nowell Nowell Street	Farmer Farmer s W. Dancey	Street Street Hunt	Dorey Dorey Hunt	W. Dancey W. Dancey Dancey
BOX HILL .... 3 6 Wednesday 6.45	Hacker Hacker s W. Dancey	Spurway Spurway Dancey	Hunt Hunt Hunt	Dorey Dorey Street	Park Park Hobbs	Dancey Dancey s Stowers	Nowell Camp Meet. L	King Porter Hunt	W. Dancey W. Dancey Dancey	Fisher Fisher Bailey	Dorey Dorey Hunt	Hobbs Hobbs Street	Spurway Spurway Hobbs	Bailey Bailey W. Dancey
P.M., Sunday Morning 9	Lane	Dancey	Neate	W. Dancey	Lane	Dancey	Neate	W. Dancey	Lane	Dancey	Neate	W. Dancey	Lane	Dancey
KINGSDOWN .... 3 6 Thursday 7	Nowell Camp Meet. LA	Hobbs Hobbs PM	Farmer Farmer Hobbs	Spurway Spurway PM	Sleigh Sleigh Street	SSA SSA PM	Dorey Dorey Hunt	Hunt Hunt PM	Camp Meeting W. Dancey	Street Street PM	Fisher Fisher Hobbs	Nowell Nowell PM	W. Dancey W. Dancey Bailey	Dancey Dancey PM
P.M., Sunday Morning 9	Angell	Brown	Bailey	Hawkins	T. Stowers	Butt	S. Stowers	Fletcher	Brown	Hawkins	Bailey	Angell	S. Stowers	Butt
WADSWICK............ 3.15 6 Thursday............ 6.45	Farmer Farmer	Dorey Dorey	Hobbs Hobbs	Street Street	Porter Porter	W. Dancey W. Dancey	Fisher Fisher	Spurway Spurway	Dancey Dancey	Dorey Dorey	Spurway Spurway	Bailey Bailey	Fisher Fisher	Hunt Hunt

PREACHERS AND RESIDENCES.

"Preach the Word."—2 Timothy iv. 2.

J. FOULGER ......99, Calton Road, Bath.
B. TURVEY ...Brook Leigh, Lockabrook.
I. J. NOWELL, 1, Lower Borough Walls.
W. H. WEST............2, Bathwick Villas.
D HOBBS ....Box Hill.
H. SPURWAY ....York Street, Bath.
G. DANCEY ....Box Hill.
J. HUNT...Box.
J. H DOREY...Upper Bristol Road, Bath.
E. STREET ....Wadswick, Box.
W. DANCEY.................................Box Hill.
T. BAILEY ....Kingsdown.
J. FISHER...Bath.

ON TRIAL.

S. STOWERS.. ....Kingsdown.

AUXILIARIES.

H. SMART ....Claverton.
P. BENNETT.........Box Cottage, Staplehill.
F. SMITH..................................East Twerton.
F. RUSSELL ....Bath.
H. HACKER ......7, Dorchester Street, Bath.
J. E. GEORGE . ...Bath.
A. MILLARD 3, Beaumont Villas, Oldfield Pk.
W. BARTLETT, 112, Coronation Rd., Bristol.
W. WILLIAMS ....Bath.
W. D. PORTER ....Batheaston.
J. GODING..Bath.
W. H. HUNTLEY..Bath.
A. GLENDALL ....Bath.
R. FARMER ....Bath.
W. E. KING..Bath.

Hope Chapel Anniversary July 15th; Tea Meeting 16th, at 6 p.m. Camp Meetings will be held at Kingsdown July 1st and Aug. 26th; Box Hill, Aug. 12th Wadswick Aug. 19th. Sunday School Anniversary at Kingsdown Aug. 5th; Tea Meeting Aug. 6th, at 5 p.m.

CIRCUIT OFFICERS.

Circuit Steward—J. MARTIN Newark Street, Bath.
„ Secretary—E HARDING 12, Cheltenham Street, Bath.
„ Missionary Treasurer, and Secretary—I. J. NOWELL, Lower Boro' Walls.
„ Preacher's Secretary—B. TURVEY, Brook Leigh, Lockabrook.

CIRCUIT COMMITTEE.

H. COX, S. DUDFIELD, S. PERRY, J HUNT, D. LOBBS, G. DANCEY, S. STOWERS, J. HALES and the Circuit Officers.

SOCIETY STEWARDS.

Bath—W. H. DAVIS, Lorne Terrace, Twerton.
Box—H. NEATE, Clock House, Box
Box Hill—W. LANE, Box Hill.
Kingsdown—J. MILLARD, Shockerwick.
Wadswick—J. HALES, Wadswick.

NOTICES.

The Offertory system will be continued for the present at Hope Chapel, to be taken at the door in the Morning, and by public collection in the Evening, of each Sunday, in lieu of Lighting and Cleaning and Circuit Collections.

Bible Classes are held at Hope Chapel on Sunday Afternoons at 3 o'clock, as follows: Young Men's Class conducted by Mr W. H. West. Young Women's Class, conducted by Mr. E. Blake. Young Men and Women are heartily invited.

The Magazines, Hymn Books, and Chant Books, of the United Methodist Free Churches, can be obtained from the Rev. J. Foulger. Plans may be obtained of the Chapel Keepers, at the Chapels.—Price Twopence

The Circuit Quarterly Meeting will be held at Box Hill on Sept. 5th at 6.0 p.m. Preachers' Quarterly Meeting at Hope Chapel on Sept. 1st, at 6 p.m. (Chairman, I. J. Nowell, Secretary, B. Turvey). Plan Committee Meeting at Hope Chapel on Sept. 10th, at 7 p.m.

The conveyance leaves Mrs. Noble's, at Box, at 8-15 each Sunday night when required.

C A. signifies Chapel Anniversary; C.C., Circuit Collection; C.M., Church Meetings; C.R.F., Chapel Relief Fund; H.C., Hospital Collection; H.H.C., Horse Hire Collection; H.T.S. Harvest Thanksgiving Services; J.MM., Juvenile Missionary Meeting; L., Lovefeast; L.C.C., Lighting and Cleaning Collection; L.M., Leaders' Meeting; P.M., Prayer Meeting; R.T., Renewal of Tickets; R.S., Revival Services; T.S., Temperance Sermon; S., Sacrament; S.S.A., Sunday School Anniversary.

The Stewards are requested to have proper notice given of the Sacraments, Lovefeasts, Collections, etc., on the previous Sabbath; also, to have all Circuit Contributions brought to the Circuit Quarterly Meeting.

Baptism will be administered at the various places, when required.

Each Preacher is expected to fulfil his own appointment, or if unavoidably prevented, *himself* to provide an accredited substitute.

MARRIAGES SOLEMNIZED AT HOPE CHAPEL, BATH; & AT BOX HILL.

BROWN AND CO., PRINTERS, BATH.

The United Methodist Free Church Plan for July to September 1888. It would seem that the Rev J Foulger had left the Circuit and his successor not appointed to take any services. The Plan contains several Camp Meetings.

tion or assistance; and that we will not allow their wicked slanders to detract from the esteem and confidence we feel towards those against whom such attacks are directed." By 1849 most had signed. Some refused on grounds of conscience or for other reasons. Amongst those who refused were three minsters who were suspected of being the authors. They were expelled. Another of those who refused to sign was the popular minister at Walcot, the Rev. James Bromley.

The responsibility inevitably fell upon the District to deal with him following the receipt by the Rev. John Rigg of a letter from London which was dated the 1st February 1850, that letter contained these accusations:

> The Rev. J. Bromley has by certain recent proceedings violated the great principles of our Connexional Union, namely that when any question has been discussed and decided by the Conference, the minority shall quietly submit to the majority, or possibly retire from the Body.
> He has made himself the public apologist of, and has openly abetted, the slanderers of his brother ministers.
> He has grossly aspersed the public acts and principles of his ministerial brethren.
> He has broken the pledges given by himself to the last Conference, in consideration of which the judicial proceedings in his case were arrested.

A special District Meeting of ministers was convened. Backed by the Trustees at Walcot, Mr Bromley declined to attend, demanding a "mixed court" of ministers and laymen. He also delivered a series of sermons conveying in no uncertain terms his scorn of the kind of discipline to which he was being subjected. There was great support for Mr Bromley locally as there was nationally for others like him. On 7th March a public meeting was called at Bath's Guildhall to enable Mr Bromley's supporters to make their views known to the public. Amidst continual applause, and hissing towards the Methodist hierarchy, comments were made of which this is typical:

"Conference has been intolerant and cruel, expelling three distinguished ministers, degrading a fourth, and oh how I dislike the word, it is so humiliating, suspending a fifth. Our Reverend friend, my opinion is settled that we are right and the Conference is verily in the wrong. The Revs. Jay, Owen, Wassell, Gillson, Hobson, and Ripon came to our rescue. Their pulpits were thrown open when our own were shut against our Pastor." (The ministers named represented the Independent, Huntingdon, Baptist and Primitive denominations).

According to contemporary reports there were 1,000 present. By some miracle tea was served. The statistics-conscious reporter claimed that 65 ladies were needed to achieve it! Before the meeting was over 100 guineas was promised "to place him above pecuniary want, if expelled." Mr Bromley said the money would be a sort of "premium for discontent" but for the wise proviso about being expelled first. He feared circumstances would compel him to throw himself on their generosity. He was right. He resided at 10 Hanover Street after moving out of the chapel-house. The Rev. William Willan moved in.

Mr Bromley and his followers, in 1850, hired the upper floor of a building in Broad Street used as a coach manufactory. The 1851 census — about which more later — tells us that it seated 680, and that the actual attendance on census day was high, being no less than 600 in the morning and 556 in the evening. In December 1851 the Walcot Trustees accepted the resignation of ten of their members and relieved them of financial responsibilities. They passed a resolution "regretting that Conference is not disposed to listen to the reasonable demands of the people . . . or to restore peace and harmony to our distracted Societies". In fact by this time the Wesleyan Reformers as they were known occupied 11 places of worship in the Bath area with a total attendance of 2,808, compared with the Wesleyans who in 16 chapels attracted 3,035. So the bizarre outcome of the Flysheets affair for Bath was the virtual halving of the Wesleyan adherents and their income. The membership of Walcot stood at 315 in 1848; in 1850 it was 186 and it continued to fall until 1857 when it reached 132 before beginning to climb again. It must be emphasised that the national picture was quite different. The 1851 census totals for attendance were:-

Wesleyans .....1,544,528 Wesleyan Reformers 91,503

Mr Bromley had, by 1857, removed his congregation to the

resplendent domed room at 9 Quiet Street known as "The Bazaar" because it had previously been used for auction sales. It had also temporarily housed the New King Street congregation while their new chapel was under construction in 1847.

In 1861 any association with the Methodists appears to have been terminated, for the name "Independent Congregational" was adopted. However in 1869, when Mr Bromley died, it was decided to join the United Methodist Free Church at Hope Chapel, and the Quiet Street premises were vacated.

The New Connexion

Before we turn our attention to larger matters there is one other dissident Methodist Society in Bath whose story must be told. As long ago as 1797 a break-away group demanding greater democracy in Methodist affairs had been formed nationally under Alexander Kilham and was known as the Methodist New Connexion. Never numerically of any great consequence they first appeared in Bath about 1855. They met initially in a room off The Corridor, and moved into the Quiet Street chapel in 1869 when the Bromleyites moved out. Some of the congregation however remained at the Corridor until 1874 under the Rev. Thomas Anthony and called themselves "The Independent New Connexion".

The Society was never large or influential enough to be free from financial embarrassment; their ministers were too constantly being switched around; the choice often lay between experienced married ones whom they could not afford or unmarried fledglings whom they preferred not to have. When one minister was taken ill the President of the New Connexion, the Rev. C. D. Ward, attended as supply. His stint finished, he expected to be paid. The local Society declined as they were in debt and suggested the Committee which sent the sick minister was responsible. Ward's reply advising them to seek a grant is a gem: "Any brother however healthy when appointed might have broken down; therefore Providence and not the Missionary Committee should be recognised as the Author of this Visitation."

With membership fluctuating around 55 it was obvious that they could not afford to build a new church and when the owners of the Quiet Street chapel gave them notice to quit they were too demoralised to argue. After 26 years of survival the little society ceased to meet on 9th June 1881. The Wesleyan Quarterly Meeting considered the propriety of inviting them to join New King Street or Walcot and left it that "each member of the meeting, as the opportunity arose, to invite them to either place." Most of the members from Quiet Street chose, however, to go elsewhere, mainly to Hope Chapel. In doing so they anticipated the national unification of New Connexion and United Methodist Free Church which eventually occurred in 1907.

9

Helping the Poor 1790 onwards

A Nation-wide Movement

THE STRANGERS' Friend Society was founded in 1786 by a Cornish exciseman named James Chubb. Living in Bristol he worshipped at the New Room. His journal for September 1786 reads: "I was called to visit the sick. My friends and I agreed to search for poor, sick, distressed creatures. Each visitor subscribed weekly towards the relief of those in great want. These visits also done good to our own souls and kindled a flame in our Society." In 1790 John Wesley visited Bristol. Chubb records: "Rev. John Wesley met the Visitors of the Sick and appointed me and Thomas Delve Stewards and called us 'The Strangers' Friend Society'. We now went on our way rejoicing." John Wesley himself wrote that the organisation was "instituted wholly for the relief, not of our society, but for poor, sick, friendless strangers." Societies were quickly formed in London, Liverpool, Dublin and Manchester. The society at Bath was founded in 1790.

Unfortunately detailed records do not exist of the early years. The general rules specified that

1. The Visitors meet every Sunday Morning at 10am at New King Street.
2. Treasurers and two secretaries look after the books.
3. Books may be inspected by Subscribers and the public.
4. Visitors to be of unblameable character, capable of instructing those visited in the way of righteousness and praying with and for them.
5. They diligently and impartially seek for those in greatest need and relieve them according to their necessities.

> 6. Whatever relief is granted be given to the persons themselves.
> 7. No person to be relieved previously to being visited.

We know that by 1875, the Society was dealing with some 900 visits a year, but spending only about £45 which represents only 1s each time. Mr F. Shum pointed out that unlike other charities, the SFS gave relief only to these known personally. Another speaker at the AGM in 1891, under the Mayor's chairmanship, said that economists were trying to eliminate poverty; they were considering compulsory insurance. His serious suggestions for work to give the unemployed, based on Parisian ideas, make fascinating reading;

> Rags make paper; broken glass pounded coats sandpaper; bones make nail-brushes, tooth-brushes and fancy buttons; little wisps of women's hair carefully unravelled do duty for false hair. Men's hair collected outside barbers' shops serves for filters through which syrups are strained; bits of sponge cut up may be used for spirit lamps; bits of bread if dirty can be toasted, grated and sold to restaurants for spreading on hams and cutlets, or made into tooth powder.

With the introduction of Old Age Pensions in 1909, much of the burden was taken over by the State. However, even as recently as 1954, nine people were each receiving grants of 5s per month. In 1955 occurred the first grant to an organisation, namely Stratton House (Methodist Home for the Aged) which received £1.1s.0d. Soon all grants were going to good causes and the whole character of the fund was irrevocably changed. Eventually, with investments of £1,100, it was taken over by the Bath Circuit Social Responsibility Committee.

The Poor's Fund

An insight into the plight of some of the early Methodists can be gained from studying the work undertaken by the Committee of the Poor of the Methodist Society in Bath. This was a comparatively low key organisation which distributed the collections taken at Communion Services and Love-feasts, after deducting expenses. Gifts from well-wishers swelled the sums available for distribution. We know that £36.19s.0d was received in 1800; by 1817 receipts in the year had risen to £67. Mr Joseph Pearson was the indefatigable secretary and treasurer from 1815 to 1820, a time when he was also much committed to Sunday School work, particularly at Walcot.

There were 27 persons in 1809 each receiving 2s per month (a few got 3s). By 1815 the number of needy folk was growing and a new system was required. The Committee consisting of Messrs J. Pearson, J. Shum, M. Shum, Orchard, Jenkins and Hartnell divided the list into three categories. Those in Category 1 were paid 2s every month; Category 2 every quarter; and Category 3 less often. The records show the names, ages and addresses of recipients, the span of church membership, parish relief and a note about their condition.

Let some of these entries basically recorded in 1815 speak for themselves:

Category	Name	Age	Church (years)	Comment
1	Amy Sims	76	13	Lame. No friends. No meat. Parish pays 2s.
1	Jane Slip	83	21	Nearly blind. Past working. Parish nil.
1	Sarah Cullin	76	45	Sells oranges. Trade bad. Seen better days
1	William Dukes	69	47	Widower. Asthma. Maintains granddaughter, an orphan. (Later, in 1818, arrived in America).
1	Sarah Wheeler	36	4	Dropsey. Cannot help herself (died 1817).
1	Jas Mills	79	6	Worked on roads. Past work in winter. Infirm.
3	Thos Goodenough	46	2	A chairman. Three small children
2	Chas Cottle	63	3	Nearly blind. Cannot work. Address: "Behind the prison in a little hut" Parish 1s.
3	Jane Lear	?	?	Ill lately. A bad woman.

1	Mrs Bolwell	71	45	Asthma. Seen better days. Parish 3s.
1	John Hackler	94	14	Bedridden. Parish 2s.6d. (died 1818).
1	Eliz Membury	37	4	In decline. Parish 4s. (died 1816).
1	Diana Sweet	70	23	Quite infirm. Parish 2s.6d. Friend gives 6d weekly.
3	Mary Spencer	36	3	Weakly. Poor. Three children. Parish 5s.
1	Thos Mitchell	71	9	Asthma. Infirm. No friends. Parish 2s.6d. (At peace 1821).

Casual payments were made to meet specific needs eg:

> Mr Dukes towards wife's funeral 5s.
> Susan Walford in dying circumstances 4s.
> Ann Gain towards child's funeral 3s.

An appeal went out in 1821:

> "There are 42 poor persons belonging to the Methodist Society in Bath, 27 of whom are aged and most past work, the remaining 15 are all poor and stand in need of relief, beside cases of great distress and a number of occasional poor which are visited regularly by members of the Committee. Many of the above persons have been 20, 30, 40, and 50 years in our Society and have seen better days. On their behalf the Committee would beg all our Christian friends to lend some aid to this good work".

The Shums were always amongst the lists of subscribers. From 1823 onwards the category of "3rd Poor" was dropped. Also the record book ceased to give any information about specific individuals who were helped. From 1826, some of the responsibility devolved on class leaders. "Paid the poor in part, some of the leaders having paid their own; others who had no poor in their classes subscribing."

From 1830 the accounts fail to tell us anything beyond the cost of the wine etc and the amount of money distributed.

From 1866, donations to the fund ceased. In 1887 there was a "Society tea for poor members costing 6s.6d". By 1941 the last tiny allocation of money to "the poor" ceased. In 1950, after a long debate and in answer to the chairman's question: "Does anyone know of anyone worthy of assistance?" donations to organised charities were authorised as the proper way to maintain the work of the fund.

10

Statistical Evidence 1851 and 1881

The Mid-point in our Story

THE GREAT Ecclesiastical Census took place on 30th March 1851. This was probably a wet day and may have influenced attendance. All places of worship were invited to complete a Return giving details of their accommodation, and the number of worshippers.

Before looking at the Bath figures in detail, it may be interesting to examine the way the census revealed the expansion of non-Conformity over a wider area during the previous 50 years. In *Christianity in Somerset,* Robert Dunning has analysed the reported dates of foundation of societies in Somerset, including Bath, revealing the following pattern:

Denomination	before 1801	1801–11	1812–21	1822–31	1832–41	1842–51	No date
Congregationalist	36	6	4	14	25	21	1
Baptist: Particular	14	4	8	10	13	10	3
Undefined	3		4	4	7	7	2
Quaker	9		1	1	1	3	
Unitarian	8						
Methodist:							
Original Connexion	19	13	27	31	47	44	21
Primitive	7	1	2	2	3	11	7
Bible Christian	5	2	1	5	11	15	5
Wesleyan Assocn				1	2	1	
Wesleyan Reform	4	1	1		1	5	14
Lady Huntingdon's Connexion	1		1			2	
New Church					1	1	
Brethren	2	1	1	1		3	4
Catholic Apostolic				1	1		
Latter Day Saints	1				1	2	2
Isolated Congregations	6					3	1

We now turn to the figures for the Bath Circuits. Because the Registration Districts were based on Poor Law Unions, it was necessary to extract information for the widespread Bath Methodist Circuits from Tables 253, 258, 325, 326 and 327. The figures include, or sometimes show separately, Sunday School scholars who worshipped with the adult congregation. Hence "SS" in the figures.

Name Place	Built	Sittings Free	Other	Attendance AM	SS	Aft	SS	Eve	SS	Average am	pm
PRIMITIVE METHODISTS											
Dunkerton Carlington Lane	1841	80	45	40	94			90		150	
Wellow Single Hill	1847	60	50	40	51			90		NR	
Twerton Not recorded	1846	70	71		40	100	40	140		NR	
Westgate (House to Chapel)	1845 1849	127	305	400	37			500	30	NR	
Saltford (Cottage kitchen)	NR							50		NR	
Priston (House used for 6 yrs)	NR							35			15
WESLEYAN METHODISTS											
Wellow Cottage	NR	30				17		21		NR	
Hinton NR	1814	120	40					50			70
Midford NR	1837	80		46				65		46	65
Twerton NR	1816	80	220	42	46			100		110	170
Combe Down NR	1821	40								NR	
Faulkland NR	1842	25	96	60	20	65	20	88	19	50	70
Walcot NR	1815	320	600	300	50			400		NR	
		(Day & Sunday School under chapel)									
Larkhall NR	1832	72	108	25	36			35		99	48
Milk St NR	c1815	100			80			70		NR	
New King Street NR	1847	265	850	340	55			370		NR	

Name	Place	Built	Sittings Free	Other	Attendance AM	SS	Aft	SS	Eve	SS	Average am	pm
WESLEYAN METHODISTS (continued)												
Batheaston	NR	Pre 1800	64	48	32				61		NR	
Swainswick Spa Chapel	NR	c1837	30	60	37				35		NR	
Corston	NR	1842	60	70	15	23	19		40		50	75
Tunley-Camerton Parish	NR	1834	78	40			48		95			55
Priston (Room in private house		1831	40	30 #					30			18
Freshford Sharpstone	NR	NR	106*	104*	146*				114*		NR	
WESLEYAN REFORM												
Dunkerton	NR	NR	270		100		50		200		NR	
Wellow Shoscombe	NR	NR	60		40				40		55	
Wellow	NR	1808	95	69	40				150		40	150
Wellow Twinney		Pre 1800	30				20					20
Twerton Old Poor House		NR	110	70	110				150		130	170
Twerton	NR	NR	70	70	145				125		NR	
Combe Down 2 Byfields Buildings (Part dwelling house)		c1815	15	30	30		17		34		NR	
Bath Broad Street (opened 1850 over coach manufactory)		NR	300	380	600	60			556		550	650
Widcombe Temperance Hall (not used exclusively)		NR	150	61	50		70				NR	
Corston Room in cottage		NR			30				70		35	
Box Ebenezer		1834	160		40		18		70		NR	
WESLEYAN METHODIST ASSOCIATION												
Bath Bridewell Lane		1842	80	140	47	48			89		65	110

\# Indicates standing room only
* Estimated by Registrar
NR Not Recorded

It may be helpful at this stage to examine how the other denominations were faring in Bath at this time, what facilities they provided in the way of free and rented seats, and how attendance compared with the Methodists. This time the area covered in our summary of Census figures is confined to the City limits.

Denomination	Churches	Free seats	Others	Attendance
Church of England	28	9163	10477	26415
Independent	2	470	960	2640
Particular Baptist	5	574	1730	3033
Friends	1	300		68
Unitarians	1		300	295
Mormons	1	300		890
Wesleyan Methodists	5	787	1618	1833
Primitive Methodists	1	127	305	967
Wesleyan Association	1	80	140	184
Wesleyan Reformers	2	450	441	1336
Lady Huntingdon's	3	520	550	1590
New Church	1		300	150
Brethren	1	40		82
Isolated Congregations	3	970	250	1550
Roman Catholics	3	70	50	1395
Catholic & Apostolic	1	77	153	206
Saints	1	250		440
Jews	1	10	30	72
Total	61	14188	17304	43146

The Census of 1881 in Bath

On a fine, warm autumn Sunday in 1881, a second religious census was taken in the City of Bath. To avoid criticisms made of the 1851 figures, notice was not given, and the enumerators were all employed by *Keene's Bath Journal*. Before examining the Methodist statistics in some detail it may be helpful to look at a summary of all the denominations in order to observe any big changes in 30 years. The City population was still about 52,000. Children are again included in the figures.

Denomination	Churches	Free seats	Others	Attendance
Church of England	30	10731	9887	21257
Congregational	3	520	1800	2224
Baptists	6	672	1928	2620
Friends	1	150		63
Unitarians	1	50	300	182
Wesleyan Methodists	6	870	1666	2587
Primitive Methodists	2	250	575	1267
Free Methodists	1	100	330	242
Lady Huntingdon's	1	100	500	375
New Church	1	60	200	300
Brethren	3	840		634
Disciples of Christ	1	60		58
Gospel Hall Snow Hill	1	200		122
Mission Dolemeads	1	300		200
Moravian	1	200		148
Odd Fellow's Hall	1	60	70	80
Salvation Barracks	2	800		1354
Roman Catholics	5	290	1006	1697
Catholic & Apostolic	1	200		181
Jews	1	20	20	12
Total	69	16473	18282	35603

(When a third, afternoon, service was held the figures have been omitted from this summary)

The main general observation to be drawn from these figures is more seating but an overall drop in attendance during the intervening years. This is a tendency which will be reflected in our continued study of the life of the Methodist churches in the latter half of the 19th century. However we must not forget that some of the 1851 figures were thought to have been boosted above average by those anxious to present a good picture. Some were also accused of herding in their congregations!

We will now take a closer look at the Methodist figures. It has become a much simpler pattern than in our last review. The "Protesters" are now joined into one small congregation at Hope Chapel. The country areas of the Bath circuits are excluded from this survey. This cuts out Twerton and Weston for they were then outside the city boundaries.

Seats	Church	Attendance Morning	Evening	Total
	Wesleyans			
900	New King Street	549	435	984
1002	Walcot	530	594	1124
230	Larkhall, Dafford Street	87	83	170
124	Milk Street Mission		108	108
80	Widcombe, Temperance Hall	55	68	123
200	Holloway, Workman's Hall		78	78
	Primitives			
700	Westgate Buildings	330	760	1090
125	Claremont	85	92	177
	Free Methodists			
430	Hope, Lower Borough Walls	122	120	242

This census had been taken on 6th November. Four weeks later a further count was organised, this time of children attending Sunday School. The results so far as the Methodists were concerned are summarised as follows:

Teachers Male	Female	Total	Church	Children Male	Female	Total
			Wesleyan			
20	20	40	New King Street	159	193	352
15	12	27	Walcot	103	161	264
4	6	10	Holloway	24	44	68
NR	NR	6	Larkhall	NR	NR	75
7	16	23	Milk Street	67	75	142
1	3	4	Temperance Hall	10	20	30
			Primitive			
8	4	12	Claremont	35	42	77
10	7	17	Westgate Buildings	51	78	129
			United			
8	5	13	Hope	27	49	76

11

Routine Development in Wesleyan Circles 1850–1900

Life at New King Street

AFTER ALL the problems and rifts, the three surviving branches of the Methodist Church settled down to their different ways of working. The New King Street congregation had watched the James Bromley affair with some detachment; very few of their membership transferred their loyalty to the new cause. On Boxing Day 1850 a tea meeting was held which 500 attended. "Delightful harmony prevailed. The Spirit-stirring character of the meeting has never been surpassed. There was a hearty and united determination to support Methodism as it is." Sustained efforts were made to reduce the debt on the new chapel. Many thought that 1853 was a boom year when legacies and gifts enabled £1,500 to be raised for the cause.

Michael Shum and Family

In 1872 the redoubtable John Michael Shum died. For 64 years he had conducted musical worship at New King Street on Sundays and weekdays with talent and devotion. During the week he managed his drapery and menswear shop in Union Street. In 1819 he had married Mary Hall, whose family in Bristol had been Methodists for long enough for her to claim to be a fourth generation Methodist. The Shums (see the line drawing) showed great hospitality in their home at No. 15 Norfolk Crescent to distinguished ministers and young people of the congregation alike. For 55 years without a break they accommodated the annual Missionary deputation. Michael Shum was a composer as well as a player of hymn tunes. He

Mr and Mrs John Michael Shum. Line Drawings by Stan Roe.

was also said to be obstinate at times; for instance if given the wrong number of a tune, nothing would induce him to play another whatever words were sung! He even achieved notoriety by stirring up criticism at the Methodist Conference of 1834 in London. An innovation was reported from Bath. "A whole verse was sung at once at the request or dictation of the organist." Dr Jabez Bunting objected to the organist "dictating". But it was decided that "the middle hymn, if well known, might be sung without being given out". This referred to the practice of reading each line before singing to help illiterate congregations.

Mrs Mary Shum was a collector for Missions for 75 years, starting even before the Missionary Society had been formed. One of her daughters, Caroline Meta Shum, married the Rev. Luke H. Wiseman in 1874 as the marriage certificate shows; her stepson, Dr F. Luke Wiseman, was President of the Wesleyan Conference in 1912 and of the Methodist Conference in 1933. Yet another of her daughters, Mary, married the Rev. G. F. White; their grandson the Rev. Dr Wilbert F. Howard was President in 1944. The third daughter, Sarah, married the Rev. Wm. Davison; their son the Rev. Dr W. T. Davison was

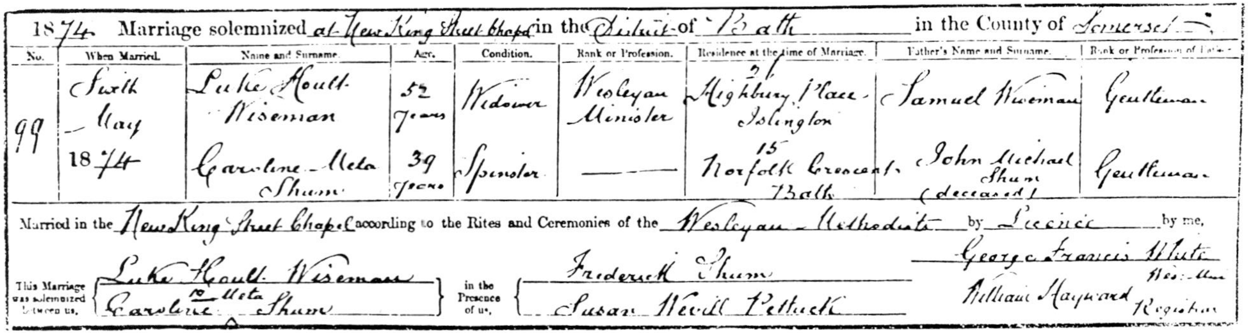

1874. Marriage solemnized at New King Street Chapel in the District of Bath in the County of Somerset

No.	When Married.	Name and Surname.	Age.	Condition.	Rank or Profession.	Residence at the time of Marriage.	Father's Name and Surname.	Rank or Profession of Father.
99	Sixth May 1874	Luke Hoult Wiseman	52 years	Widower	Wesleyan Minister	21 Highbury Place Islington	Samuel Wiseman	Gentleman
		Caroline Meta Shum	39 years	Spinster	—	15 Norfolk Crescent Bath	John Michael Shum (deceased)	Gentleman

Married in the New King Street Chapel according to the Rites and Ceremonies of the Wesleyan Methodists by Licence by me, George Francis White

This Marriage was solemnized between us, Luke Hoult Wiseman, Caroline Meta Shum

in the Presence of us, Frederick Shum, Susan Nevill Pettuck

William Hayward Registrar

The Certificate recording the marriage of Luke Hoult Wiseman to Caroline Meta Shum. Sadly he died 9 months later. The officiating minister, George Francis White was Caroline's brother-in-law.

elected President of the Wesleyan Conference in 1901. In 1893 Michael's son Frederick and grandson Ernest were both elected Bath City councillors.

Moral and Political Issues

As the years passed, and debts were cleared, the Wesleyans turned their attention to social affairs. They reacted strongly when matters of immorality came into the limelight. One such involved the revelation that prostitution was rife at the very centre of Bath. The vicar of St James's, the Rev. Jay Bolton, had discovered that some 60 prostitutes were operating in the vicinity of the *Bell Inn*, which was only a stone's throw from his church. He tried in vain to get the police and the City Council to take action. Eventually in 1884 he published a 22 page pamphlet (of which the cover and first page are reproduced) describing the whole business in the hope that public opinion would enforce action.

The Wesleyan Circuit Meeting recorded approval of "the valuable services of those gentlemen who have risked their reputation in the cause of justice, morality and purity, and expresses its sympathy with them. . ." When, three years later, the brothel keeper was brought to justice the Wesleyans expressed their pleasure.

The Salvation Army established itself officially in Bath in 1882 alongside the independent supporters of that cause. Many young people, fascinated by the lively marching and general commotion, forsook their Sunday Schools. Consequently staid Christians including many Methodists became averse to the new movement and observed its activities with great suspicion.

World affairs penetrated Circuit thinking. In 1894 support was registered for the efforts of the British Anti-Slavery Society in their attempts to stop slavery in Zanzibar. Two years later a resolution was passed urging the Government to act in ameliorating the sufferings of Christians in Armenia. During the year 1897 money was collected in aid of famine relief in India; and following that food was sent to the families of miners on strike in Wales. Temperance movements were supported; by 1898 the Wesleyans in Bath had eight Bands of Hope with 767 members who had signed the pledge.

ST. JAMES'S COURT, BATH:

A

NARRATIVE OF EVENTS.

BY

THE REV. W. JAY BOLTON,

Vicar of St. James's, Bath.

"And Jesus said unto her, Neither do I condemn thee: *go, and sin no more.*"—(John viii. 11.)

PRICE 2D.

BATH:
MARTIN WOOD, PRINTER AND STATIONER, OLD BOND STREET.
1884.

The cover and first page of the Rev W Jay Bolton's pamphlet concerning the "plague spot" in his parish.

St. James's Court, Bath.

A

NARRATIVE OF EVENTS.

To my Parishioners and Christian Friends,—

THE burden of issuing another Circular upon this very pressing and very painful subject, is again laid upon me.

Misstatements require correction: information sought must be supplied. Friends ask what has really been achieved during the past two years, and at what expense? Others are naturally anxious about the unfortunate women who have been dislodged or rescued. Some inquire as to the prospect of re-constructing the Court, when fully purchased. Whilst all should know that the evil though much abated, is not eradicated, and needs fresh aggression and self-sacrifice.

Thus it seems due, not only to my own position as Minister of this Parish, but to the Sacred Cause we all have at heart—the suppression of immorality, especially in this particular spot—that I should report progress and offer suggestions.

The essence of the Parochial system and the only hope of a depressed neighbourhood, is for clergymen and their people to trust one another and unite together for good purposes. What power,—I mean chiefly moral—a Parish has, if it would only rise and use its influence aright! To point this out is one of the objects of this paper. And for this end I must beg to be allowed to speak my mind freely, believing as I do, that concealment of facts and principles leads to half the mischief in the world.

I.—The first thing to be considered is

OUR DUTY.

This arises from the common reputation of these places. Mayors and Magistrates have frequently alluded to St. James's Court as a plague spot, and a disgrace to the city. Each of my predecessors here have protested against its continuance as ruining body and soul. The inhabitants have memorialised the Town Council in years past, I understand, and now again lately, though without success. It is only too clear that a nest of houses of this sort, kept open for profligates from other parts of Bath, and from surrounding towns, *must* be a public nuisance, and have a

In 1892 the Circuit felt able to increase the complement of ministers from two to three. At the turn of the century there were 701 members distributed as follows;

New King Street, 186; Larkhall, 28; Midford, 5; Walcot, 177; Batheaston, 15; Sladebrook, 6; Weston, 38; Corston, 23; Milk Street, 15; Oldfield Park, 85; Hinton, 20; Kingswood, 66; Twerton, 26; Inglesbatch 11. Sladebrook was destined to close shortly. The house-owner wanted the room back!

The Down-town Mission

A foothold had been maintained in Avon Street — of fond memory to Bath Methodists — and a room was in use there certainly from 1825 onwards as a "Mission" amongst the poorer adults and their children who would be happier there than in the more affluent New King Street church.

During 1844 while a search was being made in the Old Bridge area for some land on which to build a chapel to serve the Widcombe and Holloway district, it was discovered that a chapel situated in Milk Street, parallel to Avon Street, was available at a modest price, and was more commodious and airy than the Avon Street premises. The new building was purchased and the school transferred there. A Day School was later established, but this ceased in 1879. By 1899 there were 183 Sunday School scholars on the books with an average attendance of 108, and a library for their use. There was also a Band of Hope, a Mothers' Meeting, a "Girls' Parlour" open two evenings a week and a similar one for the boys described as being smaller and with an average attendance of 12–15. The mission also ran a "Penny Bank" which took in up to £4 per week.

A typical group of Avon Street residents in Victorian times is portrayed in the photograph.

During the summer there was open-air preaching in Milk Street and Corn Street in which the New King Street Mission Band participated; many people were converted and joined the fellowship. Money was raised by appeals for the many sick and poor in this slum area of Bath. There was said to be "cordial co-operation" with other churches in the neighbourhood. Alas this did not extend to some of the local lads. In 1900 windows

Avon Street dwellers gather to be photographed in mid-Victorian times.

were being constantly broken by "the boys in the street". It was then decided to ask one of the trustees, Mr T. Cox, to speak to the Chief of Police "without referring to the Mission" about the need for more police supervision. That plea has a familiar ring about it! In 1909 the matter was placed in the hands of solicitors as the letter to the landlord, Mr J. B. Bowler reveals.

Kingswood School

By 1845 John Wesley's school at Kingswood, Bristol, was finding itself cramped and unable to improve sufficiently to match the standards expected of good Public Schools of the day. James Wilson, the architect, advised the Governors that the late William Beckford's estate at Lansdown, Bath, was coming onto the market, and that it included an ideal site for a school. This was soon secured for £1,050. Wilson designed the fine "H" shaped Tudor style building of Combe Down stone and work began in 1850. The total cost was £16,000; provision was made to accommodate initially some 130 boys. A chapel was not included and so the boys attended morning worship at New King Street (Seniors), and Walcot (Juniors). In 1921 a

War Memorial chapel was erected but the weekly trek down the hill continued, at least until 1929, when the Headmaster, Mr A. B. Sackett, decided to stop the practice.

The Circuit has always benefitted from the support given by Kingswood School, particularly from members of staff who have served as local preachers, organists and circuit officials.

The full story is admirably recounted in Mr A. G. Ives' book *Kingswood School in Wesley's Day and Since* published in 1970.

The school of 1850 is shown in the reproduction of a contemporary engraving.

TIMMINS & TIMMINS
Solicitors
J. A. TIMMINS.
J. T. B. TIMMINS.

5, Henrietta Street,
Bath, 25th August, 1909.

Dear Sir,

I have received complaints from Mr Toone, the caretaker of Corn Street Chapel, with regard to the behaviour of some of your tenants in Corn Street. The tenants of whom he complains are Mr & Mrs Tandy of No 15. The annoyance has continued for some considerable time and Mr Toone informs me that it has at last become unbearable. I feel sure that you will speak to your tenants on the first available opportunity and do your best to persuade them to cease annoying Mr Toone.

I am, dear Sir,

Yours faithfully,

J Buckley Timmins.

Mr J. B. Bowler,
Great Corn Street.

Letter of complaint in 1909 concerning damage to the chapel. The mark in the centre shows that the original was filed on a spike!

Kingswood School, Lansdown, Bath as it appeared when first constructed. This engraving dates from 1850.

12

The Primitives Tackle Problems, 1860–1900

Domestic Issues

BY 1862 the membership of the Bath Primitive Methodist Church stood at 306. The Circuit Meeting passed the following resolution, which has rather a self-satisfied ring about it: "That our circuit be considered in a very prosperous state, there being an increase of members, many having been converted." Their minister since 1859 had been the Rev. J. P. Bellingham, who was clearly very popular. It was unusual at this time for a minister to stay long at one place and when the Circuit Meeting learned that a change was likely to be forced on them, they sent a note to each delegate to Conference asking them to get Bro. Bellingham retained. "We will not receive another." But they did!

The Rev. A Mottram was appointed and was destined to stay for six years. He was paid 22s per week while his young colleague, Mr Beswetherick, received only £5 per quarter.

Mr Mottram's first Circuit Meeting was faced with a directive from the General Committee to collect money for the distressed cotton manufacturing districts. They declined on the grounds that:

(a) the worst period of distress had not arrived.

(b) "our giving means are sufficiently taxed."

This contrasts strangely with the statement of prosperity pronounced only six months previously. By November however the circuit did agree to collect cast-off clothing for Lancashire. A month later the London 1st Circuit was informed: "We cannot entertain your case of chapel-begging on account of our own necessity."

Country affairs came to the fore in 1863. It was reported

Stanton Prior Chapel and "manse" in 1989.

RULES FOR THE CHOIR

OF THE

PRIMITIVE METHODIST CHAPEL,

BATH.

I. That the name of this Choir shall be as follows:—"THE CHOIR OF THE PRIMITIVE METHODIST CHAPEL, *Westgate buildings* BATH.

II. That the Choir shall be conducted and sustained for the purpose of leading and supporting the singing services in the above Chapel; the Members of the Choir, from time to time, agreeing to devote their services gratuitously for this object, that GOD may be glorified, and that the praises of His holy House may be conducted with order, harmony, and effect.

III. That the Choir shall invariably consist of persons of good moral character, and chiefly of Members in Society who take an interest in congregational singing, are regular attendants on divine worship, and who possess voices of a suitable capacity for singing in a Choir.

IV. That the Officers of the Choir shall consist of a Leader and Organist, and a Secretary, elected by a majority of all the Members from time to time, and removed from office or re-appointed, as may seem to a majority of all the Members of the Choir expedient and necessary.

V. That all the Members of the Choir are required to attend at the commencement of all the services (during which the Choir is expected to conduct the singing,) on every Lord's Day, and at the Week-day Evening services when it is practicable.

VI. The Choir shall meet in the Chapel for practice at least once a week; the evening of meeting to be mutually agreed upon by the Members and Officers of the Choir, and subject to alterations as circumstances may require.

VII. The Choir shall from time to time, fix its hours of meeting and breaking-up as may be most convenient, having regard to proper hours and to family arrangements at the several Members' homes.

VIII. The Secretary shall keep a current list of the names of all the persons composing the Choir, and at a suitable period, every practice night as may be from time to time agreed upon, he shall call over all the names; any Member not present when his or her name is called shall be fined One Penny; if not present the whole of the evening the fine shall be Twopence; and if any Member shall be absent for three practice nights successively without assigning any satisfactory reason, such person shall be considered to have left the choir; but in case any Member can satisfactorily account for his or her absence on any occasion, on the grounds of distance, personal or domestic affliction, business engagements, or other unavoidable circumstances, in such case no fine shall be inflicted.

IX. It shall not be considered lawful for any Member of the Choir to leave the singing gallery during practice hours without the consent of the Members present. Every Member violating this Rule shall be fined One Penny for each offence; but if any Member should require to leave earlier than the time appointed for the Choir to break up, such Member may be allowed to do so if it is really necessary.

X. That as it would not be decorous or becoming to enforce attendance on the Lord's Day by the infliction of fines, it is laid upon the conscience of each Member of the Choir as a binding obligation to be present at each service on that holy day; and it is hereby agreed that in case any Member shall neglect his or her duty in this matter, such Member shall be called upon to account for the same immediately after each occasion of neglect by one of the Officers of the Choir, either at one of the practice nights or privately. After the fourth neglect within the space of three months, such Member shall be excluded from the Choir, provided however, that *absence* shall not constitute a case of *neglect* on any occasion, if it can be satisfactorily accounted for on any of the grounds stated in Rule 8.—And no person shall be excluded under this Rule until he or she has been officially communicated with in reference to his or her absence or neglect, as the case may be.

XI. That it shall be the duty of the Secretary to enforce the Rules, keep a current list of the Members' and Officers' names, receive the fines, and keep account of all moneys received or paid, of all transactions of business, minutes and resolutions of the Choir, and of all changes in the appointment of Officers or otherwise.

XII. It shall be the privilege of each Member of the Choir to propose any person to become a Member whom he or she may deem suitable, but such person shall be received only by a majority of all the Members of the Choir.

XIII. The moneys collected in the Choir for fines or otherwise, shall be applied once every quarter as a majority of the Members may think fit.

XIV. All the books belonging to the Choir shall be under the care of the Secretary, and shall not be removed from the singers' gallery without his consent.

XV. The Members of the Choir shall meet to transact its business once every quarter, but in cases of emergency any of the Officers may call a Special Meeting, should the regular Quarterly Meeting not be at hand.

Signed in behalf of the Choir,

JOHN WEST, *Leader.*
WILLIAM VAUGHAN, *Organist.*
JOHN COWARD, *Secretary.*

Approved by the Bath Circuit Committee,

RICHARD OSMOND, *Chairman.*
FRANCIS W. HUNT, *Secretary.*

July 14th, 1864.

J. Francis, Printer, Kingsmead Street, Bath.

Rules for the Choir, 1864. The space for hand-written insertion in paragraph one suggests that these rules were designed to be adopted by other local Primitive Methodist choirs.

that Mr W. Hooper was building "a beautiful new chapel" at Stanton Prior without charge except cleaning, lighting etc. The circuit agreed to provide a harmonium. The chapel and adjoining preacher's house still look spruce though no longer used for religious purposes. Our photograph shows it today. At Farleighwick there was a problem. "After repeated trials the people have once more forsaken the preaching services", so further services would not be arranged there. From Corston came the news that Bro. Alexander had joined the Wesleyans "ostensibly because it was inconvenient to attend our service".

The second minister at this time was Mr Hawkins. He suddenly announced that he wished to marry without giving the usual notice. This meant he expected the "immunities and salary" of a married man without awaiting District and Conference approval. The matter was referred to the General Committee in London on whose behalf the Rev. Moses Lupton replied saying that Mr Hawkins would have to wait a year. The Bath circuit response was predictable. As they could not afford two married men, Mr Hawkins must go. So go he did, to be replaced by the Rev. J. Harding who lodged at Keynsham with a "respectable family" at 2s.6d per week.

Expansion was still the order of the day. The offer of a chapel at Claremont for £10 per year was snapped up quickly; the Independents at Argyle Street were also after it! At Saltford "four perches of land" for a chapel were bought for £15. A preaching room in the slum area of Bath, Corn Street, was taken over; also one in Entry Hill.

There had been ructions amongst the choir members at Westgate Buildings. Some had resigned including the leaders; a harmonium used in the Assembly Rooms, to which the congregation had moved temporarily, had something to do with the trouble. So bad had things become that it became necessary in 1864 to ask the Circuit Meeting to approve a new set of ground rules. These are reproduced in full. There is a reference in paragraph 13 to fines and we are fortunately told on what basis they were levied. It is amusing to record at this point that some years later a lady officiating as assistant organist resigned "due to uncomplimentary remarks passed on her playing". Critics in church life can be very harsh!

Discipline was still being exercised over recalcitrant preachers. In 1865 Brother Pond was removed from the plan having become "disaffected in his mind towards our Society", and for neglecting his appointments. A warning was given at the same time to all persons at Twerton and elsewhere who absented themselves from class that they risked losing their membership.

Young single ministers must have been attractive to the predominantly female population of Bath. In September 1865, Mr Harding announced his intention of getting married, nor was he willing to "waive the enjoyment of the privilege to which he was entitled". The Circuit Secretary offered furnished lodgings in his own house at 6s. per week. Four voted in favour, several had left the meeting, and "a large majority did not vote and were silent". That was not the end of the affair. Next month's minutes tell us: "Due to the alarming deficiency of funds, owing to the impending marriage of Mr Harding, it was agreed to write him a kind Christian letter . . . desiring him to desist from marrying for the next few months . . . as we fear the consequences to him and Mr Mottram will be serious. If he accepts our friendly advice . . . we will present him with a handsome donation when he leaves the circuit."

Before he left the circuit the following summer it was reported that "Mr Harding is still £2.8s.10¼d deficient despite utmost efforts to make up his salary. Perhaps he has received private donations which could liquidate his claim on the circuit?" This all suggests that the attempts to get him to put off his marriage were unsuccessful.

About this time (ie early 1866) the General Committee appointed a date to be observed as a Day of Humiliation on account of the cattle plague. And an application to "lend" Twerton Chapel for a phrenological lecture was refused.

Westgate Buildings

Despite improvements made from time to time the chapel at Westgate Buildings was a constant source of worry. Things came to a head in 1862 when it became impossible to accommodate properly all those wishing to attend the Anniversary services. The ventilation was hopeless and people feared the

Sunday School above the main chapel would "suddenly fall through onto their laps"! The danger of the supporting beams giving way under the weight of the 120 children plus their teachers caused those in the church below to be "filled with serious apprehension and alarm". Furthermore the building was far from watertight. Various efforts were made to locate a suitable site for a new church but without success. Two years passed. Adjoining the chapel on the north side stood a "very peculiar building", partly occupied as apartments and part the studio of Arthur Murch Esq. Eventually the whole complex was bought for £630. It was necessary to appoint a new Trust to see the matter through for only two members of the earlier Trust were available. The new Trust comprised: Messrs R. Osmond, W. Vaughan, J. Coward, F. W. Hunt, G. Humphries, J. Horner, G. Chappell, H. Hacker, H. Knight, J. Thorley, T. E. Revell, W. Brass, G. Salisbury, J. Dorey, J. Hunt and H. Coward. The new building was designed by Mr J. T. Irvine, for which he charged only £12. The foundation stone was laid by Councillor Mr J. W. Templer on 30th April 1866. Then tea for 500 was served in the Guildhall, after which there was a public meeting. Proceeds for the day totalled £130.

After postponements due to building delays the chapel was opened on 21st November 1866. It was licensed for marriages soon afterwards. The insured value of the premises was £2,700, comprising: Chapel and school-room £1,500, Organ £150, Fittings £400, House No 1 £300, House No 2 £300, Library £50. The two houses were sold in 1879 for £450 each. In that year the envelope system was introduced. The new organ gave trouble for years, and eventually in 1880 another one was purchased for £185 from a Mr Clarke.

The Circuit kept pleading poverty as a reason for not wanting two married ministers. By 1870 the membership was 260 and falling, but in 1873 a new chapel 30 feet × 20 feet was built at Freshford.

The New Broom

During the year of 1875 the circuit rejoiced to learn that the Rev. Murray Wilson had agreed to become their new Superintendent after completing an American tour. He would be paid £25 per quarter, his unmarried assistant £13.10s.0d. Mr Wilson immediately set about a review of the membership statistics which he suspected were to prove to be unreliable. The following is what he discovered:

> Bath — 30 down. Some had not met for two years, others less.
> Claremont — Less than reported. One missing three years, others less.
> Twerton — No class meeting.
> Keynsham — Class attendance quite good.
> Saltford — No class meeting.
> Stanton — No class meeting.
> Dolemeads — No society.
> Corston — No society.

"The present ministers are not responsible for the deplorable state of our societies generally," he wrote. After this implied criticism of his predecessors Mr Wilson decided to visit all the local preachers to urge them to take their responsibilities more seriously. Some were found to be conducting baptismal services, and were warned that this was contrary to Connexional discipline. They were relieved of preaching appointments but their names were allowed to stay on the plan. It was decided to sell the Twerton Chapel. A site was picked for a new chapel at Claremont. By 1877, despite 49 conversions, no total overall rise in effective membership had taken place because so many never attended class, and so could not strictly be included in the figures.

Mr Murray Wilson stepped out of line in 1879 for the circuit record is endorsed: "We express disapproval of Rev. M. Wilson's method of entering the circuit accounts for June 1878. A statement to that effect will be entered in the Account Book". By 1880, there were only 234 members; there was a debt of £103 and some were outvoted in their attempt to reduce the complement to one minister. By 1882 the new chapel at Claremont had been opened and the decision was taken to form two separate circuits, each supporting one minister. In 1883 Keynsham was transferred to Bristol 2nd Circuit, and the privately owned chapel at Stanton Prior closed.

When the Westgate Trust membership was reviewed in

1886 it was discovered that in the intervening 23 years eight had died and three had left the Primitive Methodists, so replacements were appointed. The occupations of the Trustees are worth recording: miller, clothier, boot maker, compositor, gentleman, coal merchant, railway inspector, grocer's assistant, wheelchairman, railway porter, painter, builder, baker and postman.

13

Obituaries in the Nineteenth Century

The Policy

VICTORIAN RELIGIOUS obituaries were frequently accounts of the lives of pious persons whose last moments were of great significance. Indeed an almost morbid interest was taken by those attending the dying in securing confirmation that "all is well". It sometimes seems that the signatory was seeking publicity for his own efforts to this end.

One aspect of policy for Bath Methodists was laid down in the minutes of the New King Street Leaders' Meeting on 2nd December 1839: "Funeral sermons are uncalled for except for those long-standing in the church. But how shall we publicly recognise the death of all members? In future Leaders are to furnish the Secretary with a written report of the death of any member, containing a brief account of their conversion, but more particularly their experience in the immediate prospect of dissolution. All are to be read at the annual Watch Night Service."

A Poignant Case

This example, somewhat shortened, which just pre-dates the above Wesleyan directive, is taken from the *Primitive Methodist Magazine.* It is of interest not only because it confirms the above comments, but also by virtue of the social and religious background it reveals of a devout servant girl moved from the countryside, like so many, to find employment in the City of Bath:-

> Died, Jan 18, 1838, at Bath, aged twenty-four, Rachel Wootton. She was born Jan. 7, 1814 at Sandy Lane, in the

parish of Calne, in Wiltshire. Her parents are members of a religious community. After a sermon on: 'Remember now thy Creator in the days of thy youth', she retired into a wood and poured out her soul to God. But after this her serious desires weakened.

At the age of 16 she left home and went into service in the city of Bath. Curiosity led her to the PM place of worship. She had a deep sense of guilt. But her soul was soon blest with the pardoning love of God. In Sept 1833, she joined our society, and ornamented her profession to the close of her probation.

Servants in Bath cannot always attend the means of grace. But Rachel valued the golden opportunities too highly to allow any wilful neglect. Her class leader, Mrs Feare, says her attendance was as regular as possible, her experience scriptural, and her Christian life a practical illustration of a renewed heart.

Jan. 2, 1838, she complained of a pain in her head; and her illness soon rapidly increased. Her disorder was an inflammation on her lungs; her medical attendant pronounced her incurable. On the 10th I conversed and prayed with her. She told me she was not afraid to die; that her prospects of a future and happier state were clear. The day before her death, while Brother Haywood, local preacher, prayed, she exclaimed: 'Glory! glory! glory!'

The class leader visited many times. Rachel said if it was the Lord's will she would rather die than live. 'Tell my class mates to meet me in heaven.'

She wished me to preach her funeral sermon from the text she was first impressed with.

On the day of her death, being asked how she was, she said, 'Happy'. A friend asked her to lift up her hand as a sign if she was happy at departing. She lifted up her hand in token of victory, and said 'Happy', and her spirit took its flight to the mansions of bliss.

Henry Pope

14

The Twentieth Century Dawns 1900–1930s

The General Situation

THE WESLEYAN Circuit had begun the 19th century with 30 places of worship; due to schisms and a slackening of Victorian standards of church attendance there were barely a dozen a century later. The Primitive Methodists, divided into two small circuits, had only five, while the United Methodists, after starting with such a flourish, found themselves with only five as well. Most of the Societies were in a poor financial state, some still struggling to pay off building loans. With just over 1,000 members in all, something needed to be done. When membership numbers were high it had been possible to indulge in the luxury of break-away movements; surely the time had now come to put all that aside? As we shall see it was to be a slow and wearisome process before the three branches would unite. In the meantime the burden of maintaining independent witness continued to sap the resources and energies of so many earnest, well-meaning Christian men and women. Let us first see how the Primitive Methodists were coping.

The Primitive Methodists

At Westgate Buildings, the 20th century began with a Sunday School attendance of 175 scholars and 25 teachers. Within ten years figures were 121 and 16 respectively. With upheaval of the war the 1918 figures became 63 and 13. Throughout this time the records show it was very much "business as usual". Sunday School outings continued annually to such places as Burnham, Frenchay, Lacock and even Weymouth. A small concession to expense one year led to a visit "by electric car" to

Newton only a couple of miles out of town; another year they combined with Oldfield Park.

During 1907 we are told that the Band of Hope numbered 90 in total; and that 12 boys had joined the Anti-Cigarette League, thereby pledging not to smoke until 21. The fall in overall attendance by 1912 was attributed to the handicap of a schoolroom situated beneath the chapel "dull and heavy and having an awkward entrance". In 1915 the explanation was: "the streets are so quiet, the passing through of transport vehicles, the presence of large numbers of HM Forces, the publication of more newspapers on Sundays . . . all make scholars less regular in attendance and excites them so they become less reverent. The call to the colours has played havoc with the numbers of teachers."

Research is handicapped by absence of records concerning the main church activities in the immediate pre-1914 war days. Membership was 109 in 1913, and was much the same in 1921. There was only one Primitive circuit again. Some adjustments to church life were occasioned by the war. Lighting restrictions caused the Sunday evening services to be shortened in the winter of 1916; the previous year there were disturbing noises from the adjoining skittle alley at the Empire Soldiers' Club. An offer was made in 1921 by the Labour Party to purchase Westgate Buildings for £5,000. This was declined following an emergency meeting of Leaders. Seventeen years later the Bath Co-operative Society, whose principal Bath shop adjoined, also attempted to secure the premises. They offered, in part exchange, land on Hollow Road with a frontage of 320 feet. But the next war intervened before the matter could be resolved.

During the 1920s fund raising was of prime importance. There were constant appeals for personal giving, the re-introduction of the envelope system, garden parties, even a plea in 1924 to the Sunday School to make a grant to Society funds. The basis was that during the year the Mayor and Corporation had attended the Sunday School Anniversary and presumably boosted the School's income. Things got so bad that there was one joint account for Trust, Society and School funds. One evening collection in 1926 was sent to support the families of striking miners in the Radstock area.

The cover of the Wesleyan Circuit Magazine, The Myrtle, as it appeared in 1916.

Sunday preaching appointments by the one minister available were based on a strict "ability to pay" basis. Thus in 1926 the circuit received attention on the following scale:

	1st Qr	2nd Qr	3rd Qr	4th Qr	Assessment £ s d
Westgate	12	12	11	12	46.10.0
Claremont	6	5	6	5	22.10.0
Oldfield Park	3	3	3	3	7. 0.0
Freshford	1	2	2	1	2. 5.0
Saltford	-	-	-	1	15.0

The 1932 depression led to an application for the use of the Westgate Buildings schoolroom by the unemployed, but this was turned down. By 1938 the membership had fallen to 68.

Freshford chapel was sold in 1936 for £170.

Oldfield Park Chapel was a "tin tabernacle" in Shaftesbury Road, opposite the Scala cinema (later converted to a supermarket). It was sold in 1940 to Bath City Council for £600 including the large plot of land on which an air-raid shelter had already been built.

The Wesleyans

Meanwhile we return to the Wesleyans. In 1900 they rejoiced in a circuit membership of 702. The circuit magazine, *The Myrtle,* was launched in 1902. The title, which was not universally admired, sprang from Isaiah 55 verse 13: "Instead of the brier shall come up the myrtle-tree". The 1916 cover is shown in our picture. The buildings illustrated are: Walcot, Kingswood, Batheaston, New King Street, Inglesbatch, Oldfield Park and Weston.

During the pre-1914 war years, protests were recorded about the outrages in Macedonia, Chinese labour in South Africa, atrocities in the Congo, Sunday entertainments and military exercises in Britain. At a time when anti-German feelings were high in Bath, and it was considered almost treasonable to suggest any dealings with these expected invaders, the Wesleyan Methodists in 1909 were a lone and courageous voice calling for goodwill.

The Circuit meeting on the 13th December unanimously supported appeals to all classes in both nations to promote a mutual spirit of goodwill and friendship. They maintained that sections of the Press tried to foment strife between the nations; and expressed the desire that the bond of peace between the two peoples might be preserved and strengthened.

The setting up in 1908 of a Wesleyan "Old Age Pensions Committee", to help those seeking to take advantage of the new legislation, serves as a reminder that Civic Authority was gradually taking over much of the social work previously undertaken by churches and other charities. It was no longer necessary for people to continue to work until they dropped; a new body of pensioners was now emerging. The churches were also having to react to the thrusting movements for Women's Suffrage which were powerfully expressed in Bath.

Female preaching had long been a feature of Primitive Methodism. Women had served on the Circuit Quarterly meetings of the Wesleyans since 1895, the first participants being Mrs Hunt, Mrs Reece and Mrs Stow. Women's names were also appearing in the lists of Trustees. The possibility was explored of appointing a deaconess to serve New King Street and Milk Street in 1909 but nothing came of it.

The Wesley Guild Movement was flourishing. The 1908–9 programme for instance reveals that weekly meetings were held at each church, with the Guild's standard four sections, Devotional, Literary, Christian Service and Social being represented in each month's itinerary.

Here are some of the subjects which interested the members 80 years ago:

> "The Essentials of Success"
> "England 1,000 years ago" (with limelight views)
> "Are Christianity and Socialism antagonistic?"
> "Daylight Saving Bill"
> "Wesley's various visits to Bath"
> "Our Cycle Tour, Westward Ho!" (with limelight illustrations)

The regular weekly meetings at New King Street around this time comprised:

Sunday — Services at 11am and 6.30pm.
Men's Own at 3pm.
Sunday School at 10am and 2.45pm.

Monday	—	Junior class 6.30pm. Band of Hope 7.15pm. Mixed class 8pm.
Tuesday	—	Women's class 3.30pm. Girls' class 8pm. Men's class 8.15pm.
Wednesday	—	Preaching service 7pm. Mixed class 8pm. Girls' class 8pm. Men's class 8.15pm.
Thursday	—	Women's class 7pm. Wesley Guild 8pm.
Friday	—	Church prayer meeting 8pm.

Recognition had come by 1912 that in the Bristol District, of which Bath was a part, membership figures were falling to an alarming extent. Synod directed that attention be paid to the following areas;

1. Open-air services.
2. Sunday Schools as the nursery of the church, and the urgent call for efficient workers.
3. A soul-winning campaign on the basis of one individual bringing another to the Lord Jesus.

The local implementation of this policy was considered by the Quarterly Meeting of June 1913. It was decided that after prayerful preparation there would be open-air work at the five principal churches "in conjunction with the Anglican Church". The Chairman, the Rev. A. E. Shooter, hoped that "the mission would not be a beginning and ending in itself, but that the attack on the strongholds of Satan thus begun might be continued and maintained". After a month of prayer the mission was pursued as planned, initially in the city churches. First reports were promising, and there was evidence of increased membership. Although the War was to put an end to these grand endeavours, enough was done to show that given leadership and inspiration, the Wesleyans still had the ability to make their message heard in the City.

There is no evidence of opposition to the war effort. September 1914 saw that the Quarterly meeting "observed with gratification the number of young men responding to their country's call for the war". A list was compiled by the Superintendent of those volunteering. Sunday, 30th December 1914 was officially designated as "Peace Sunday". Superficially this appeared to reflect the widely held view that the war would be over by Christmas. Actually the event to be celebrated was 100 years of peace with the United States! As the war dragged on Rolls of Honour were drawn up by all churches. By 1918, 378 members of the Wesleyan Circuit were serving, including ten women as nurses in France. The United Methodists had 124 young men on active service by 1916. At one stage they recorded their strong disapproval of the harsh treatment of conscientious objectors. Many hundreds of Methodist soldiers passed through the Bath war hospitals, and every endeavour was made to offer them welcome and succour. Soldiers billeted in Bath were offered the facilities of a "Soldiers' Institute" at New King Street which was open every evening. Armistice Day was celebrated with a great circuit meeting at New King Street when the speaker was the Rev. O. S. Watkins, Senior Wesleyan Chaplain to the Forces.

15

Seeds and Fruit of Union From 1920 onwards

The First Stirrings

WITH THE ugliness of The Great War a thing of the past the Wesleyans were anxious to see "Revival"; vigorous activity was centred in the Wesley Guild Movement and public meetings. They also sought to improve the attractiveness of public worship deciding this could best be achieved by raising money for church improvement and extension. Within two years a target of £1,000 had been reached.

The early '20s saw the first tentative moves towards Methodist Union manifesting themselves in Bath. Contacts were few, such as the odd combined temperance demonstration, the occasional exchange of pulpits, and from 1922 the use of *The Myrtle* by all three denominations with the publication therein of all three preaching plans. Our photograph of the cover in 1927 shows that Claremont, Beechen Cliff, Westgate Buildings, and Box have been added. A committee of representatives of the three bodies met in 1921 for exploratory talks. Whatever happened is not recorded, but the Wesleyans were not persuaded to expect any radical plan. On receiving their representatives' report, the following was resolved:

> This Quarterly Meeting is of the opinion that owing to the seriously divided views of all three churches, especially the Wesleyans, the time has not arrived when with safety a complete scheme of 'Methodist Union' by fusion can be adopted.

The voting was by no means unanimous, 41 voted in favour of the resolution, 36 against and two were neutral. To test the water a more simple resolution was put two years later:

The Myrtle, now "The Organ of Bath Methodism", in 1927.

"Are you in favour of organic union between the three denominations?"

Again opinions were divided but this time the majority swung the other way. The vote was 53 for, 30 against and three neutral. The United Methodists in December 1924, having been told it was "an opportunity that may never occur again in your lifetime", also voted favourably on a similar resolution: 22 for, eight against and nine neutral. Unfortunately we do not have any figures from the Primitives. All this suggested that a majority of Methodists wanted union but on their own terms. In 1925 the Bath Wesleyans sent a "memorial" (proposal) to Conference asking that all members be given the opportunity to vote on the matter. There was little national support however due perhaps to uninformed prejudices. Life in the Bath Methodist churches returned to normal.

A Practical Demonstration

After four years had passed without any progress having been made towards union the Primitives became impatient. They were anxious to break the impasse. They suggested that once more a joint committee be set up, this time with the firm objective of preparing the way for the smooth working of Methodist Union when this was finally achieved. The "United Council" was formed and consisted of six representatives of each denomination plus circuit stewards and ministers. The Council met on the 17th January 1930 and immediately got down to serious business. Two brilliant ideas surfaced which achieved universal support. The first was to hold the Quarterly meetings of each of the participating denominations on the same evening at the same venue but in separate rooms. After each meeting had dealt with its business they would all join together for fellowship and praise. This did happen on 13th March at Walcot, preceded by the inevitable tea.

The whole event was an unqualified success.

The second idea which came out of that meeting in January 1930 was to arrange a public display of unity and this was entitled a "Methodist Conversazione" and the venue was the fashionable Pump Room. This was held on 20th March and received good support from the Methodist people. It commenced at 7pm with a musical programme chaired by Mr W. W. Bell in the Concert Hall. After refreshments and "Methodist Community singing" there was a rally chaired by Alderman C. H. Hacker, a prominent Primitive Methodist layman and Local Preacher, "a born optimist with a fine sense of humour".

Dr Ferrier Hulme was the principal speaker. In his address he called for "our youth to be haunted with the presence of God. In all our work and play we need to be conscious of His presence. Some have asked: 'What are we going to get out of it?' I ask: 'What are we going to put into it and accomplish by it?' Our divisions may have been historically necessary, but no-one is interested in them now. We can serve the present age better together than by ourselves. We have seen the day of one Methodism in Bath. Surely we ought to have a function like this once a year at the Pump Room." The photograph shows the prominent ministers and laymen who attended.

Pump Room Conversazione, 1930. The front row comprises (L to R): — Revs A Hanley Smith, W S Green, James Goudie, Dr T Ferrier Hulme, Thomas Banks, William J Heaton. The young ministers in the second row are Revs E Ralph Bates and Arthur H Jerx.

The practical outcome of the discussions was disappointingly restricted to:

United services on Good Friday
Interchanges of pulpits
Better joint use of *The Myrtle*
A central Temperance Council

Lethargy Returns

The United Council met again on 25th April. The enthusiasm had gone. "Only a moderately representative gathering assembled." There was a feeling of "not being alive to the fact that for Methodism this is a great day of God. Has a deadly torpor *(sic)* crept on unawares?" Instead of getting down to brass tacks and deciding how a combined circuit would be organised the meeting left matters in the hands of the ministers. Why? The truth of the matter was that the laymen could see no way through the prejudices and suspicions which still lurked beneath the surface. The Pump Room meeting, though hailed as a success, was in fact supported only by a minority of members. It would have been easier for the Primitives and Uniteds to go along with the Wesleyans if either of them had a City building which was attractive and capable of accommodating united gatherings. So nothing happened. Individual congregations followed the attitude of the ministers and decided that the time was premature for the formation of one circuit for Bath. Two years passed.

National Directives

The next move was prompted by Conference decisions coming down from all three Connexional Headquarters and following the celebration of legal union by a gathering in the Royal Albert Hall in London. This was reflected in a service at Westgate Buildings on 3rd October 1932 "to celebrate the recent great and all-embracing union of the Methodist Churches." By all accounts it was a great success. Unfortunately the lights fused just as the service began! As the newspaper reporter put it: "Out of the darkness came the light of human voices raised in hymns of praise." Alderman Hacker described the emotional scenes he had witnessed at the Albert Hall where 10,000 people had celebrated the union when it became an established fact. But still there was little impetus in Bath. The Primitive Methodists put forward a tentative idea whereby in any re-organisation Westgate Buildings would become a Central Mission with the appointment of a minister "specially adapted for this work". They further suggested that the work at Claremont should be extended and the building improved, the cost being covered by the sale of the Oldfield Park chapel. As time passed the United Methodists became restive too and endeavoured to stir the Wesleyans into doing something. At last the United Council was re-convened to face the task of forming one circuit from the 751 Wesleyans (13 churches), 277 Uniteds (five churches) and 168 Primitives (four churches). Its recommendations were accepted by each of the participating Circuit Meetings. Nothing very dramatic emerged. Though there would be one circuit "the oversight of the work shall be continued as at present". There would be one Superintending Minister but certainly no redundancy! Concentrated efforts were to be made towards strengthening Suburban churches which were handicapped by lack of accommodation and ministerial oversight. The need was recognised for a new church in the Southdown area and for a review of the most effective working of the City churches. The new combined preaching plan listed the Societies in the following order:

New King Street	163 members	ex-Wesleyan
Westgate Buildings	71 members	ex-Primitive
Beechen Cliff	147 members	ex-United
Walcot	183 members	ex-Wesleyan
Claremont	70 members	ex-Primitive
Larkhall	22 members	ex-Wesleyan
Batheaston	31 members	ex-Wesleyan
Oldfield Park	196 members	ex-Wesleyan
Oldfield Park (Shaftesbury Road)	22 members	ex-Primitive
Weston	88 members	ex-Wesleyan
Twerton	57 members	ex-United
Inglesbatch	5 members	ex-Wesleyan

Corston	3 members	ex-Wesleyan
Hinton	5 members	ex-Wesleyan
Midford	2 members	ex-Wesleyan
Milk Street	3 members	ex-Wesleyan
Bathampton	10 members	ex-Wesleyan
Freshford	5 members	ex-Primitive
Box	39 members	ex-United
Box Hill	17 members	ex-United
Kingsdown	17 members	ex-United
Kingswood School	40 members	ex-Wesleyan

The first meeting of the newly formed Circuit Quarterly Meeting took place at New King Street on 12th September 1935 under the chairmanship of the Rev. E. A. Spear. Other ministers were Revs. W. T. Healey, A. A. Thomas, A. J. Trebilco, Thomas Oakley, and A. R. Bates. Messrs E. W. Bladwell and Ivan Sheppard were elected Circuit Stewards. The total membership was reported to be 1,140.

The amalgamated circuit shown on the 1936 Circuit Plan settled down quite easily and one wonders why it had taken so long to make the change. Area committees were set up to study how to extend the church's influence to the new housing estates which the City Council was building on the southern boundary. In June 1938 authority was granted to secure an option on any suitable building site which might become available. As a result the Southdown site was acquired in 1939.

The importance of giving a boost to Sunday School work generally was also recognised. Competition between schools was to be encouraged by presenting shields for the best school "in the matter of attendance etc". The ground rules were never clearly defined! Every teacher was to be encouraged in the work by being sent individual letters. Parents' associations were to be formed with social meetings at least once a quarter. Evangelistic campaigns were planned to be held at New King Street and Westgate Buildings with the "Crusaders" in attendance. Alas, as in 1914, world events were to take over and all these schemes were doomed to come to nothing.

The September 1938 Circuit Meeting unanimously passed the following evocative resolution drafted by Mr F. S. Cook,

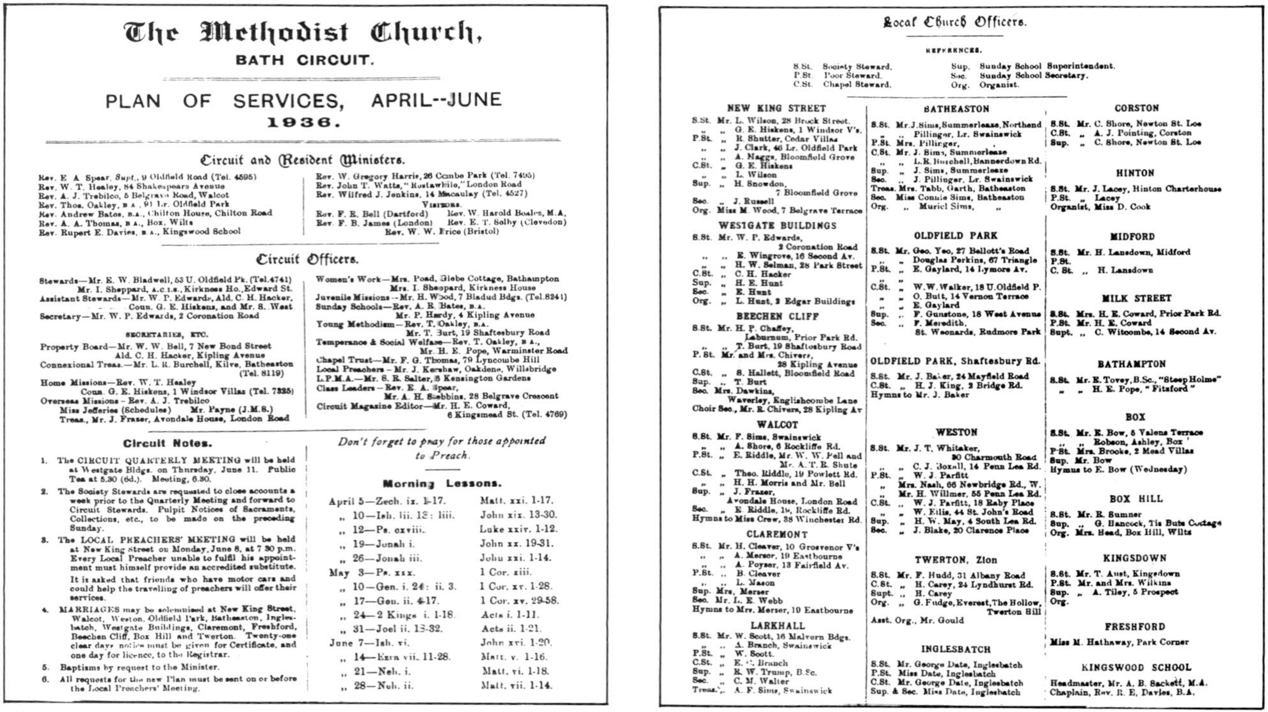

The Methodist Church,

BATH CIRCUIT.

PLAN OF SERVICES, APRIL--JUNE 1936.

Circuit and Resident Ministers.

Rev. E A Spear, *Supt.*, 9 Oldfield Road (Tel. 4595)
Rev. W. T. Healey, 84 Shakespeare Avenue
Rev. A. J. Trebilco, 5 Belgrave Road, Walcot
Rev. Thos. Oakley, B.A., 91 Lr. Oldfield Park
Rev. Andrew Bates, B.A., Chilton House, Chilton Road
Rev. A. A. Thomas, B.A., Box, Wilts
Rev. Rupert E. Davies, B.A., Kingswood School

Rev. W. Gregory Harris, 26 Combe Park (Tel. 7495)
Rev. John T. Watts, "Rustawhile," London Road
Rev. Wilfred J. Jenkins, 14 Macaulay (Tel. 4527)

VISITORS.

Rev. F. R. Bell (Dartford) Rev. W. Harold Beales, M.A.
Rev. F. B. James (London) Rev. E. T. Selby (Clevedon)
Rev. W. W. Price (Bristol)

Circuit Officers.

Stewards—Mr. E. W. Bladwell, 53 U. Oldfield Pk. (Tel.4741)
Mr. I. Sheppard, A.C.I.S., Kirkness Ho., Edward St.
Assistant Stewards—Mr. W. P. Edwards, Ald. C. H. Hacker, Coun. G. E. Hiskens, and Mr. S. West
Secretary—Mr. W. P. Edwards, 2 Coronation Road

SECRETARIES, ETC.

Property Board—Mr. W. W. Bell, 7 New Bond Street
Ald. C. H. Hacker, Kipling Avenue
Connexional Treas.—Mr. L. R. Burchell, Kilve, Batheaston (Tel. 8119)
Home Missions—Rev. W. T. Healey
Coun. G. E. Hiskens, 1 Windsor Villas (Tel. 7325)
Overseas Missions—Rev. A. J. Trebilco
Miss Jefferies (Schedules) Mr. Payne (J.M.S.)
Treas., Mr. J. Fraser, Avondale House, London Road

Women's Work—Mrs. Poad, Glebe Cottage, Bathampton
Mrs. I. Sheppard, Kirkness House
Juvenile Missions—Mr. H. Wood, 7 Bladud Bdgs. (Tel.8241)
Sunday Schools—Rev. A. R. Bates, B.A.
Mr. P. Hardy, 4 Kipling Avenue
Young Methodism—Rev. T. Oakley, B.A.
Mr. T. Burt, 19 Shaftesbury Road
Temperance & Social Welfare—Rev. T. Oakley, B.A.,
Mr. H. E. Pope, Warminster Road
Chapel Trust—Mr. F. G. Thomas, 79 Lyncombe Hill
Local Preachers—Mr. J. Kershaw, Oakdene, Willsbridge
L.P.M.A.—Mr. S. R. Salter, 8 Kensington Gardens
Class Leaders—Rev. E. A. Spear,
Mr. A. H. Stebbins, 28 Belgrave Crescent
Circuit Magazine Editor—Mr. H. E. Coward, 6 Kingsmead St. (Tel. 4769)

Circuit Notes.

1. The CIRCUIT QUARTERLY MEETING will be held at Westgate Bldgs. on Thursday, June 11. Public Tea at 5.30 (6d.). Meeting, 6.30.
2. The Society Stewards are requested to close accounts a week prior to the Quarterly Meeting and forward to Circuit Stewards. Pulpit Notices of Sacraments, Collections, etc., to be made on the preceding Sunday.
3. The LOCAL PREACHERS' MEETING will be held at New King Street on Monday, June 8, at 7 30 p.m. Every Local Preacher unable to fulfil his appointment must himself provide an accredited substitute.
It is asked that friends who have motor cars and could help the travelling of preachers will offer their services.
4. MARRIAGES may be solemnised at New King Street, Walcot, Weston, Oldfield Park, Batheaston, Inglesbatch, Westgate Buildings, Claremont, Freshford, Beechen Cliff, Box Hill and Twerton. Twenty-one clear days notice must be given for Certificate, and one day for licence, to the Registrar.
5. Baptisms by request to the Minister.
6. All requests for the new Plan must be sent on or before the Local Preachers' Meeting.

Don't forget to pray for those appointed to Preach.

Morning Lessons.

April 5—Zech. ix. 1-17.		Matt. xxi. 1-17.
,, 10—Isa. lii. 13: liii.		John xix. 13-30.
,, 12—Ps. cxviii.		Luke xxiv. 1-12.
,, 19—Jonah i.		John xx. 19-31.
,, 26—Jonah iii.		John xxi. 1-14.
May 3—Ps. xxx.		1 Cor. xiii.
,, 10—Gen. i. 24: ii. 3.		1 Cor. xv. 1-28.
,, 17—Gen. ii. 4-17.		1 Cor. xv. 29-58.
,, 24—2 Kings i. 1-18.		Acts i. 1-11.
,, 31—Joel ii. 13-32.		Acts ii. 1-21.
June 7—Isa. vi.		John xvi. 1-20.
,, 14—Ezra vii. 11-28.		Matt. v. 1-16.
,, 21—Neh. i.		Matt. vi. 1-18.
,, 28—Neh. ii.		Matt. vii. 1-14.

Local Church Officers.

REFERENCES.

S.St. Society Steward. Sup. Sunday School Superintendent.
P.St. Poor Steward. Sec. Sunday School Secretary.
C.St. Chapel Steward. Org. Organist.

NEW KING STREET
S.St. Mr. L. Wilson, 28 Brock Street.
,, ,, G. E. Hiskens, 1 Windsor V's.
P.St. ,, R. Shutter, Cedar Villas
,, ,, J. Clark, 46 Lr. Oldfield Park
,, ,, A. Maggs, Bloomfield Grove
C.St. ,, G. E. Hiskens
,, ,, L. Wilson
Sup. ,, H. Snowdon, 7 Bloomfield Grove
Sec. ,, J. Russell
Org. Miss M. Wood, 7 Belgrave Terrace

WESTGATE BUILDINGS
S.St. Mr. W. P. Edwards, 2 Coronation Road
,, ,, E. Wingrove, 16 Second Av.
,, ,, H. W. Selman, 28 Park Street
C.St. ,, C. H. Hacker
Sup. ,, H. E. Hunt
Sec. ,, E. Hunt
Org. ,, L. Hunt, 2 Edgar Buildings

BEECHEN CLIFF
S.St. Mr. H. P. Chaffey, Laburnum, Prior Park Rd.
,, ,, T. Burt, 19 Shaftesbury Road
P. St. Mr. and Mrs. Chivers, 28 Kipling Avenue
C.St. ,, S. Hallett, Bloomfield Road
Sup. ,, T. Burt
Sec. Mrs. Dawkins, Waverley, Englishcombe Lane
Choir Sec., Mr. R. Chivers, 28 Kipling Av

WALCOT
S.St. Mr. F. Sims, Swainswick
,, ,, A. Shore, 6 Rockliffe Rd.
P.St. ,, E. Riddle, Mr. W. W. Pell and Mr. A. T. R. Shute
C.St. ,, Theo. Riddle, 19 Powlett Rd.
,, ,, H. H. Morris and Mr. Bell
Sup. ,, J. Fraser, Avondale House, London Road
Sec. ,, E. Riddle, 19, Rockliffe Rd.
Hymns to Miss Crew, 38 Winchester Rd.

CLAREMONT
S.St. Mr. H. Cleaver, 10 Grosvenor V's
,, ,, A. Merser, 19 Eastbourne
,, ,, A. Poyser, 13 Fairfield Av.
P.St. ,, B. Cleaver
,, ,, L. Mason
Sup. Mrs. Merser
Sec. Mr. L. E. Webb
Hymns to Mrs. Merser, 19 Eastbourne

LARKHALL
S.St. Mr. W. Scott, 16 Malvern Bdgs.
,, ,, A. Branch, Swainswick
P.St. ,, W. Scott.
C.St. ,, E. C. Branch
Sup. ,, R. W. Trump, B.Sc.
Sec. ,, C. M. Walter
Treas. ,, A. F. Sims, Swainswick

BATHEASTON
S.St. Mr. J. Sims, Summerleaze, Northend
,, ,, Pillinger, Lr. Swainswick
P.St. Mrs. Pillinger,
C.St. Mr. J. Sims, Summerleaze
,, ,, L. R. Burchell, Bannerdown Rd.
Sup. ,, J. Sims, Summerleaze
Sec. ,, J. Pillinger, Lr. Swainswick
Treas. Mrs. Tabb, Garth, Batheaston
Sec. Miss Connie Sims, Batheaston
Org. ,, Muriel Sims, ,,

OLDFIELD PARK
S.St. Mr. Geo. Yeo, 27 Bellott's Road
,, ,, Douglas Perkins, 67 Triangle
P.St. ,, E. Gaylard, 14 Lymore Av.
,, ,,
C.St. ,, W. W. Walker, 18 U. Oldfield P.
,, ,, O. Butt, 14 Vernon Terrace
,, ,, E. Gaylard
Sup. ,, F. Gunstone, 18 West Avenue
Sec. ,, F. Meredith, St. Weonards, Rudmore Park

OLDFIELD PARK, Shaftesbury Rd.
S.St. Mr. J. Baker, 24 Mayfield Road
C.St. ,, H. J. King, 2 Bridge Rd.
Hymns to Mr. J. Baker

WESTON
S.St. Mr. J. T. Whitaker, 30 Charmouth Road
,, ,, C. J. Boxall, 14 Penn Lea Rd.
P.St. ,, W. J. Parfitt
,, Mrs. Nash, 66 Newbridge Rd., W.
,, Mr. H. Willmer, 55 Penn Lea Rd.
C.St. ,, W. J. Parfitt, 18 Raby Place
,, ,, W. Ellis, 44 St. John's Road
Sup. ,, H. W. May, 4 South Lea Rd.
Sec. ,, J. Blake, 20 Clarence Place

TWERTON, Zion
S.St. Mr. F. Hudd, 31 Albany Road
C.St. ,, H. Carey, 24 Lyndhurst Rd.
Supt. ,, H. Carey
Org. ,, G. Fudge, Everest, The Hollow, Twerton Hill
Asst. Org., Mr. Gould

INGLESBATCH
S.St. Mr. George Date, Inglesbatch
P.St. Miss Date, Inglesbatch
C.St. Mr. George Date, Inglesbatch
Sup. & Sec. Miss Date, Inglesbatch

CORSTON
S.St. Mr. C. Shore, Newton St. Loe
C.St. ,, A. J. Pointing, Corston
Sup. ,, C. Shore, Newton St. Loe

HINTON
S.St. Mr. J. Lacey, Hinton Charterhouse
P.St. ,, Lacey
Organist, Miss D. Cook

MIDFORD
S.St. Mr. H. Lansdown, Midford
P.St.
C. St. ,, H. Lansdown

MILK STREET
S.St. Mrs. H. E. Coward, Prior Park Rd.
P.St. Mr. H. E. Coward
Supt. ,, C. Witcombe, 14 Second Av.

BATHAMPTON
S.St. Mr. E. Tovey, B.Sc., "Steep Holme"
,, ,, H. E. Pope, "Fitzford"

BOX
S.St. Mr. E. Bow, 5 Valens Terrace
,, ,, Robson, Ashley, Box
P.St. Mrs. Brooke, 2 Mead Villas
Sup. Mr. Bow
Hymns to E. Bow (Wednesday)

BOX HILL
S.St. Mr. R. Sumner
Sup. ,, G. Hancock, Tis Buts Cottage
Org. Mrs. Head, Box Hill, Wilts

KINGSDOWN
S.St. Mr. T. Aust, Kingsdown
P.St. Mr. and Mrs. Wilkins
Sup. ,, A. Tiley, 5 Prospect
Org.

FRESHFORD
Miss M. Hathaway, Park Corner

KINGSWOOD SCHOOL
Headmaster, Mr. A. B. Sackett, M.A.
Chaplain, Rev. R. E. Davies, B.A.

Combined Preaching Plan 1936. All the Bath Methodist Churches and their officials appear together for the first time. The appeal is included: "Don't forget to pray for those appointed to preach".

The Bath Methodist Circuit Plan, 1936.

Places and Hours of Services		April 5 Palm Sunday	April 12 Easter	April 19	April 26	May 3	May 10 Synod	May 17	May 24 Ascension	May 31 Whit Sunday	June 7 Trinity	June 14	June 21	June 28
*NEW KING STREET Wednesday	11.0 6.30 7.30	Oakley Spear Good Fri., 11	Spear s Watts s Spear	Trebilco Spear Spear	Trebilco Spear Spear	Bates A Cook A Spear	Healey Spear s Synod	Trebilco Stebbins Spear	Spear SSA Spear SSA Mon. SSA	Oakley Spear Spear	Spear s Trebilco Spear	Oakley Harris Spear	Spear Trebilco Spear	Selby Spear Spear
*WESTGATE BDGS. ... Tuesday, C.E. ...	11.0 6.30 7.30	Bates King Bates	Lucas Bates	Tucker Head Bates	Lynham Bates s Bates	Spear Salter Bates	Bates SSA Bates SSA Synod	Shute Tidswell Bates	Price Price Bates	Stockwell Bates s	Bates Barnes Bates	Pillinger Bates Bates	Bates Rutherford Bates	Oakley Bates s Bates
*BEECHEN CLIFF ... Tuesday	11.0 6.30 7.45	Healey Healey s Good Fri., 11	Healey s Healey Healey	Spear Healey Healey	Healey CA Healey CA Healey	Healey Foster Healey	Oakley Healey Synod	Salter Thomas Healey	Bates SSA Bates SSA Healey	Healey Healey s Healey	Healey Healey Healey	Healey Wilkinson Healey	Healey Healey Healey	Healey Huntley Healey
*WALCOT ... ... Friday, ...	11.0 6.30 7.0	Trebilco Salter Good Fri., 11	Oakley Trebilco s Trebilco	Bell CA Bell CA Bell (Tues.)	Spear Trebilco Trebilco	Trebilco A Spear A	James SSA James SSA Mon. SSA	Barnes Trebilco s	Harris Oakley Trebilco	Watts Trebilco	Trebilco A. T. Davies Trebilco	Coward Trebilco s	Trebilco Spear Trebilco	R. Davies Selby
*CLAREMONT ... ... Wednesday	11.0 6.30 8.0	Tucker Bates Bates	Bates s Hewitt	Mrs. Gibbs Bates Bates	Armstrong Wilkinson Bates	Packer Bates Bates	Barnes Pillinger Synod	Bates s Bates SSA Spear (Mon.)	Laytham Laytham Bates	Spear Selley	Mitchard Bates s Bates	Bates Salter Bates	Howard Brown Bates	Bates Lucas Bates
*LARKHALL ... ... Tuesday	11.0 6.30 7.30	Burge D.H.S. Trebilco	Coxon Shute	Branch Tucker Trebilco	Stockwell Supply	Howard A Webb A Trebilco	West Mitchard	Walter Ashman Trebilco	Bishop Packer	Cook CA Watts CA Trebilco	Oakley Lucas	Mrs. Gibbs C. Webb Trebilco	Gifford Crew	Brinkworth Wilkinson Trebilco
*BATHEASTON ... ... Tuesday	11.0 6.30 7.30	Salter Wilkinson	Trebilco s Pillinger Trebilco	Mitchard Lynham	G. Tett A Coxon A Trebilco	Oakley SSA Trebilco SSA	Foster Mellor Trebilco	A. T. Davies Spear s	Shute R. Davies Trebilco	Head Armstrong	Burt Cook Trebilco	Tidswell CA Healey CA	Packer Stockwell Trebilco	Barnes King
*OLDFIELD PARK W. Wednesday	11.0 6.30 7.30	Spear Trebilco Oakley	Watts Oakley s	Oakley Tidswell Oakley	Shute Harris Oakley	Musson A Oakley A s Oakley	Beales SSA Beales SSA Mon. SSA	Stebbins Oakley	Oakley Howard Oakley	Trebilco Oakley	Coward Spear Oakley	Huntley Oakley Oakley	Oakley s Snowdon Oakley	A. T. Davies Oakley Oakley
*OLDFIELD PARK ... Shaftesbury Road Monday	11.0 6.30 8.0	Mrs. Gibbs Mitchard Bates	C. Webb Armstrong	Bates Walter Bates	Selley Blake	Burge Lucas Bates	Brinkworth Stockwell	Thompson Thompson Crew	Branch Sis. Lillian	Bates Blake	Coxon King	Crew Gifford Bates	Burt CA Bates CA s	Bishop Shute
*WESTON ... ... Friday	11.0 6.30 7.30	Cook Oakley Harris	Tidswell Spear s Harris	Foster Armstrong Harris	Bates SSA Oakley SSA Mon. SSA	Tucker A Harris A Harris	Spear Lynham Harris	Oakley Musson Harris	Head Trebilco s Harris	Snowdon Harris Harris	Watts CA Oakley CA Harris	Trebilco Rutherford Harris	Pillinger Oakley s Harris	Spear Salter Harris
*TWERTON, Zion ... Wednesday	11.0 6.0 7.30	Head Raymont Healey	Selley Stockwell Healey	Healey s Wade Healey	Foster Pillinger Healey	Crew Healey s Healey	Hardy Salter Synod	Coxon Davis Healey	Healey Robinson Healey	Wilkinson Hacker Healey	Baguley SSA Baguley SSA Healey	Robinson Cook Healey	Burge Armstrong Healey	Snowdon Healey s Healey
INGLESBATCH .. ... Thursday	11.0 6.30 7.0	Musson Musson	Cook Cook Spear	Shute Shute	Oakley Snowdon	E.G.Davis A E.G.Davis A Spear	Watts Watts s	Mitchard Mitchard	Salter Salter	Tidswell Tidswell	Lynham Lynham Q.M.	Russell Russell	Tucker Tucker	Stebbins Stebbins
CORSTON .. ... Tuesday	6.0 7.0	Walter	King	Short Oakley	Bishop	D.H.S. A	Branch	Long	Shore Oakley	Brinkworth	Howard	Webb	Coxon	Mitchard Oakley
*HINTON .. ... Thursday ...	6.0 7.0	Lynham Oakley	Lacey	Oakley s	Brinkworth	Head A Oakley	Lacey	Selley	Mellor	E. Webb Oakley	Snowdon	Short	Burge	Pillinger Oakley
MIDFORD ... .. Thursday ...	6.0 7.0	Pillinger	Brinkworth	Mellor	C. Webb Oakley	Burge A	Oakley SSA	Gifford	Stockwell Oakley	Walter	Armstrong	D.H.S.	Long Oakley	Lacey
MILK STREET ...	6.30	Burge	Coward	Beer	Mrs. Gibbs	Coward	West	Armstrong	Crew	Coward	Branch	G. Tett	Mellor	Selley
BATHAMPTON ... Thursday ...	6.30 7.0	Tucker	Tett	Trebilco SSA	Wootton	Wilkinson	Burt	Pillinger	Beer	Milne s	Watts	Shute	Foster	Barnes
*BOX ... ... Wednesday ...	11.0 6.30 7.30	Ashman Thomas s	Thomas Sis. Lillian Thomas	Thomas Blake	Mellor West Thomas	Thomas Tucker	Hughes Thomas Thomas	Thomas King	Thomas Healey Thomas	Bow Thomas s	Raymont Raymont Thomas	Sis. Lillian Thomas	Thomas Hardy Thomas	Martin SSA Martin SSA
*BOX HILL ... ... Thursday ..	6.0 7.15	Spear (3) SSA Snowdon (6) ,,	Thomas s Thomas	Hardy	Laytham Thomas	Thomas	Walter Thomas	Raymont	Stebbins Thomas	Edbrook	Thomas s Thomas	Musson	Burt Thomas	Wade
KINGSDOWN ... ... Tuesday 3.0 &	6.15 7.15	Gifford Thomas	Bow	Davis Thomas	Thomas s	Ashman Thomas	Webb	C. Webb Thomas	Raymont	Hardy Thomas	Sis. Lillian	Brinkworth Thomas	Thomas s	Walter Thomas
FRESHFORD ... ... Monday	6.0 7.0													
KINGSWOOD SCHOOL	11.0 7.0							Spear	Trebilco					

PREACHERS

1877 H. J. Lucas, 11 Walcot Parade
1880 H. Bolett, 21 Stall Street
1881 J. W. Charter, Williamstowe, Combe Down
1885 J. Kershaw, Oakleene, Westbridge, Bristol
1885 W. Rumming, 3 Hensley Park
1886 S. Gifford, Bay Cottage, Bathford
1886 W. Mellor, 9 Moorland Road
1886 Mrs. C. Street, The Wharf, Box, Wilts
1886 Major T. Grenfell, 30 Marlborough Bldgs.
1889 C. H. Hacker, Westleigh, Kipling Avenue
1890 H. K. Hunt, 3 Edgar Buildings
1893 A. Beer, 10 Pulteney Mansions
1894 A. Ashman, 23 Longfellow Avenue
1894 A. H. Stebbins, 28 Belgrave Crescent
1896 W. A. Wilkinson, 19 Shakerpeare Avenue
1896 R. Armstrong, 9 Rockliffe Avenue
1897 E. Bow, 5 Valona Terrace, Box, Wilts
1897 J. H. Kent, 6 The Vineyards
1898 H. E. Pope, Fitzford, Warminster Road
1899 H. A. Musson, Tregenna, Bloomfield Park
1899 E. Ruddick, 23 Faulkland Road
1901 J. Lacey, Hinton Charterhouse
1902 H. E. Coward, Lilac Cottage, Clarendon Rd.
1902 W. H. Foster, 2 Milton Avenue
1905 H. Snowdon, 7 Bloomfield Grove
1905 E. Webb, Nightingale House, Grosvenor
1907 W. Harris, 10a Monmouth Place
1907 Sister Lillian E. Lamb, Box, Wilts
1909 C. Vaughan, Pickwick, Corsham, Wilts
1910 M. Harwood, 108 Kellaway Av., Bristol
1911 S. E. Read, 15 Moorland Road
1912 T. S. Burt, 19 Shaftesbury Road
1912 H. G. Fear, 9 Sydney Place
1912 S. R. Salter, 6 Kensington Gardens
1913 H. J. King, 3 Bridge Road
1913 J. Raymont, 7 Lyncombe Hill
1914 A. Hughes, 33 Fairmead View, Box, Wilts
1914 A. E. B. Wade, 18 Rockcliff Road
1915 F. S. Cook, M.A., Burton House, Lansdown
1915 E. V. Selley, 65 Triangle
1915 H. H. West, 1 Cambridge Terr., Widcombe H.
1917 Mrs. A. K. Gibbs, 27 Eastbourne
1919 J. H. Barnes, M.A., Kingswood School
1922 H. J. Stockwell, Windy Ridge, Odd Down
1926 A. D. J. Milne, B.A., Kingswood School
1927 S. G. Head, 4 Longfellow Avenue
1927 A. Packer, 11 Johnstone Street
1929 R. I. Redfern, M.A., Kingswood School
1929 A. T. R. Shute, 1 Highbury Villas, Walcot
1929 H. H. West, jun., 1 Cambridge Terrace
1931 A. T. Brinkworth, 3 Chatham Row
1932 Sidney W. Pillinger, Lower Swainswick
1933 C. M. Walter, Kaleigh Croft Cott., Lansdown
1933 A. T. Davies, B.A., Kingswood School

ON TRIAL.

H. F. Howard, B.A., Evelyn Road
E. G. Davis, 33 Prospect Pl., Up. Weston
A. F. Mitchard, Y.M.C.A.
D. H. S.
D. B.

HELPERS.

R. C. Branch, Swainswick
H. Burge, 42 Brook Road
L. F. Lynham, Norfolk Crescent
W. I. Tidswell, M.A., 4 Northfields, Lansdown
Coun. J. Hewitt, 3 Eastbourne Villas
C. Shore, Newton St. Loe
F. Crew, 38 Winchester Road
W. H. Bishop, Brooklyn Road, Larkhall
F. Russell, 111 Wellsway
G. Weekes, 3 Livingstone Terrace
E. Tucker, Brent Knoll, Bathampton
C. Webb, Mellstock, Twerton Hill
Rev. F. P. Thompson, 45 Herbert Road
T. Fox, 155 Wellsway
P. Hardy, 4 Kipling Avenue
E. Tovey, B.Sc., Bathampton

N.B.—Each preacher is expected to take his own appointments, or, if unable, to provide an accredited substitute. No appointment may be set aside without consent of the Superintendent, and preacher concerned.

References.—

C, Circuit Fund; CT, Chapel Trust Fund; H, Hospital; SSA, Sunday School Anniversary; CA, Chapel Anniversary; FM, Foreign Missions; HM, Home Missions; E, Education Fund; GC, General Chapel Fund; MK, Maintenance & Education of Ministers' Children Fund; A, Auxiliary Fund; TM, Training of Ministers Fund; CF, Connexional Fund; LP, Local Preachers' Mutual Aid; GS, General Sustentation Fund.

MA,(of Kingswood School). It reminds us of National feelings at the time:-

> This meeting records its deep thankfulness for the courage and initiative of the Prime Minister in travelling to Germany for a personal interview with its Leader. It earnestly prays for success in his efforts for peace, and that his example may begin a period when no diplomatic convention or tradition, and no personal or national pride shall stand in the way of our common humanity and common responsibility for the world's peace.

The Second World War

The coming of war was not altogether catastrophic for church life in Bath. While some members were drafted away, there was a big influx of Admiralty staff and evacuee children from London. These, lacking normal home life, found a ready welcome in the social activities provided by the churches and in the homes of the members.

Once the "phoney" war was over the people of Bath were constantly reminded of its savagery by witnessing the frequent and lurid night-time bombing of nearby Bristol.

Bath's turn to suffer came in April 1942; in retaliation for British raids on Lübeck the Luftwaffe turned its attention to Bath. During the nights of Saturday and Sunday 25th and 26th April German bombers concentrated on the city. The full story of this tragedy has been told in other books; suffice to say that great damage and loss of life occurred all over the city and its suburbs of which the Methodists took their due share. Their principal casualty was New King street church which was almost completely destroyed. Westgate Buildings was also damaged. Though it took several months to arrange, eventually the two Societies combined, holding services initially in the school-room beneath Westgate Buildings.

The latter church was eventually repaired sufficiently for the congregation to move upstairs. The membership of Westgate Buildings which had fallen below 70 by 1938 was now 162 and it became undeniably the Methodists' chief City Centre church.

New King Street Church, April 1942, showing bomb damage which led to the complete demolition of the building.

Post-War Contraction

Peace came, but for many reasons the pioneering spirit had been weakened by adverse influences. In many villages decline had set in before the Great War and this trend in the reduction of population intensified between the Wars. Rural Methodism, faced with falling attendances and heavy maintenance bills, lost heart. Even the evangelistically enthusiastic were frustrated. One after another the country chapels closed down and were sold off to become storehouses, workshops or private residences. Eventually Box was the sole rural survivor, being large enough to absorb losses and collecting new support when the neighbouring Societies ceased to meet. It was a similar story in and around the City. By the mid-sixties only Walcot, Beechen Cliff, Oldfield Park (ex Wesleyan), Claremont, Weston, Twerton, Batheaston and Bathampton remained; added to which Southdown had been built. By 1947 losses on *The Myrtle* had caused publication to cease and after that preaching plans were sold separately.

The trouble with Westgate Buildings was its gloomy appearance both outside and in. By 1946 the membership had dropped to 135, but, nothing daunted, the Trustees secured Chapel Committee approval to spend £715 on the construction of an organ composed of New King Street's and Westgate's combined. It was guaranteed to last 25 years and to be capable of transfer to a new church. But it was not to be! Within ten years complaints were rife. In 1958 a new electronic organ was installed. Thanks to legacies the church was declared free of debt in 1950. The records show only five attending the 1958 Leaders' Meeting, only 16 at the Annual Society Meeting, and membership down to 93. The following year only ten attended the Society Meeting, though to be fair it was snowing. Mission was however still in the air. A week of special services included open-air witness outside the Stothert & Pitt Engineering Works led by the Rev. Andrew Crawford.

In 1960 the Society declared its inability to meet its assessment and difficulty in filling the church offices. But with stoic determination, still they carried on, trying "Popular Services", a cinema service and a renewed youth club. Soon the Sunday School was down to 20, the youth club reduced to ten. An

The entrance to the "gloomy" Westgate Buildings Chapel photographed in 1964 at the time of closure.

attempt to form a Central Methodist Youth Club in partnership with Walcot failed. The Church members were ballotted about the future. Some 29 wanted to carry on, only ten voted for closure. Eventually in 1963 a Connexional Commission visited Bath and recognised that £30,000 was needed if modern premises were to be built on the site and certainly that sort of money was not available.

When it was viewed from the other angle, the sale of this valuable commercial site would provide the funds for badly needed extensions and improvements in other Circuit churches. The inevitable decision to close was taken, the last service being held on 30th August 1964 at which time the photograph was taken. The balance of Society funds was sent to the Ivory Coast Appeal, and the membership dispersed to other Methodist churches. Rev. Willie Edmundson, Superintendent Minister published the following spirited riposte to those who saw the closing of Westgate as evidence that Methodism was on the wane:

> Numerically and spiritually it is as strong as in most places. All churches are faced with the problem of the maintenance of their work and witness in city centres. It is the change of social pattern. Our Methodist membership is 1,109 in the City. There will not be another church on the site; the church was outmoded and dilapidated, but now extensions in other churches will be possible.

It is sad that visual evidence of the existence of the Westgate Buildings church does not exist today and shops stand in its stead.

The New King Street site was sold in 1952. Percy Boys' Club was erected in its place. In December 1979 two plaques were unveiled there; one, the original from New King Street church, stating the connection with John Wesley, the second explaining what had happened since. The original plaque had been unveiled in December 1927 by Madame Sarah Grand, Mayoress of Bath, during the Superintendency of Rev. F. G. Gatehouse on the 150th anniversary of the foundation-stone laying of the former church. It was the 52nd tablet erected by the city's Mural Tablets Committee.

The November 1989 statistical state of the Bath Circuit with its four full-time ministers, was as follows:

Membership 731 Active Local Preachers 19					Community Roll 2353 On trial 6	
					Average Morning Attendance	
Individual churches	Built	Members	Community Roll	Young	Adults	Children
Beechen Cliff	1907	161	408	111	106	25
Bathampton	1972	15	37	5	18	—
Oldfield Park	1892	111	450	75	79	18
Southdown	1952	30	80	40	18	10
Twerton	1852	25	89	12	20	9
Walcot	1816	151	520	86	142	31
Box	1897	30	79	18	29	14
Weston	1891	128	400	130	69	41
Claremont	1882	46	200	70	36	6
Batheaston	1876	34	90	10	21	—

Many changes in grouping under individual ministers have been tried over the years, the current arrangement being:

Oldfield Park, Southdown and Twerton
Walcot, Box and University chaplaincy
Weston, Claremont and Batheaston
Beechen Cliff and Bathampton

The Future

How does the future look in the light of all that has gone before? The present Superintendent Minister of the Bath Circuit. The Rev. Ian G. Cramb, sees it this way:

> "What a rich and varied story the foregoing pages represent. It began with John Wesley and here we are 250 years later with a religious scene very different from that of 18th century Bath. We have moved through the divisions of Methodism after Wesley's death and on to the Union of 1932; we have seen the closure of chapels, especially in the villages around the city. Our Circuit of ten churches is much smaller geographically today, and membership figures are one third less than they were even 20 years ago. All this has happened against a background of contemporary history — including two world wars — which saw

the destruction of at least one of our buildings, but more importantly, the death of a number of our people. The experience of war and revolution of thought and ideas in the modern world has presented a challenge to our churches which we have not always accepted.

What of the future? As we read the Bible it is tempting to think that it was obvious in those days what God was doing and what His people should do. The truth was they acted "in faith", and so must we. We do not know how the events of coming days will affect our work; but that is the world in which our Circuit must develop its mission.

With no major developments in our area we have no plans to build new churches though some of the present ones will be enlarged and upgraded. They are well sited but all could be more effective. We live in the days of increasing ecumenical co-operation, and maybe our 'future' lies even more with our fellow Christians than in the past. Meanwhile *'we'll praise Him for all that is past, and trust Him for all that's to come'."*

16

Bathampton

The Background

BY THE 1920s the suburbs of Bathampton, Englishcombe and Twerton were being developed. The Wesleyan Circuit set up a commission to look into the possibilities of establishing chapels in each. A meeting of commission members was held at New King Street on 9th February 1926 under the chairmanship of the Rev. F. G. Gatehouse to discuss the matter. As the Baptists had shown considerable interest in Bathampton it was decided to leave that field open to them. However a small number of people at Bathampton had different ideas. It was the tenacity of these few which won the day. In November 1929, Mr W. H. Padfield conveyed a plot of land adjoining the main Warminster Road to the Bath Wesleyan Circuit. A prefabricated chapel was built there. A new chapel was built in Holcombe Lane in 1972; the old chapel is still in use as a Scout hut. Pictures of both buildings are shown.

A Very Personal Story

Few records remain of those early years but we do have the memory of Mr Kelvin Thomas MBE, who was a boy in those days, and whose family have been involved in the chapel at Bathampton throughout its history. The chapel is known affectionately to some as St Thomas's! Here is his very personal account of the work at Bathampton:

"It was in the year 1926 that the family left South Wales, not by choice but due to the General Srike which forced so many to seek employment in other parts of the country. My mother's parents lived in the hamlet of Bathford, and provided a home for us during this distressing time. Our family consisted of four children, two boys and two girls, (my younger

The original chapel at Bathampton which in 1990 is used by the Scouts. Line drawing by Stan Roe.

Bathampton Methodist Church built in 1972, photographed 1989.

sister Hilary was to be born in Bathampton some three years later).

The Calvinistic Church of Wales, Grangetown, Cardiff, was our spiritual home where we were to be found every Sunday morning. Boots polished on Saturday night of course, together with our weekly dose of syrup of figs or senna pods. Sunday School was at 3pm. In the morning we sat with our parents on very hard wooden benches, form-like with one long rail on which to rest our back, and plenty of room for my father to give us a poke should we dare to make a noise. We enjoyed going to chapel. There was singing, and giggling; and for the one who was the youngest, that delectable time when just before the sermon mother would take us on her lap and we would have the enormous pleasure of caressing her fox fur, and we believed the little head of the fox enjoyed it too.

The old Ford Tourer which brought us to Bathford, with side screens made of perspex material, wended its way through the Forest of Dean and Gloucester (no Severn Bridge of course) and took a full day to accomplish the journey.

Bathampton was soon visited, and we as children were allowed to accompany our parents to see the new house which was only partially built, No 6 Down Lane. I can hear now the echoing footsteps as we climbed the stairs, and the view from every window, seeing fields tall with mowing grass and quiet noises of men mixing mortar, and a pick-axe gently thudding on the virgin soil.

Bathampton boasted a Parish Church but no Chapel, and we were Chapel people. One would have thought that my father and mother had enough to concern them what with work to find and four children to feed and clothe, and that little time and energy would be left to explore means and ways of establishing a chapel at Bathampton.

No way could be found to interest the Wesleyan Methodist Church in building a chapel in the village, and there it may have rested had it not been for a group of people: Mr Wilfred Padfield, Canal Farm, Bathampton; Mr Picket, Down Lane; and my father and mother, Charles and Lena Thomas, "Penhevad" 6, Down Lane Bathampton. "Penhevad" is the name of a little piece of Wales they brought with them, for our previous home was at 6, Penhevad Street, Grangetown, Cardiff. This name was painted in gold lettering upon a Welsh black gate to remind us of our origin.

Mr and Mrs Padfield had two girls and one boy. They too had not originated from this part of the country but their roots were in the Wesleyan Methodist church and they also felt a need for a chapel in Bathampton. For my father money was at a premium, for he had started a Coal Business from scratch with an old "T" Ford with pneumatic tyres on the front axle and hard rubber tyres at the rear. The lamps were oil lit, the windscreen wiper manually operated, and the cab very draughty as I was later to find out.

As I recall it was in 1930 or thereabouts when Mr Padfield, my father and I walked around the parcel of land under the lea of Hampton Downs which Mr Padfield was going to give to the new church. The ground would be prepared and levelled to take a fabricated building, asbestos clad and lined with timber. The building duly arrived and was erected. My father and Mr Padfield stood surety for the bank loan which was to take some 20 years to repay. No affiliation with the Wesleyan Church was made; this was to come later. Contact with lay preachers, who would give us their time and services, was made and worship commenced. The first officers were: Sunday School teacher, Mr Padfield; organist, Mrs Lena Thomas; Steward, Mr Charles Thomas. We knew we would have a small congregation, Mr Padfield's family of five; our own family of six; and Mr Picket.

It should be mentioned here that prior to the chapel on the hill being built we worshipped around the Billiard Table in the Old Barn in the village, opposite the Post Office and store, by the courtesy of Harbutt's Plasticine, the owners. Earlier still (not in my time however), a group of Christians met behind Chapel Row, just off the High Street in one of the cottages.

The Wesleyan Methodist Church, Bath Circuit, was impressed by the fortitude and singleness of purpose shown by the small church, so much so, that some five years after its formation they declared their willingness to support this young society. Bathampton was included on the Plan and enjoyed the occasional visit by an ordained minister.

I remember with pride the wonderful Harvest Festival teas, the beautiful decoration of the overhead beams which lent themselves so adequately to "Old Man's Beard". I remember how hot the chapel was during the height of summer, how cold in the winter with only six small water-filled, gas-ignition, cast-iron radiators. Frost on the inside of the windows was a common sight. A small harmonium demanded from the organist physical strength to supply sufficient air by constant movement of the foot pedals, whilst employing the knees to side swells, added to which a row of stops had to be manipulated along the length of the keyboard; the instrument was now ready to be played!

I remember wonderful Sunday School treats, as they were called; a special pleasure was given to the children: the privilege of riding Mr Padfield's horse. This animal was a real friend of the family and had never experienced the use of a whip. It was a common sight to see Mr Padfield riding in his trap, the reins loosely held in his hands, with an occasional word to his four-legged friend which can only be described as conversation.

The Sunday School grew, new families came to the village and each played a part in carrying on the Christian fellowship, to name but a few, Mr Ernest Tovey, Mr William Welch, Mr and Mrs Marcel Northway and all branches of the Thomas family."

Further Information

There are two references to Free Church preaching places at Bathampton in the 19th century. The Wesleyan Local Preachers' Minute book for 1840 records that it was agreed to put Bathampton "on the plan". Where the services were held, or for how long, is not related.

The 1851 census shows that there was at that time a "Zion Chapel" which comprised two cottages which had been joined together in 1845. There were 65 "Free Sittings" and the congregation at the evening service was 24. The figures were reported by "James Charmbury", but no denomination was mentioned. This may have been the cottage meeting place mentioned in Mr Kelvin Thomas' account.

The Editor of this book preached his very first sermon in the old Bathampton chapel on 6th October 1940. By the 1960's that chapel was not big enough to cope with the various needs of the different groups attached to the church. In 1972 the new chapel was erected, indeed it is the most recent to be built by the Bath Circuit.

One of the great assets brought to Bathampton by the Thomas family was the now world-famous Silver Ring Choir. Its formation stemmed from a rehearsal in 1951 in the chapel for an anthem for the next Sunday's worship. The choir grew from strength to strength both in size and success. They have travelled to many parts of the world; won countless awards in national and international competitive fields; appeared on radio and television and marketed many records. In 1956 Kelvin Thomas wrote: "Did ever art so grace the human race as doth the singer's song."

17

Batheaston

The First Chapel

THERE IS a well-founded tradition that John Wesley preached in Northend, but identification of the exact spot still eludes us. It is described variously as a farmyard, a builder's yard, Mr Bartlett's yard; and two present members of the Society have received the tradition as "in the yard of Lower Northend Farm" and "in the yard where 'Greensleeves' now is". Perhaps John Wesley visited the area more than once and these traditions recall different occasions. What is of greater importance is that from these beginnings came the jubilant faith which inspired the building of the first Methodist chapel in Batheaston and has sustained its people ever since — through good times and bad.

It was an act of faith for a little group of village people to rent a plot of land and "to build one good and substantial chapel . . . in a firm, good and lasting manner with sound and good materials to cost £100". But these people had heard John Wesley speak to them and they were in close touch with the Methodists in Bath some three miles away, whose support — both spiritual and material — they enjoyed. Of the first trustees of the new chapel, 14 were members of the Society in Bath, four being pork butchers and only the remaining three lived in Batheaston. These three were Thomas Lewis a carpenter, William Sainsbury a fuller, and Isaac Gale, a clothworker.

The plot of land they rented on a 999-year lease is that upon which the present chapel stands and the ground rent of £1 per year "of good and lawful money of Great Britain" is still paid to the landowners. But we don't know whether the original lessor ever availed himself of the clause which permitted him "to raise fruit trees against the wall of the chapel so as such trees be not suffered to grow in such manner as to obstruct or hinder the light of the said Chapel."

Of immeasurably greater significance to these early Methodists would be the conditions of the assignment of the chapel to the first Trustees "for the purpose of therein preaching and expounding God's Holy Word provided always that they allow to be preached no other doctrine than is contained in Mr Wesley's Notes upon the New Testament and four volumes of Sermons". By early 1797 the Batheaston Society of the people called Methodists was in being and the Bath Circuit Account Book records the receipt of Batheaston's first quarterly assessment of one guinea; it was then called quarterage. We do not have any information about these very early members of the Society, nor have we any drawing of their chapel. What we do have, however, is a description of it as it was in the last years before its replacement by the present chapel. In 1923, Mr J Grant Melluish writing in *The Myrtle*, recalled his boyhood in Batheaston, and of the old chapel he said:

> "It was a plain structure with no ornamentation whatever, standing in modest seclusion. One can recall the old pews with their doors and the row of pegs along the side walls for hats and coats. The large square pulpit faced the door and had a commodious cupboard underneath; alongside was the old-fashioned family pew which was capable of accommodating more than the average sized family, for in this pew the Communion service was held. In the middle of the chapel stood the stove, around which on forms in cold weather the congregation sat for warmth. The gallery was at the entrance . . . The clock was in front of the gallery and faced the pulpit."

(This clock is now in the schoolroom and is in working order — the only surviving relic of the first chapel.)

The same writer also gives us the names of some of those who regularly attended the services during the middle years of the 19th century: "Mr James Bryant whose duty it was to start the singing; Mr John Rich, a dairyman (see photograph) who played the harmonium, died in 1923; Mr and Mrs Crouch from Saint Catherine; Mr and Mrs Butler from Oakford Farm; Mr Beeker; Mrs Dew; Granny Woodman in her Meth-

Mr John Rich.

odist bonnet and long cloak; Miss Bartlett, who as a small child had heard John Wesley preach; Mr Brinkworth; Mr James Lewis, whose duty it was to snuff the candles; Mr James Melluish and his son Mr Dan Melluish and his family". The first pastor, in 1834, was the Rev. Peter Duncan.

The New Chapel

The old chapel was nearing the end of its useful life by the year 1875 and the question of its replacement was the subject of "conversation" at the Circuit Quarterly meeting. December of the same year saw the decision to re-build taken, and £230 had been promised towards the estimated cost of £400. By June 1876, the new chapel had been completed and it was registered as a Place of Worship. Marriages were authorised in 1878.

The Register of Baptisms begins in July 1876 with the entry for Rosaline Emma Reed, the daughter of a family whose name appears for many years among the members and benefactors of the chapel. The Reeds were paper-makers at Bathford. (See Chapter 24 for more information).

Other names from the period before 1900 are Courtney, White, Mungeam, Hackman, Yates (James and Lucy brought ten children for baptism between 1878 and 1888), Gale, Bath, Maslen, Scott, Seymour, Shute, Pottecary, Rawlings and Willis.

The earliest Seat Rent Ledger still available commences in 1878 and names the families who worshipped regularly and who must have been most actively involved in the work of the new chapel. We owe them much and it seems fitting that their names should be recorded here:-

Richman, Ferris, Beale, Rich, Melluish, Maslen, Yates, Packer, Hodder, Mulligan, Cobb, Wilson, Reed, Grant, Brinkworth, Gothard, Beeker, Lovell, Burge, White, Mungeam.

As the years passed names disappeared from the records, and others appeared for the first time; Hobbs, Batt, Wiltshire, Sims, Slade.

The early years of the present century seem to have been lean, but by 1912 things were looking brighter, numbers were increasing again and, during the next ten years, names of many who have served the society devotedly into our own times are first recorded; Coates, Padfield, Tabb, Burchell, Ponting, Pillinger, Willcox, Hunt, and Dawe. The congregation during these difficult years, though small in numbers, played an active part in Circuit affairs. *The Myrtle* records Batheaston's donation to Conference expenses in 1905 when Conference met in Bristol, to the hospital, and to foreign missions, and includes reports of Sunday School anniversaries and treats, Christmas parties, and Guild visits exchanged with Oldfield Park. We sense that though numbers were low, faith was strong and the Society maintained its witness and cared for its young people.

The walls by 1907 were "in a very bad condition" but with a balance of only 18s, action had to be deferred. It was 1911 before the necessary work could be afforded and then the job was done by a Batheaston firm — Hewlett and Appleby — whose tender of £22 for the "cleaning, repairing and painting of the premises" was the lowest of those received. In this year there was also trouble with the organ which was "badly in need of repair and should be replaced by a more modern American organ". However, repairs were effected and the old organ continued to lead the singing.

> 1913. Balance — £1.2s.7d. The Trustees resolved to contribute annually to the Worn Out Ministers' Fund.
> 1914. The old boiler was worn out and leaking; repairs were authorised to cost no more than £10.
> 1915. A new boiler was installed at a total cost of £7.10s.0d and there was still a balance of £1.3s.6d.

The period of financial stringency was passing, membership was increasing and there was a growing Sunday School. With the ending of the War in November 1918, members who had served in the Forces were welcomed home; church and village were looking to the future. And what an encouraging picture presented itself! There was a Men's Bible Class led by Mr Leonard Burchell, a Guild, and a Sunday School with 95 scholars. The only building which the Society had for all these activities was the chapel itself. The difficulties of teaching 95 children (ranging in age from four to 14 years) in the chapel which had fixed pews, were enough to deter any but the most stout-hearted and devoted of teachers!

Further Expansion

A piece of land alongside the chapel was purchased in 1920 and, under the leadership of the Rev. A. G. Tuck, plans were put in hand for the building of a schoolroom. The Committee which was appointed to oversee the project consisted entirely of members from the Batheaston Society. Mr Mowbray A. Green, the renowned Bath architect and author of the definitive book on the city's Georgian buildings, was appointed to design the schoolroom. Donations flowed in from the churches of the Bath Circuit and friends in the district and even farther afield, all of whom wished the project well.

When members and friends gathered for the laying of the foundation stones on 22nd June 1921, over £856 had been received towards the estimated cost of £1,000. Batheaston's own contribution was £460. The details of the stonelaying are recorded on a wall tablet in the schoolroom. According to the *Bath Chronicle* "glorious weather favoured the Wesleyan Methodists in Batheaston" on the occasion. The ceremonies were followed by "tea in the chapel to which a large company sat down". We applaud the ladies of that day who evidently coped magnificently with the catering under difficult conditions.

Now the building could proceed. Mr J. Rawlings was the builder and Mr W. Moss was responsible for the woodwork. By the end of 1921 the new schoolroom was in use, but there was still an outstanding debt to be paid. Some of the local efforts which helped towards clearing the deficit were: A Garden Fete at Canal Farm, Bathampton (the home of Mr W. H. Padfield, a prominent member of the Society. See Chapter 16). This was a really big affair and was reported at length in the Bath press; a Sale of Christmas fare at which "all the requisites for the Christmas board may be had"; a Concert by Oldfield Park Concert Party, charges for admission — Adults 6d, children 3d and a few reserved seats at 1s; and in a more serious vein, the Oldfield Park Sunday School Choir presented a sacred cantata *The Story of Jesus*.

Sunday School outings were a regular feature. Our photograph of one such was taken around 1925.

Charabanc outings were a popular attraction. The Batheaston School is pictured at Cheddar around 1925.

During the 1920s there is a mention of the "choir and choirmaster" and the "organs". The organ in the church seemed to be frequently in need of attention, and is the one which is still in use. In those days the blower sat alongside the organist on the bench by the wall and operated the long wooden handle of the bellows — for which service he received 3s. 6d per quarter. The second instrument was an American organ which at this time was in the vestry. Unfortunately it has not been possible to discover when these two instruments were first purchased. It was during the year 1929 that the organ in the church was dismantled, thoroughly overhauled, various "bits" replaced, cleaned, re-assembled and tuned for a total charge of £5. Further major work was required ten years later and the cost then was £10.

The schoolroom continued to be the scene of much activity and was frequently used by organisations outside the church for meetings, concerts and classes and at the outbreak of the Second World War in 1939, Air Raid Precaution and Keep Fit Classes were added to the number. The following brief entries from the Stewards' accounts are reminders of wartime activities:

	£. s.d
Received from the Rural District Council for Evacuees	1.10.0
Paid for a stirrup pump	1.0.0
Paid for War Risk Insurance	9.0.0
Paid for wood for the blackout	1.6.0
Received from "B" Platoon of the Home Guard for use of room	10.0

The schoolroom was also used for film shows in support of the War Savings Movement, the Russian Red Cross and the Merchant Seamen's Charities.

Post-War Progress

A new Trust was formed in 1945 which included senior members of families who had served the church for many years, and among whose children are numbered two who entered the Methodist ministry — Stanley Pillinger and Michael Hucker. The work and witness of the church had continued all through the dark days of the War. Batheaston had escaped many of the rigours of the war and now faced the future with humble thankfulness. Records tell of the continuing activities of the Youth Club, the fellowship meetings and the Sunday School, and in September 1945 the first meeting of the Women's Happy Hour. Much work was needed to be done on the premises to make good the dilapidations of the war years. The iron railings around the front of the church had been requisitioned during 1942 in the drive for scrap metal for armaments and were now to be replaced. The government compensation was £14.15s.0d and the new railings cost £108! The heating system needed attention and much other work was necessary. An appeal for funds was, as always, generously met, and in 1948 a Gift Day raised £114 and a Sale of Work another £132.

The gift in 1950 by Mrs Mary Hick of a strip of land behind the schoolroom was received by the Trust, who gladly accepted the proviso that they "allow Mr Godwin to continue in occupation of the land until such time as they should require it and should then, at their own expense, move Mr Godwin's fowlhouse."

The land immediately to the north of the schoolroom was purchased in 1953 ready for future building extensions. In the meantime a great deal of work on the chapel itself had been proceeding and on 1st October of the same year it was re-opened for worship. The new work included the pulpit which was given in memory of Mr Henry S. Tabb whose death in 1951, after many years of devoted service, had been such a sad loss to the Society. The church was re-opened by Mrs C. M. Tabb and the service of dedication was conducted by the Rev. Lionel Brayton, the Superintendent of the Bath Circuit, assisted by the Rev. T. Griffith Rees, who was the minister at Batheaston.

Mr Leonard Burchell.

This line drawing by Stan Roe shows Batheaston Schoolroom with the Chapel beyond.

Approval was obtained in 1954, for the use as a car park, of the land to the north of the schoolroom. Three years later saw the inauguration of an organ fund which made possible the expenditure of £123 on renovation and repair work. The need of the Sunday School for extra accommodation was met by the building of two new classrooms behind the schoolroom.

The long blue velvet curtains — the gift of Mrs Blanche Bence — were, in 1956, hung on the east wall of the church behind the pulpit. There is a rose window behind the curtains through which the morning sunlight streams. It used to light the church with radiance but made it quite impossible for the congregation to see the preacher! Mrs Bence's gift provided a beautiful solution to this problem and now on sunny mornings the congregation can see as well as hear those who lead the worship.

A survey of 1966 revealed an infestation of woodworm in the timbers and flooring of the church. Professional help was immediately sought, the trouble dealt with, and the congregation returned to worship in a church odorous with the smell of insecticide.

Perhaps it was the sight of the ladies on their knees washing dishes which prompted a gift to the Trust for the improvement of the kitchen accommodation. This resulted in the transformation of one of the small schoolrooms into a spacious and very workable kitchen, and the building underneath of a new long schoolroom with access from inside and outside the main buildings. The new extensions were opened on 30th September, 1967.

The time had now come when it was possible to provide the youth club building which was so desperately needed. This building, set on a portion of the car park, was opened in 1972 by Mrs Mary Burchell and named The Leonard Burchell Room in memory of her father (at the special request of youth club members). Mr Leonard Burchell had served the church from 1913 to 1971 and we include his photograph.

18

Beechen Cliff

How it all Began

AT THE TURN of the century the United Methodist Free Churches of the Bath Circuit occupied five preaching places, namely: Hope Chapel, Bath; Box; Box Hill; Kingsdown; and Zion Chapel, Twerton.

Because Oldfield Park was being developed as a new suburb of Bath a site was earmarked there in 1899 by the United Methodists for a new chapel. The Beechen Cliff Estate at Bear Flat was to be the next housing development. In a large mansion near the cliff edge, Esher House, lived Mr F. W. Spear, the Secretary of the Bath and District Sunday School Union. He watched the new estate being built and soon realised that the children living there did not have a Sunday School within easy reach. He therefore opened a school in his own house. Mr Spear persuaded the Sunday School Union to "hint" to the Bath Free Church Council that a Sunday School should be built in the area. The United Methodists were offered the opportunity.

About this time the Baptists had set about erecting a Church and schools at The Triangle, Oldfield Park, which was within a few hundred yards of the United Methodists' site, thus to some extent pre-empting their proposed development (the Wesleyans had been well established just across the road since 1892). It was without much reluctance therefore that the United Methodists transferred their attention to the Beechen Cliff area. Mr Robert Bird, JP, of Cardiff, the Connexional Treasurer, offered money for the purchase of a site.

The now familiar and admirably situated Shakespeare Avenue site was secured in May 1905 with a loan from Headquarters of £1,500, and the plot at Oldfield Park was abandoned. Once the site had been dedicated an architect had to be appointed, and a builder selected. In less than two years all these preparations were completed and the new Church was constructed and opened its doors.

The Rev H Walker Blott.

The Circuit Superintendent Minister from 1903 had been the Rev. H. Walker Blott (see photograph). It was his task to manage the whole Bath United Methodist Circuit without any ministerial assistance until April 1907. Under his guidance nearly 1,000 houses on the new estate were canvassed by a small group of enthusiasts from Hope Chapel. For 13 consecutive months they distributed *The Beechen Cliff Magazine* to every house.

Stone-laying

The stone-laying ceremony was held on a mercifully fine day, Tuesday, 17th July 1906. Unfortunately the Rev. John Moore, Connexional Home Missions Secretary, who was to have conducted the ceremony, could not attend. His place had to be taken by the Chairman-elect of the Bristol District, the Rev. W. Locke Smith.

Here are the names and representation of those who laid the 13 foundation stones:

The Connexion: Rev. Edward Boaden (Chapel Secretary), Mr Robert Bird, JP, (Treasurer).

Bristol District: Mr W. H. Butler, Mrs T. Butler, Mr A. E. Chivers of Radstock.

City of Bath: Mrs Walter Pitt, Mr Sam Hallett, Mr William Webb (the builder), Mr George Townsend (foreman of builders).

Bath Circuit: Mr Enoch Harding (Circuit Secretary), Mrs A. P. Monks, Miss Dorothy Hallett (aged 16), Master Kedgwin Turvey (aged 8, son of Mr G. K. Turvey, Church Steward of Hope Chapel. He was also present when the church's 75th anniversary was celebrated in 1982).

Among those present was Mr F. W. Spear of Esher House. He also donated £50.

The Treasurer, Mr Jacob Tucker of Twerton, expected the church to cost £3,915, towards which £540 had been promised, and "the workmen were subscribing towards the building themselves".

Open Air Preaching

It was necessary to sustain the momentum by holding open-air services on the site until the church should be built. A special Quarterly Meeting held at Hope Chapel on 12th March 1906 decided to introduce these weekly services from Whit Sunday, 3rd June, at 8.15pm. The first such service was conducted by Mr A. P. Monks (the Preachers' Secretary) with the Rev. H. W. Blott preaching the sermon. At the Circuit Preachers' Meeting at Box on 14th June 1906 Beechen Cliff was placed on the next quarterly Plan. Amongst the names of the preachers appointed for Beechen Cliff on that first Plan, the term "Supply" features 13 times! This suggests that open-air speakers were hard to find since no preacher could be named for these appointments at the time the plan was drafted. These outdoor services ceased on 7th October 1906.

The first official church meeting on record was held at the Manse, 28 Austin Villas, Wells Road, on 18th April 1907. Those present were: Rev. H. Walker Blott (in the chair), Mrs Blott, Mrs Swain, Mrs Blake, Mrs James, Messrs Swain,

James, Blake and Keen. Church Officers were appointed. They decided that pews would be rented and free alternately and unlabelled. Front pews could cost 2s a quarter for one sitting, 8s for five; and double these amounts would be charged for the back seats. The attraction of "sitting at the back" was thus recognised from the outset!

Beechen Cliff Methodist Church as sketched by the architect, Mr W H Dinsley, 1907.

The offertory would be paid into the bank on Monday mornings, thus "lessening the interest on the overdraft". Sunday School would meet at 3pm; Superintendent: The Rev. H. W. Blott; Deputy Superintendent: Mr McCheyne; Secretary and Treasurer: Mr A. Blake; Teachers: Mrs Blott (who was in charge of the Primary Department), Mr McCheyne, Mr L. James and Mr C. P. Keen.

An International Bible Reading Association branch would be formed, Mr L. James being the Secretary. A Junior Christian Endeavour would meet on Wednesdays at 6.30pm and a Singing School on Tuesdays at the same time.

And so the pioneer leaders were on station with the initial policy decisions taken.

The New Church

The church itself was opened a week later on Thursday 25th April 1907 by His Worship the Mayor of Bath, following one year and five days physical labour. It had been designed by an architect "well-known in Methodist Circles", Mr W. Hugil Dinsley of Chorley, whose sketch of the premises is reproduced. Its specification reads: "Gothic style to seat 500, church parlour for 60, vestry, school hall and classrooms, three of which 'may be thrown into the hall', which would then seat 400. The other classrooms to be stone-walled all round, and so designed that a second storey of classrooms could be added over the first." At the time of the opening, only the church, parlour, vestry and a row of classrooms had been completed. The hall and the rest of the classrooms were due to be added later. The main building was erected by Mr W. Webb, builder, the heating installed by Messrs W. Parham, and the lighting by the Bath Gas Co. The sum of £671 was sanctioned for the purchase of an organ.

The Mayor, Alderman S. W. Bush, JP, with some foresight "hoped they might find there a haven for the storm-tossed sons of men", and "prayed for the time when all the churches would become one, and there would be only one army fighting against sin and against Satan". Rather curiously, and before unlocking the door, he handed over 10s "sent by a communicant of the Church of England". The throng of well-wishers, ministers, trustees, etc, then entered the church behind the Mayor and Mayoress. The dedicatory sermon was preached by the Rev. D. Irving, President of the United Methodist Church. He said: "Some might find sermons in stones, books in brooks and good in everything, but those who found great spiritual uplifting were those who went where Scripture was read and expounded."

There was a tea (tickets sixpence), after which a public meeting enabled the local clergymen to have their say. The Rev. Blott announced that £648.13s.4d. had been raised towards the total cost of £4,000 and that the afternoon offertory had raised a further £22.3s.0d. The Rev. J. Turner Smith (Argyle Congregational) said the building was one in which it was easy to speak and easy to hear. Churches were of little use unless everyone could see and hear well. This place of worship was planted in the midst of homes clustering upon the hillside. He prayed God to richly bless all who worshipped Him there. The church at present did not have any history. They would, in fact, be making history. Mr Spear announced that without the lapse of a single Sunday there would be a Sunday School now meeting in the church. We can see clearly therefore that Mr Spear's "hint" had been realised.

The Trustees

The original Trustees were: Messrs R. Bird, D. Irving, J. McCheyne, A. S. Bryant, J. M. Bell, G. Carey, A. P. Monks, S. Hallett, T. Butler, E. Harding, W. Swain, O. S. Gullick, J. B. Butler, J. Martin and W. L. Stone.

The Trust was subsequently re-formed and increased in number several times. The last of the original trustees, Mr Enoch Harding, died on 29th December 1939, aged 87. One milestone was the appointment in 1952 of the first lady trustees, Elsie Taylor, Maud Reakes and Constance Meredith. However the next renewal on 11th May 1964 saw in all-male membership once more.

The Sunday Services

It was some time before any settled pattern was adopted. The "church meeting" dictated many aspects of the conduct of worship. For instance, before 1907 was out these decisions were taken: To stop singing the Lord's prayer. To stop the preacher descending from the pulpit for the offertory prayer. To stop the singing of Amen after prayers. To hold "adult school" early on Sunday mornings instead of a prayer meeting . . . then . . . To stop holding the "adult schools", instead to hold a Bible Class in the afternoon. To hold Sunday night "socials" once a month instead of prayer meetings. To hold a special service once a month (except August), thus:- January: New Year. February: Missions. March: District Extension Fund. April: Trust Anniversary. May: Sunday School Anniversary. June: Flower Service. July: Chapel Loan Fund. September: Harvest. October: Local Preachers' Mutual Aid. November: Hospital and Temperance. December: Christmas.

During the week

Good use of the premises was essential to raise funds for reducing the colossal financial debt with which the church was encumbered. On 21st, 22nd and 23rd May, 1907, a "May Fair" was held which raised £82. There were stalls behind the church under a canvas awning and all the churches in the circuit, as well as other Free Churches, manned them. Each evening the May Queen (Doris Swain) was crowned. The Lady Mayoress of Bristol (Mrs A. J. Smith) opened the proceedings on the first day. The Lord Mayor said he thought the Rev. Blott was "a very go-ahead sort of man". Mr Blott assured his audience that those attending the church during the first four weeks were not drawn from other churches. Mrs. S. C. L. Fuller opened on the second day. On the third day the ceremony was performed by representatives of the various United Methodist Free Church Sunday Schools in the circuit: Master Teddy Blake from Hope, Miss Dorothy Sheppard from Box (happily still with us in 1990), Miss Ada Vivash from Box Hill, Miss Gertrude Butt from Kingsdown, Miss Florence Cook from Twerton and Master Tom Swain from Beechen Cliff.

There was a warning about the selection of May Queen: "Any canvassing will disqualify." When war came in 1914 the annual May Fair became the "Red, White and Blue" Fair.

The Daily Round

As early as the middle of 1908 the Minister's wife drew attention to "the small amount collected at the services," and she proposed that "open receptacles be used". A decision to use wood platters, rather than baskets, was straightway taken. They are still in use today. A "Church Building Society" was tried, but so little was invested that it was wound up in 1910. Later that year an envelope scheme was introduced. Rather ominously, any who did not join would be interviewed by Section Leaders "to ascertain their feelings". It was to be 1924 before the church could claim to be debt-free. In 1944 the envelope numbering system was introduced whereby the donors would be unknown to the stewards.

It is interesting, and perhaps sad, to record this general impression gained from reading the minutes of church meetings: Whereas initially the emphasis had been on spiritual achievement, reports gradually changed in character until the financial results in meticulous detail became the most important and sometimes sole means of recording the state of affairs. In the early days it had been customary for the Section Leaders and Stewards rather than the Minister to report on the "spiritual state" of the various organisations. On one occasion we read that all was well except for the Bible Class "which needs stimulating". A yet later phase in the minute books revealed the over-riding importance of appointing people onto various committees. Some meetings seemed to be concerned with little else. The early enthusiasm for insisting that such representatives reported back to main committees soon disappeared altogether.

New members were admitted by election at the Leaders' Meetings and received at the Annual Convenant Services, held from 1909 onwards on the first Sunday evening of the calendar year. To encourage and get to know visitors, socials were held after some evening services. On at least one occasion the Church Steward announced the last hymn so that the Minister was released in time to catch visitors leaving the church.

During the year 1911 there were complaints that the church services were "not hearty enough". Members agreed to silence would-be critics by entering more fully into the work and by

Reception, 29 January 1914, after wedding of Edward Roberts and Dorothy Hallett at Beechen Cliff Church.

becoming "a zealous and peculiar people". Around this period the Leaders were meeting monthly, and all the church members quarterly, to debate church affairs.

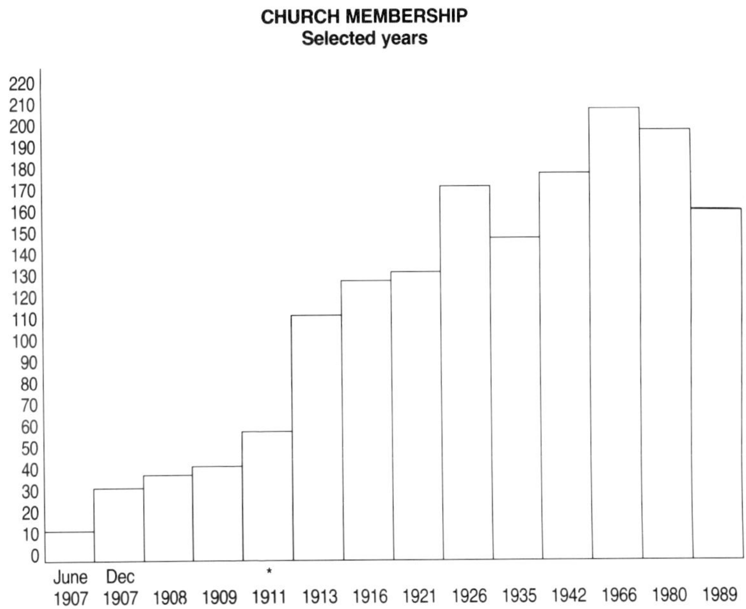

* Hope Chapel closing 1911.

Prayer meetings were a vital part of church life and were held at various times on Sundays starting at 7.30am and also during the week. The stewards recommended that people should engage more in open prayer; that there should be more singing and less pauses. One lady spoke of the great difficulty she found in praying openly; one man thought this kept people away. Some suggested they should finish the preceding service earlier. Mr Blott undertook to shorten his sermons! Just 20 years later (1930) similar discussions led to the formation of twelve "Groups" within the congregation with a leader for each.

A winter programme for 1927 shows the following as regular week-night activities: Monday — Scouts, Tuesday afternoon — Women's Missionary Auxiliary, evening — Fellowship,

Wednesday — Male Voice Choir, Ladies' Guild, Friday — Choir Practice.

Our photograph shows a wedding group in 1914 which involved several prominent families. The minister was the Rev. J. M. Ward.

Musical Matters

Inevitably this was a delicate subject. Committees recorded decisions "that the meeting ask the Trustees to seek a change of organist" or "complaints were received re the strong voice of one of the members of the choir". The Secretary was instructed to intimate to that member that his services could now be dispensed with. In December 1910: "The choir seemed to be a little bit receding . . . should like to see a little more punctuality and enthusiasm." One assumes that initially the choir accompanied only the evening service, for in December 1909: "the members of the choir were requested to endeavour to be present at the morning service."

The organ was always a problem child. In 1911 the Trustees were considering buying an American organ. When Hope Chapel finally closed in 1913 however, their organ was moved to Beechen Cliff. Organ blowers were not always reliable; as recently as 1944 it was reported that the organ was silent because there was no one to blow. In 1945 the choir raised £65 for an electric blower. The organ was dismantled and thoroughly overhauled in 1980 at a cost of £5,000, after a demonstration with electronic organs had failed to woo the leadership.

Pews superseded chairs in the choir and at the sides of the church in 1913. Seven years later Mr G. K. Turvey, using his talent as monumental mason, gave the War Memorial. He also carved the text over the choir arch: "Let us come boldly unto the throne of grace that we may obtain mercy and find grace to help." (Hebrews Chap 4, v 16).

Work Amongst the Young

Clearly many organisations in the church waxed and waned and were sometimes eclipsed, but the Sunday School went from strength to strength. It was led by devoted staff and, from all the evidence, was advanced in its methods. A report published at the end of the first 12 months is one of the most stimulating church documents one could hope to read as the following extracts reveal:

> We present our first annual report . . . we can give you statistics . . . but that can never adequately convey any idea of the moral and more lasting work done . . . We trust that the children's lives may show forth both now and in the years to come the lessons they have learned in this place, and thus witness that our efforts on their behalf have not been in vain . . . Our school is run on strictly systematic lines . . . The scholars feel that by lack of attendance, or neglect of duty, not only themselves but their whole class are involved . . . We very seldom have a scholar absent . . . Our work with the children does not end with Sunday . . . We have a girls' working guild, a singing school, a junior Christian Endeavour Society, a cricket club, outing and parties . . . Our primary department . . . is a new departure . . . we have had a number of visitors engaged in similar work . . . We started this year with 22 scholars and nine teachers. We now number 70 scholars and 15 teachers . . . we are far from satisfied . . . we believe in small classes and plenty of teachers . . . we have persistently endeavoured to strengthen the connection between school and church.

The teachers were themselves meeting monthly after school for prayer and to prepare their lessons.

The Rev. Blott had been President of the Bath Sunday School Union and had visited many of the Sunday Schools in Bath. In 1907 he retired from that office "in order to step back into the ranks of Sunday School teachers". There is ample evidence for affirming that his and Mrs Blott's leadership were largely responsible for laying such excellent foundations for the youth work at Beechen Cliff. Mr Blott relinquished the Superintendency in May 1909, and Mr C. P. Keen succeeded him. The second annual report revealed that the school was recognised as a pioneer in Primary education in the city, and that others were following their example. The minimum age of entry was fixed at four "so successful was the Department".

Various methods were tried to improve attendance and punctuality. "YOU ARE LATE" cards were hung in conspicuous positions after opening time. Three late marks were equivalent to one absent mark. Class marks were made dependent upon written work as well as attendance. Elaborate quarterly awards were dropped during 1910 in favour of annual ones. Collecting cards for school funds were distributed. Those scholars filling their cards were honoured by being chosen to take up the Anniversary offertories.

The 1910 annual report announced that none had left "to join that large throng who fritter away the golden hours of the Sabbath in aimless and fruitless pleasure-seeking". Some local residents were courting disapproval by sending their children to Beechen Cliff "only till they are of fit age to be transplanted to their proper denominational soil". Lack of teachers was handicapping the work, regular preparation classes were being held, and the first teacher "promoted from the ranks" had been welcomed. There were 86 scholars and 20 teachers. Nine scholars had unbroken attendance records since the school opened.

In May 1913 the new school hall and classrooms were opened by W. H. Butler, Esq, JP, (impressive rows of foundation stones bore the initials of 35 scholars). These buildings cost £1,111 and the debt was cleared two years later.

Around this time the total school membership with staff was about 130, a figure probably never attained again. Sunday School outings were a regular feature of the year's work. The following summary indicates the most popular venues. 1908, Clevedon; 1909,10,11, Weston "on a date when the tide serves"; 1912, Upper Weston by special car, and walk to Loud's Farm for tea and games; 1913,14, Farleigh Castle by motor and horse; 1915, Upper Weston; 1917, Bathampton (by train); 1919, Weston; 1920, Steeple Ashton, Edington and Bratton, 108 went in three motor charabancs on 23rd June, tea at Edington, boating on the lake, cricket and games. Started at 1.30pm, back at 9.30pm; 1923, Weston by three charabancs from Red Charabanc Company; 1924, Weston by train, 43 scholars and 17 adults. The Primary Department went to Clifton Zoo; 1925, Edington; 1929, Edington. Primary went to Glasshouse Cafe on another day.

Youth Organisations

Mention has already been made of the week-night activities sponsored by the Sunday School in the early years of their existence. The year 1907 also saw the founding of an Institute for Boys' and Men's Physical Culture. Boxing was however stopped in 1910, although at that time there was little popular outcry against the sport.

An interesting comment was made in 1909 by Mr Blott who, reporting that a Young People's Society had been formed for all over 13, regretted that it was chiefly females who attended and hoped young men might be induced to join. About this time the children's singing school was abandoned "leaving Mr Blott to spend the evening to the best possible advantage".

It was decided, on the 23rd October 1914, to recommend "the formation of BP Boy Scouts and Girl Guides in connection with our Church and School". Surprisingly on the 14th November it was reported that the Guides had already started with 12 girls, but there were not enough boys to get the Scouts going. "If the Scouts are not started soon the Physical Culture class will return." The Band of Hope, which in 1909 was attended by 60, ceased about this time. Three years later it is known the Scouts were running under Mr Hamish O'Hara. It is recorded that in 1918 when the Sunday School library was being overhauled, the "useless books" were given to the Guides! During the year 1919, the Guide Company won three shields. These were for racing, singing and cobbling.

An Abstainers League was formed in 1921. Six years later there is mention of the Badminton Club. The Cubs appear to have started in 1924, but it was 1929 before there was talk of a Brownie pack. As recently as 1946 the Leaders decided that "for the good of the devotional work of our church" permission could not be given for young people to dance in the church hall, although a Methodist Conference resolution of 1942 had in fact permitted this (and card playing).

"Special Consideration" for Beechen Cliff

In 1910 Beechen Cliff felt they could afford to pay for more of a minister's time than they had hitherto been getting. It was from the following resolution passed at the Circuit Quarterly

Meeting at Hope Chapel on 17th December 1910 that Beechen Cliff acquired a reputation for exclusiveness which remained for many years afterwards:

> . . . so that the Beechen Cliff church may receive the whole Sunday Services of the Rev. J. M. Ward, the church will make itself responsible for the whole cost of such services, believing that the main hope of building up a strong flourishing church in the neighbourhood depends on them having the same pulpit service every Sunday . . . there are no Methodist traditions or attachments, the people are drawn by convenience and the hope of attaching them lies in an efficient pulpit supply.

The outcome was that Beechen Cliff paid two-thirds of the circuit expenses, the other one-third being shared amongst the remaining four churches. By 1913 Beechen Cliff paid three-quarters.

A Bath Circuit Quarterly Meeting of 1946, now representing the whole range of Methodist Societies, endeavoured to end Beechen Cliff's special position, by arranging for the following resolution to be put to the Beechen Cliff Leaders' Meeting held on the 3rd September of that year:

> That this society considers the time has arrived when Beechen Cliff need no longer be treated differently from other principal societies as regards ministerial preaching appointments on the plan.

The resolution was however lost, only two people voting in favour.

The subject then lapsed.

To gauge the extent of such "exclusiveness" over the years one has only to study the figures contained in the following table. This shows to what extent during the years in question each church's "own minister" occupied the pulpit (out of 104 services each year). Principal churches which came into the reckoning after Union are also shown.

Own Ministers' Preaching

Year	Beechen Cliff	New King Street	Westgate	Walcot	Oldfield Park
1908	64	-	-	-	-
1909	87	-	-	-	-
1910	68	-	-	-	-
1911	90	-	-	-	-
1937	66	37	42	36	-
1940	64	39	39	34	-
1945	59	-	41	47	-
1950	47	-	42	38	-
1980	51	-	-	42	41
1987	45	-	-	55	31

The World Outside

The outbreak of the Great War caused Beechen Cliff Leaders' Meeting to resolve on 14th September 1914 that "all preachers be requested to make use of our Nation's hymns and to make some reference to the grave situation at every service".

Soon afterwards the (United Methodist) Circuit Meeting decided "to record admiration of the patriotism of the young men of our churches in offering themselves to fight". Each church was required to prepare and keep up-to-date a Roll of Honour of all the young men who had joined the Forces.

The Circuit Meeting of 1916 unanimously passed a resolution expressing gratification that 120 young men had joined up, but recorded strong disapproval over the harsh treatment of conscientious objectors. A copy of this resolution was sent to the Prime Minister, Mr Asquith and the War Secretary, Mr Lloyd George.

Soon afterwards the figures for all the United Methodist Churches of the Bath Circuit became known and are reproduced here for convenience:

Church	Members	Men Joined Forces	Wounded	Died
Beechen Cliff	131	28	3	-
Box	48	30	1	2
Box Hill	27	37	4	2
Kingsdown	13	14	1	2
Twerton	52	15	1	-

The area around Beechen Cliff was heavily bombed in 1942. This view shows the schoolroom and the church and the nearby devastation.

Church Logo 1989.

At Beechen Cliff the Educational Authorities made use of some of the rooms. In January 1915 "at the children's wish" the money they would have spent on prizes was donated to the Belgian Refugees' Fund. This was at the time when thousands of refugee Belgians had fled to England. In 1916 lighting regulations led to the steps being roped off during the dark evenings "to ensure the safety of worshippers leaving the church". The customary Watch Night Service had to be cancelled. After the war hope centred round the League of Nations, support for which was contained in a Circuit resolution in September 1921. Beechen Cliff decided to affiliate to the League of Nations' Union and to pay £1.1s.0d. subscription. Two years later a resolution was passed supporting the League's attitude towards Italy and Greece. In 1922 a retiring collection was taken for the distressed Cornish tin miners, and in 1923 for the Mayor's Japanese fund.

The World War 1939–45 brought the Admiralty to Bath and changed the congregation somewhat. The school premises were taken over as a First Aid Post. The church railings were removed for scrap in the spring of 1940. In April 1942, despite widespread devastation at Bear Flat and elsewhere in the vicinity from bombing, the church escaped relatively lightly. Windows were broken and some ceilings badly displaced. The photograph shows how close the church came to total destruction.

Post-war years have seen Beechen Cliff taking its full part in Circuit affairs. At the same time there has been co-operation with nearby Anglican and Catholic churches in which the Methodists have shared the initiative. House groups have sustained the fellowship, and the appointment of Pastoral visitors and "Care Links" has enabled contact to be maintained with the majority of those on the Community roll. The uniformed organisations have flourished and sometimes wavered according to the availability of dedicated leadership. Sunday School attendance has fallen. In looking back over the years it is clear that, despite the variety of competing interests, Beechen Cliff Church has been able to maintain its witness because it sees its role as a servant of this particular neighbourhood (see logo), one which contains no other Non-Conformist representation.

19

Box and District

Ebenezer Chapel

THE FIRST documentary record of Methodist activity at Box is in 1820 when Samuel Roe sought permission of the Bishop of Salisbury to use his own house for religious worship. The Bath Methodist Society accounts show quarterly payments of £1 being made from 1823, and in 1829 the strength was shown as nine persons. The first meeting place was said to have been in an old cottage at Woodstock, and later in the home of Mr Thomas Rowe.

The first chapel, Ebenezer, was built in 1834 at the instigation of Mr Rowe. The chapel, which was certainly more spacious than his house, soon attracted more members. Numbers had doubled by 1840 when the construction of Isambard Kingdom Brunel's famous Box tunnel, together with the new-found stone industry in the area, brought a great influx of labour, and therefore business and prosperity, to the village.

The increased local population, revelling in full employment and an assured income, brought problems for the authorities and a challenge to the churches with riotous living and questionable morals. Drunkenness — two more public houses opened, which made a total of five — and fighting, were the order of the day and night.

Membership fluctuated as the following figures taken from Circuit schedules, demonstrate:

1829 - 9;	1833 - 6;	1838 - 7;
1839 - 13;	1840 - 16;	1844 - 11;
1847 - 0;	1848 - 5;	1849 - 6;
1850 - 6;	1851 - onwards record do not exist.	

The reason for the chapel disappearing from the Wesleyan records was that its membership transferred allegiance to the

At Box in 1896 the stone-laying for the new chapel.

Wesleyan Reformers; they soon became part of the United Methodist Free Church Circuit. The 1851 Census states that Ebenezer had 160 seats with attendances of 40 in the morning and 70 in the evening. A separate return shows 18 "Brethren" meeting in the afternoon. The building therefore may have been shared at this time.

Revival and Expansion

Cottage meetings were held for some years in the neighbouring areas of Box Hill and Kingsdown, and eventually small chapels were erected in each place in 1867 and 1869 respectively. Both witnessed scenes of remarkable revivals and large numbers were converted. It could not be long before Box village's Ebenezer Chapel needed to consider bigger premises. So the band of Christian-minded men and women moved gladly to the task. The stone-laying ceremony in 1896, alongside the old chapel, is shown in the photograph.

Saturday, 6th February, 1897, was a red letter day in the annals of the United Free Methodists in the Bath Circuit, for on that day, to use a phrase beloved of contemporary journalists, "a neat and commodious new church" was opened. It accommodated 250 people. Lady Dickson-Poynder, wife of the Member of Parliament for Chippenham, performed the honours, as her husband was too ill to attend. She admitted that, since she herself belonged to "a different community of Christians", she could not agree with all the Methodists did and said, but she felt they all had the same aim. As a woman she felt glad that in the new church the wives, mothers and daughters of those who had worked so hard would be able to worship God in comfort. After several speeches the inevitable tea was served in the village school and a rally was held in the church at 6pm when stirring and enthusiastic addresses were given by the Revs. Dr Brook and J. J. Martin of Bristol, A. Warcup (Primitive Methodists) of Chippenham, and other friends. Mr Bow, the Secretary, explained that the building had cost £1,200, towards which £500 has already been raised. Miss Noble presided at the harmonium, and the singing of the various hymns and anthems was hearty. Solos were rendered by Mr Enoch Harding and Master Stanley Harding, of Bath.

The Rev. J. T. Hodge said they had good reason to be encouraged on account of the work of God in the country places connected with the Bath Circuit, for during the previous three years Box, Box Hill and Kingsdown, had each doubled their membership.

The Twentieth Century

The church experienced many happy and melancholy events in its history. One of the saddest was on the 14th June, 1906, when Mr J. H. Dorey — a circuit steward for 17 years in Bath, and a preacher for 50 years — died suddenly at Box Station while waiting for the train back to Bath, having addressed the Circuit Preachers' Meeting which had been held at Box. Mr Dorey spoke to the six preachers present that fateful evening on the subject: "Go Preach". Every word of his talk has been preserved. It finished, prophetically, like this:

> We sow the seed, others will come after us and reap a splendid harvest; the garners of Heaven will be filled with the faithful. From every land and in every tongue they shall join the Hallelujah chorus of the skies. Let it be our aim to induce some to join the redeemed army of God.

The school and classrooms were opened in 1907, thus creating "a noble and imposing frontage with self-contained premises within", not only affording accommodation for its several organisations, but for many village ones also. The cost was £1,057. Our photograph, taken in 1906, shows the old church and the remains of some even older cottages standing where the new school was soon to be built.

The Great War of 1914–18 brought hardship for the people of Box and its church. A high proportion of the men-folk joined the Forces. Money was short so the debt remained static for many years and it took until 1924 to be finally cleared with the aid of a small interest-free loan from the Connexional Chapel Fund.

By 1921 the Box "area" was becoming anxious at the lack of ministerial oversight as the Bath churches tended to occupy most of the ministers' time. They wanted a deaconess to be appointed, though it would cost £130 per annum. The propo-

Box United Methodist Chapel in 1906. The old chapel stands in the foreground. It was soon to be demolished to give way to the new Sunday School.

sition was lost when put to the Circuit Meeting "due to a majority of timorous and fear-to-launch-away brethren". However a subsequent attempt proved successful and Sister Lillian Lamb was appointed in 1923 after seven years service in Bristol. Her enthusiasm and earnestness achieved great success.

The Second World War saw the Royal Air Force taking over nearby Rudloe Manor in 1941. The church responded by allowing weekday use of its premises, encouraging its members to open their homes to the newcomers, and adjusting the Sunday services to allow the RAF personnel to attend Communion at a time when they were free from other duties.

Post-War activity has been steady, though Box Hill and Kingsdown have both closed in line with the decline in rural population. At Box the building has been spruced up with improved interior layout and heating, and a revitalised organ. The numbers attending worship are rising steadily and occasional evening services have been re-introduced. The Guild has been restarted and there is considerable use of the premises by the local community.

20

Claremont

The Countess of Huntingdon's Chapel

THE PRESENT day inhabitants of the popular Fairfield Park area of Bath would not take very kindly to reading that they live "in a populous suburb of Bath, where ignorance and immorality with their consequent destitution and misery are abundant". Such though, was the description contained in the *Primitive Methodist Magazine* in 1865, where it was reported that the denomination had taken over a chapel previously occupied by the Countess of Huntingdon's Connexion, and that the opening had taken place on 24th January of that year.

That original church seated 122 worshippers, and was situated at the bottom of Claremont Buildings, a steep row of 30 terraced houses built in 1825 and demolished in 1968. It abutted on to Fairfield Road and the steps leading to the main entrance reached to within a few feet only of the pavement.

The old building had a long and varied history. The earliest reference to its use for religious purposes which can be found is a Survey map for 1852–54 on which it is shown as "Lady Huntingdon's Chapel and School".

It was in 1863 that the Bath Primitive Methodist Circuit Steward, Mr Richard Osmond, brought the Mission to the attention of the Circuit. The building was owned by a Mr William Amery of 8 New Bond Street, Bath, a confectioner, and was available to let. The Independents of Argyle Street were also said to be interested in taking it. The Circuit Meeting of December 1863 agreed to rent the building at £10 per year. They tried — but failed — to get the owner to fit rail-backs to the seats as part of the deal.

As a result of the untiring efforts of Mr and Mrs Osmond an active congregation and Sunday School were established. In

1867 the building was purchased, complete with adjoining cottage and garden for £280. The Osmonds' daughter Alice was organist from 1876 to 1879. During this time she married the Rev Murray Wilson who was the Minister in charge of the Bath Primitive Methodist Circuit at the time. She died in 1891.

The work of the Mission prospered so well that accommodation began to be inadequate and the building of the present church was planned. In 1882 the old premises was sold to a Mr William Seymour, a builder, for £230 and converted into a carpenter's shop. After passing through several hands the building was given to St Saviours' Church, and eventually demolished in 1939. A shop was built in its place.

Today's Church

The Trustees had not far to look for a site for a new church. Just across the road and abutting on the corner of Eastbourne and Tyning Lane was a piece of land, belonging to Mr William Seymour, which was leased to them in 1881 at four guineas a year. In June that year plans were submitted to the Urban Sanitary Authority, for approval for a church to seat 260 people. It was to be 45 feet by 33 feet with a schoolroom at the rear 36 feet by 18 feet, with five classrooms, boiler house etc. The plans also included the unusual circular ornamental window over the main entrance (see sketch) and the four two-light windows in each of the side walls as they exist today. The roofing slates were best blue Portmadoc and the whole would be lit by gas. The Architect was Mr J. Hick and the church was built by Mr Joseph Bladwell.

On the 9th August, 1881 the Foundation Stone was laid by Lady Hayter, wife of Sir Arthur Hayter one of the two Members of Parliament for Bath at that time. During the ceremony, which fortunately was "blessed with most auspicious weather", a choir of no less than 150 voices gave strong support to the hymn singing. Memorial stones were laid by Mrs Richard Osmond in memory of her late husband, the pioneer of the Claremont Mission; Rev. Murray Wilson, Miss Kate Melluish, and Mr Handel Cossham. The latter was destined to be Mayor of Bath in 1882 and 1884; a very controversial figure who later became MP for Bristol East and died in the House of Commons in 1890. In a cavity beneath the foundation stone, at the north-west corner facing Fairfield Road, was placed a bottle containing a copy of the previous week's issue of the Bath papers; a copy of the *Primitive Methodist*; a plan of the Bath Circuit; a copy of the hand bill announcing the proceedings of the day and a list of the names of the Ministers and of the Trustees together with those of the Architect and Contractor.

The proceedings at Claremont were followed by a public tea and a public meeting at Walcot Chapel, where the large choir again sang hymns. Other memorial stones were laid in connection with the schoolroom and classrooms on the 3rd October 1881.

Claremont Chapel in 1989. Line drawing by Stan Roe.

The new church was opened for worship on Sunday, 21st May, 1882. The Preacher for both services that day was the Rev. W. Dinnick of Brighton, who, in his 40 years of ministry, had been responsible for building 23 chapels and two manses and largely clearing them of debt. It is recorded that churches generally in the south drew inspiration from his forcefulness and originality. The total cost of the building was £1,190, of which £630 was raised before opening. The cost may seem low but it must be remembered that so were wages. A craftsman earned 7d an hour, a labourer 4d. By the end of 1897 the church was free from mortgage debt.

The porch was added in 1900. The original gas lighting was replaced by electricity in 1923. The Sweetland organ which came from Hope Chapel, was acquired in 1882 and has been renovated several times since the church was built. Whilst the church is now comfortably heated the Trustees have not been without their problems in this matter. Various types of heating have been tried, originally a coke-fired hot water system, then gas fired boilers and finally the present electric night storage fan heaters. Extensive alterations have been carried out in 1951, 1966 and 1984 to bring the church into its present state.

The Sunday School was established in the old church in Claremont Buildings from the outset and helped to bring the current church into being. The role of the Sunday School in this matter is commemorated by a number of memorial stones laid by scholars in 1881, many of whom had made donations towards the building of the church. Along with the other youth activities it is still going strong after years of good work by Superintendents and teachers alike.

Mention has been made of the Rev. Murray Wilson. He was particularly associated with Claremont, and the following notes may be of interest: Born in 1828, he spent 36 years in the active Primitive Methodist ministry, and 27 years in retirement. After being superannuated in 1886 he lived in Bath at 39 Wellsway and centred his interest on Claremont Church, to which he made many generous financial gifts including the cost of the porch. He died in 1913 and was buried at Locksbrook Cemetery.

Other names connected with Claremont over the years are Mr and Mrs William Cleaver. Mr Cleaver died in 1917 at 82 years of age after serving as Trustee since the church was built. His wife, Anne, served in the Sunday School for over 25 years and died in 1905. Mr Samuel Phillips was the last of the original Trustees when he died in 1922 after 50 years in membership during which he was a teacher and then Superintendent in the Sunday School.

Attendance and youth work at Claremont tend to fluctuate; the Wesley Guild is a tower of strength.

21

Oldfield Park

Early Days

BY THE END of the eighteenth century the Spa had begun to decline and the support provided by tourism was insufficient to maintain the population. Until some industry came there was bound to be unemployment for those who had served the Spa visitors. The railway arrived in Bath early, in 1840, but it was not until a generation later that new industries had really taken root south west of the city down the Avon valley. The main industrial concerns to establish themselves in the 19th century were the railways (Great Western, followed by the Somerset & Dorset), engineering (principally Stothert & Pitt, crane makers), cloth, garments and printing. The consequence of this was that a rising urban industrial class was added to the hitherto clear social divisions of master and servant that characterised Spa life. Victorian class divisions were rigid in most of the country, and Bath was probably one of the places where social boundaries were most rigid of all.

New King Street Church, at the centre of Methodism in Bath, attracted the independent tradesmen, shop-owners, and minor officials, all of whom knew their place in the order of things — a little below the professional and moneyed classes. However Methodism has always encouraged a social conscience. Some members of New King Street were concerned for the spiritual welfare of the workers and their children who were beginning to occupy the new houses being built to the west of the large villas in Oldfield Park. At the time there were about a hundred of these new homes in Moorlands Road, Livingstone Road, West Avenue and South Avenue; more were planned.

It was to a house in Livingstone Road in the latter part of

1889 that the minister at New King Street, the Rev. W. Burchill, called a meeting to discuss the prospects of starting a local mission. Five attended — Mr Burchill and his wife, Mr Walker, Miss Palmer and Miss Kendall. Enthusiasm was apparent, so a further meeting was arranged in Mr Harry Brown's house in West Avenue. The outcome was the starting of a Sunday School at 1 South Avenue (see contemporary photograph), a corner shop known until recently as Tanners. The first Sunday, which was 16th March 1890, nine children attended. Their names were:- Alexander and Alice Painter, Fred and Evelyn Meredith, Nellie, Minnie, Laura and William Sellick, and Daisy Spencer. Services were held in the shop and later in the parlour behind.

The two founder teachers were George Vaughan and Walter Walker, the former a keen musician and the latter a rising star in Colmer's Department Store, destined by the time he

The first Methodist centre in Oldfield Park — No 1 South Avenue.

died in 1938 to be on the Directors' board. The initial progress of the school was as follows:

16 March	3 boys	6 girls
23 March	9 boys	11 girls
30 March	10 boys	18 girls
6 April	13 boys	21 girls

Following an appeal for help, two young ladies joined the teaching force, a register was procured, and house to house visitation took place. They insisted that any new recruits should not be taken from other Sunday Schools. Within a short time a make-shift extension was built onto the shop front. The campaign was too successful, for by the year's end there were 116 on the roll with an average attendance of 84. Sometimes the school spread onto the pavement! Much to the founders' dismay, newcomers had to be refused admission.

An evening service was next offered in the same premises; this was so successful that plans were made to build a proper church. The Wesleyan Conference appointed a young minister, the Rev. D. Ashby "on supply", to supervise this development to which he was able to devote considerable time and effort. It was hoped to build on the nearby Triangle Site, but the Council withheld permission because this was scheduled to remain an open space. So the new church had to be built on the rather awkward site on a hillock, possibly thrown up by the railway engineers, just to the west of the Triangle. Appropriately enough, 21 years later this quotation from *Pilgrim's Progress* appeared on the cover of the Souvenir booklet:

> Now as Christian went on his way, we came to a little ascent, which was cast up on purpose that pilgrims might see before them.

When the Baptists applied to build their church on the Triangle site they mustered enough support on the Council, much to the envy of the Methodists, for permission to be granted them, and most of the open space was lost. Two non-Conformist chapels were to stand cheek by jowl.

Oldfield Park Wesleyan Chapel as it appeared in 1892.

A Proper Church

On the 14th September 1892, within two and a half years of the opening of the original school, Oldfield Park Wesleyan Church was opened (see photograph). An additional minister, the Rev. Charles A. Duthie was appointed to the Circuit, thus increasing the complement from two to three. The cost of the premises with 350 sittings was £2,249. Attendances rose rapidly; by 1898 it was realised that more room was needed. The population of the area was growing by leaps and bounds, and this industrial suburb of Bath at the turn of the century was in many ways where the city's real wealth lay, for the artisans who manned the new industries were concentrated thereabouts. There was little difficulty in securing a loan to expand the premises by providing a west transept and choir. This was said to increase the sittings to 508, but that seems somewhat exaggerated; today the church seats 315 in comfort. The cost of the extension was £1,476. By this time the Sunday School meeting in the hall below claimed to number 268 with 27 teachers; we are brought down to earth by learning that the average attendance was only 140. The total collections from January to April 1893 were £2.2s.5d. This means that

Oldfield Park Junior Class in July 1903. The headgear of both girls and boys is fascinating!

Mr George Vaughan.

Mr Walter Walker.

childrens' individual offerings were about a farthing each Sunday, which sounds very little. The parents, though not well paid, were in fact generous towards the church in many ways. Their meagre farthing would be worth perhaps 10p by today's values.

Bursting at the Seams

By 1903, when the photograph of the Junior class was taken, the number of children attending had risen to an embarrassing extent. The main schoolroom was fully occupied. In addition 144 infants were meeting in the chapel at 2.15pm, but had to be sent home at 3pm to make room for the men's class. Practical mothers were saying it was not worth dressing up their children for such a short session! Additionally 70 Juniors were packed into the vestry; a total of over 400 children on the premises. To cater for all these children a new "tin tabernacle" was erected alongside the church. This added £280 to the debt. It was later partitioned to separate Infants from Juniors (ie all those under 11 years).

The first Sunday School "treat" of any consequence took place in 1909, when 203 children and 97 adults travelled on the Somerset and Dorset line to Weymouth. Apparently the most exciting moment came on the return journey when a lady, finding herself on the wrong train, pulled the communication chord!

George Vaughan died in February 1910. As Sunday School pioneer, harmonium player, church organist and choirmaster, also Steward, and Trust Secretary his contribution to the Church's early life was enormous.

The 21st birthday celebrations on 30th October 1910 were led by the Rev. P. B. Jenkinson, minister from 1903 to 1905. He was better known by the Oldfield Park congregation simply as "Big Brother" in the innocent days before that title assumed ominous overtones. The church was packed for both services; 350 children met at the same time in the morning in the hall below watching that classic of the magic lantern *Pilgrim's Progress*. The tea meeting next day was attended by 250. An elaborate brochure was published containing historical photographs, and the portraits of Messrs Vaughan and

Walker which we have reproduced. The building debt stood at £971, but £3,000 had been cleared over the years by a none too affluent Society. The motto at the time was: "Neither man nor church should be at full strength at 21 years".

In 1912 special missions were led by the Rev. A. E. Shooter with a week of services; every house in the district was visited, open air meetings held and public houses canvassed. Word got around that a miniature Salvation Army was being formed! There is no doubt that this was a thriving church during the years before 1914, providing a dominating influence over many people's lives in the area. In all fairness, though, it must be recognised that there were few counter-attractions: it seems that spiritual life was at a high-tide. Non-Conformity provided social facilities, education both religious and secular, music, drama and sport for those living in the growing urban areas; and Oldfield Park was no exception. As well as a very modern Sunday School with teacher training and graded classes, there was a Wesley Guild, choir, cycling club, and later Sports Club on hired land off Mount Road, Southdown, south of the Oldfield development. It was known as "Breezy Heights" where the members themselves erected a "fine pavilion".

During the year of 1911 the house next to the church, number 110 West Avenue, was acquired for £450 and opened as a caretaker's residence and Wesleyan Institute for Men, an attempt to provide an alternative to the billiard-halls and taverns of the area. The words "young men" and "young women" meant in those days boys and girls who had left school (over 12 years before 1918 when leaving age was raised to 14) and whom we should now call teenagers. The church provided many facilities for boys, but girls had to be content with sewing circles and were probably not allowed out at night.

Attendance of children at morning worship had been encouraged since 1903. By the year 1914 the organisation was termed: "The League of Worshipping Children" and later: "The Order of the Morning Star". At Sunday School time there was a fellowship for adults (over 16 perhaps), and earlier in the day, originally 7.45am, subsequently at 10.15am, a prayer meeting. This all meant a four-session Sunday for many, and plenty of exercise walking to and from church. On Sundays the Wesley Guild organised mission services at

Longmead Street, East Twerton, where a room was rented for 2s per week. Attendance numbered up to 40 on Sunday afternoons and evenings, also Thursday evenings.

Writing in 1914 Miss Ivy Goodland told of a tradition of joy in service:

> We are always happy to sing to our friends in other churches.
> We think nothing of spoiling a best hat on the top of a tram-car on a pouring wet night. Sometimes we travel in real luxury.
> We have been to Batheaston, Inglesbatch and Midsomer Norton in real motor charabancs. It is true we were very much squeezed.
> Oh what excitement and good spirits!

Between the Wars

Optimism prevailed, the church was eminently progressive, new ideas were welcomed, new ventures were tried, while change and development were accepted with enthusiasm. The War of 1914–1918 dimmed this hopeful outlook a little, but the effects were not that great apart from the casualty lists; 11 men were lost on the battlefield. A bi-monthly magazine kept those absent on duty in touch with church life at home. The opening of a new organ in 1921, which cost £425, helped to restore the original keenness. The choir has been consistently successful over the years not only on festive occasions but in strong support of the hymn singing every Sunday. Successive choir-masters and organists have been inspired to give sterling service; the names of Mr Arthur Metherall and Mr John Moore are particularly remembered by many.

A visitor to the pulpit in the early '20s remarked that none of the other local churches had so great a group of enthusiastic young men. Around 1926 there was an unfortunate schism. This was due to the popular Deputy Sunday School Superintendent not being appointed to succeed Mr Walker when he retired from being Superintendent. The minister felt that the deputy was unsuitable due to his ambiguous attitude to the drink question. He left the church, taking a large number of senior teenagers with him. Before long however new members and young people replaced those who had left.

By 1926 the debt was finally cleared and "Gift Days" began to rival annual "Sales of Work" as money-raising agencies. A toilet block was built behind the School building financed by a legacy from Mr Joseph Bladwell. The Rev. E. Ralph Bates, the contributor of the first three chapters of this book, was minister from 1928 to 1931. These were years of much encouragement. Membership topped the 200 mark for the first time, and under the pew-rent scheme every sitting was booked. But the situation was changing. Counter-attractions were growing, Sunday cinemas and easier transport in particular. By 1940, Oldfield Park was less of an industrial community than it had been in pre-war days.

The Second World War and Beyond

The arrival of the Admiralty in Bath and the bombing attacks of 1942 both affected the church. The premises were used as a Rest Centre; a great many people in the vicinity were bombed out of their homes, including the minister who had to camp out in the church building for a period. At the end of the war, the wave of enthusiasm for all kinds of youth work did not pass Oldfield Park by, and the church actively engaged in "open" youth work, i.e. it was not confined to church families. The uniformed organisations were well supported. A new youth wing was opened in 1948 at the end of the Sunday School building at a cost of £1,500, of which only £350 had to be raised locally. The opening ceremonies included a performance of *Hiawatha* by the Rangers; it was this company that eventually developed into the Bath Light Opera Group. There have been more alterations and renovations in recent years. In 1972, the church was generally refurbished and the choir and communion table area re-arranged. Ten years later, the youth wing was upgraded and transformed into a church lounge and the church roof was replaced at a cost of £16,000; that sum was raised in three years. These schemes may seem small compared with the mammoth efforts of earlier years, but there is no sign of the Society falling behind the times. The School building has once again been adapted for contemporary open youth work.

Sadly membership figures have fallen. This reflects the rising average age of the congregation and the increasing mobility of the local population. Losses of older folk and those moving away are not being replaced by the younger element now predominating in the neighbourhood. With less than 120 members, the church nevertheless still hosts a Sunday School, the Brownies, a group of younger women and various midweek fellowship groups. Ecumenical activity in the area is encouragingly cordial. There appears to be potential for growth.

22

Southdown

The Southdown Project

IN APRIL 1942, two German air raids were concentrated on Bath, and among the buildings destroyed was the historic New King Street Methodist (ex-Wesleyan) chapel. This event was to have a profound effect on the church destined to be built at Southdown, a new area of housing high up on the south west side of the city.

A site for a new Methodist Church at Southdown had been negotiated in 1938. Already an estate of council houses had been built in this hilly region, as well as a few much older housing developments, which had come as ribbon development along Englishcombe Lane and Southdown Road. Sites had been reserved for Anglican and Non-conformist churches and the Methodist Circuit already had plans for the one designated for its use. These were held in abeyance until 1945, but by the end of that year a trust had been formed and contracts had been drawn up for building to commence. The plans were prepared and were very ambitious. They encompassed a church, a hall, and a Sunday school with buildings for community use. In addition there was space for a manse and caretaker's house to be linked by a covered way, or maybe internal passage, with the main block of buildings.

Various suggestions as to the style of building were made. The General Secretary of the Chapel Department, who was also the President of Conference, felt that a steel framed building would be correct, but traditional feeling prevailed and the design task was given to J. Beresford Smith, a local architect. He had several other local churches on his board, and was also being used by the Local Education Authority.

It was decided in 1946 that funds from the destroyed church at New King Street should be used to aid the Southdown project, although it was then still envisaged that there would eventually be a new town centre church to replace New King Street, Milk Street, and possibly Westgate Buildings churches. In 1947 a timetable was arranged so that the site, described by the minister-designate as "an enormous cabbage-patch", should be cleared by March, 1948, and that between then and 1952 efforts should be made to raise a third of the money. Other funds would come from the Rank Trust, and also from sales of property in the town. The first part of the scheme: class rooms, kitchen, toilets and hall, would come to about £8,000.

Building Begins

This was merely the beginning of a series of problems concerned with finance. The slowness of the system of building licences at the time meant that financial inflation took place before a start could be made. Similarly the building fund grew very slowly, and by 1950 only £85 was in hand. The first casualty was the hall which was cut out of the first stage.

At last in 1950 building began. The foundation stone was laid by the Mayor of Bath, Miss Kathleen Harper JP on 27 May 1950. The first Leaders' Meeting was held on 8th February 1951 with Mr H. Horler and Mr T. Willavoys as Stewards. In March 1951 the new rooms were opened by Mrs E. W. Bladwell. The builder was F. J. Blackmore. The intended Sunday School room had been built with a heightened roof and this became for the time being the Southdown Church (a dual purpose building) with a kitchen, other rooms and toilets.

The minister appointed, the Rev. Charles Clark, despite looking after Weston and Oldfield Park churches and living in Lower Oldfield Park, quite a distance from Southdown, proved to be an able pioneer and motivator.

Thirteen members, with commendable missionary spirit, transferred from Oldfield Park church, and by May 1951 ten other people who lived rather nearer had joined them. There is no doubt that a small group of people was striving hard, and with commendable enthusiasm, to build up a church with all the activities that the more established Methodist churches were undertaking, and all this on top of attempting to raise money to build the remainder of this ambitious scheme.

From quite early in the history of Southdown serious financial difficulties arose. The contractor's bill in 1952 caused problems both to them and to the circuit. In addition to all this the Trust funds were barely adequate to meet heating bills; but until 1969 the church managed to meet its financial assessment, although this too, with its consistent increases in the late fifties and sixties, caused the treasurer of the time, Mr Hubert Horler, considerable headaches.

Initial Growth

Through the first 20 years or so there were publicity campaigns and special services to attract the growing population of Southdown and the newer Whiteway housing schemes. Open air services, the Home Missions caravan, door to door visitation, and publicity leaflets were all employed at one time or another, but the underlying trend revealed in the minutes of the Leaders' Meetings was that the task was very great. Various activities were started from the beginning: Women's Meeting, Choir, Guild, Sunday School and Youth Club.

There were some eight years of fairly steady growth after the opening in 1951. As expected, the Sunday School did well, having a membership of 120 by January 1952, and a waiting list had to be imposed; this was the pattern for the next decade. The decline in numbers of children in the estates around, after the mid-'60s, partly accounts for fewer children in the school.

Church membership itself rose from 36 in 1952 to 90 in 1960. In 1952 the average congregation was 30, but rose to only 50 in the same period. The Women's Meeting reached 40 fairly quickly, but that seems to have been the maximum. Youth club work, as ever, provided an intractable problem, and in line with the current fashions of the time, or the ideas of the leaders, varied from a rather uncontrollable open club, to a small fellowship of Church members' children.

The '50s and '60s were extremely difficult years for church growth in general; the "serving Church in the community" — which was the current trend at that time — depended on a large number of skilled and committed personnel, and the undivided attention of a leader. Southdown's limited resources could not measure up to this immense challenge during the second of these decades, in spite of the continued enthusiasm and hard work of the church workers.

High Hopes

Meanwhile it was time to continue with the building, and all the members were looking forward to the new church when at least the problems of dual use would not have to be faced. Plans were submitted by the architect in 1954, but these were rejected by the Chapel Affairs Committee at Manchester. "The architectural treatment seemed more appropriate for a commerical building or technical school than for a Methodist Church" they said. Attention was also called to the unnecessary amount of glass: "It appears as though somebody, the architect or someone else, had been influenced by continental architecture and justified the plan on the ground that similar treatment was successful in France." New plans were drawn up, not dissimilar to the plan by the same architect for Weston Area Church, but with a cruciform building to be built alongside the existing Sunday School. (The same architect designed St Barnabas Church at Southdown). A "choir" room also was to be added. These plans were not wholly welcomed at Manchester, and the shallow transepts, the chancel based choir, and the western position of the choir room ("In Methodism we do not have a procession of the choir down the aisle") were criticised.

With minor amendments, however, the scheme was finally approved, and Beresford Smith's present white building with square topped, narrow windows, shallow transepts and a broad square crossing tower with pyramidical cap was the result. This was built in 1958–59, the finance being available because the New King Street war damage compensation money could be transferred ('ported' was the technical word) to the new replacement premises at Southdown. This was sufficient to cover the major part of the new building, which was constructed by Messrs Geo. Yeo & Son and cost £14,500.

The foundation stones were made from material recovered from the demolished New King Street buildings. They were laid on 10th January 1959 by Mrs L. H. Poad and Mr E. W. Bladwell.

The church was opened by Mrs Charles Clark, the wife of the former Minister, on 21st September 1959. Membership stood at 80. However the new building did not provide the panacea so many had been expecting. In less than four months from the opening, complaints were being voiced about the heating and the acoustics. The latter problem was caused by the comparatively immense volume and excessive height of the central tower. The usual wrangling with the architect and the builder began, and various solutions were tried. In addition there were aesthetic problems in 1960 with the installation of the new single manual organ, the gift of Mr E. W. Bladwell. When it was formally opened, the guest organist was Rev. T. Brian Coleman, a former minister. In less than five years major repairs were needed to the tower, and these were a drain on the still very limited local finances. This problem continues to plague the Trustees.

A pleasant feature of the church is the font. This was recovered, broken, from the ruins of New King Street, then restored for continued use. A pair of valuable silver chalices, believed to have been used by John Wesley, was also transferred to Southdown. One was hallmarked 1773/4 and therefore could have been used in the Avon Street preaching house.

The Wesley Chalices photographed before their disappearance.

The other was dated 1778/9, just after New King Street opened. From 1782, with the possible exception of 1785, John Wesley administered the sacrament every year up to his last visit in 1790, presumably using these chalices. Sadly they were stolen in 1987. Our photograph records their appearance and condition.

One success story of the early period was the choir. This was established quite soon after the 1951 opening and by the time the premises were extended in 1959, was able to master some quite complicated works. They sang at the opening of the church building, and were extremely fortunate in their two choir trainers, Mrs Phyllis Marsh and later Mr Paul Selley. However, the choir only survived a comparatively short time after their second choirmaster went away to college, and the church was unable to replace him on a regular basis.

Optimism thwarted

The air of disappointment in the years after 1960 can be read into the comments in the Leaders' meetings. In spite of the fellowship between Ministers and Leaders, success seems to have eluded Southdown, and it is sad to compare communicants (22) with membership (90) in the early '60s. As financial assessment rose with membership, attempts were made during the next few years to make membership figures "more realistic", particularly when the circuit wished to increase the amount the church was to contribute each quarter.

An extension of community involvement was made in 1961 when it was agreed that the local Infant Welfare Clinic should use the premises. This has continued to the present day. In addition local uniformed youth organisations, and a mothers and toddlers club (partly a church-supported group) came into the premises. More recently a table tennis club also used the hall for its competition games.

The thwarted movement towards church unity accounted for a lack of direction in the '60s, and perhaps the '70s as well. At Southdown this aspect seems to have had a rather damaging effect. The new Anglican church, St. Barnabas, which was built almost concurrently with the Methodist church, was under dynamic leadership. When the Anglican-Methodist conversations took place, the Methodist Minister, Rev. G. Simmons, was a keen supporter of the proposals. The whole church at Southdown seemed equally enthusiastic, and went forward with him towards the union. Unfortunately the final defeat of the proposals at the Anglican Synod, came at just the time when everything seemed to point to success at last, and was obviously a bitter disappointment.

It was in 1969 that the members realised that the site would never be fully developed in the foreseeable future, and decided to sell the plots of land once intended for the manse and the caretaker's house, and which had now become eyesores. The money raised from this proved sufficient to pay for the installation of a new oil-fired heating system, and as a by-product, the general appearance of the site was much improved.

Devoted Leadership

During the next decade very little progress was made, but with small numbers Southdown was able to maintain a series of activities. The Women's Meeting led by Mrs Kathleen Swift, the Guild tirelessly championed by Mr Jim Allwork, and the Sunday School resurrected by Miss Marilyn Tricker and others, continued in spite of there being only a very limited group of committed leaders including Mr and Mrs Leslie Hompstead who have maintained constant support. The Silver Jubilee celebrations of 1976 were a time of joyful reunion. In the early eighties a house fellowship started. This had been tried in the mid-'60s, but had failed, mainly because some members were not ready to accept the idea of a religious meeting off church premises. Now the atmosphere was different, and this may be the seed which will renew the church. The first major reconstruction job has recently been done on the oldest parts. The stage was removed and the accessibility of the kitchen improved. This was a very necessary piece of work, and done by the church members themselves.

The landscaped grounds and broad central aisle have attracted many weddings, their numbers increased perhaps by Methodism's liberal attitude towards the marriage of the divorced. Despite the large numbers drawn to the church on such special occasions, very few have shown lasting interest.

Southdown, unlike other churches in the Bath Circuit, is blessed with good car parking facilities. This in turn has proved popular to those organising Circuit events. Our photograph shows the church today.

Southdown Methodist Church in 1989.

Where Southdown has failed, and where other Methodist churches up and down the country have failed too, has been in their inability to communicate with, and win over the occupants of Local Authority housing estates. Provided help comes from areas other than those immediately adjacent to the church, there is no reason why Southdown should not thrive, particularly if the ecumenical dimension improves.

23

Twerton

The Wesleyans

TWERTON WAS the name derived from Twiverton, meaning two-ford, a Saxon hamlet some two miles from Bath on the Bristol side. Dependent upon the cloth-trade it was probably where Chaucer's Wife of Bath came from. In 1847 the Carr family arrived from Penrith. They resurrected the woollen mills and took a leading part in encouraging the social life of the community. Twerton became part of the City of Bath in 1911.

Methodists were meeting in Twerton at least as early as the 1790's. Their leader in 1806 was Jasper Jones, and in 1812 their membership stood at 32. With this encouraging support and assisted by a "private collection" in the Bath Circuit, their first chapel was built in 1816 at Penny Buildings, where Marjorie Whimster House now stands. It could seat 300, and by 1838 membership had risen to 100, the highest to be recorded in the church's history. There is reason to believe that attendance was far in excess of membership, and in 1851 we know there was a thriving Sunday School and adult attendance averaging 60 in the morning and 170 at night. This is all the more surprising since the "Bromley affair", (See Chapter 8), took away a great deal of Wesleyan support in Twerton. The official Wesleyan membership figures tell their own story:

June 1850	82
September 1850	45
December 1850	18

Unfortunately we know little about the struggles which the small loyal congregation of Wesleyans must have survived through the rest of the 19th century. The building became increasingly delapidated and maintenance was sacrificed. In 1923 the appointment of a new Board of Trustees led to a proper review of the prospects. Proposals to close the chapel stemmed from "its entire lack of comfort, together with roof and floor problems. Strangers coming once are not likely to come again". The minister, Rev. J. W. Simister said that the ancient building, though out of the way and full of discomfort had enough love to make it worth while to try to keep it going, particularly as the Sunday School was a "hopeful spot". A Commission met the next year to take a decision one way or the other. The alternatives were union with the United Methodists at Zion, or a renovation scheme which would cost some £400. Several Trustees felt the financial burden to be too great. The outcome was a 7:7 vote, with the chairman casting in favour of retaining and improving the building. However a "higher authority" stepped in. Someone must have whispered a word in a certain quarter for the City Engineer condemned the premises opining that "the Trustees are running an entirely improper risk in keeping them open".

Despite some last-ditch attempts to the contrary, the decision was eventually taken in 1926 to sell the premises. The building lingered on until 1933, when a local builder agreed to demolish it in return for keeping the stones. The site was eventually sold to the Council for £15. The Trust was wound up in 1949 with the transfer of £139.8s.0d to the Southdown church fund. A few illustrious names appear in the list of Trustees: Stephen Fox Andrews, grocer; William Mitchell, draper; Sidney Edward Reed, watchmaker; Luther Wilson, chemist.

The Primitive Methodists

We now return to the early days, back in fact to December 1845. The Circuit Meeting of the Primitive Methodists decided to "beg money to buy stone and land for a chapel at Twerton measuring 25 feet x 20 feet".

The chapel was duly erected at Prospect Buildings in 1846 at a cost of £124, and the initial membership was 38. It could accommodate 140, and at first attracted an attendance of 60 on Sundays and 25 in the week. This rose in 1851 to over 100

— perhaps aided by the Bromley affair. In 1867 the Trustees were authorised by the circuit to instal a harmonium. There was a gradual falling off in support, the signs being that there were no strong local leaders. By 1876, the Circuit was proposing to offer the chapel for sale, though hoping to get a "more eligible site". They hoped to sell it for £175 but there were no suitable offers so repair work was authorised provided funds could be raised. However December 1878 saw the ominous appointment of a committee to dispose of the place.

The church was without, it was said, any members in 1879, and only a small congregation, plus a debt of £75. Activities must have come to an end for in 1882 "disposal of 'the things' from Twerton was proceeding". The chapel was converted to cottages, and these were subsequently demolished. Thus ended any evidence of Primitive Methodist witness in the village of Twerton.

The United Methodists

The only Methodist Society to survive at Twerton until the present day, was established as a result of the 1850 upheaval. At first the Bromleyites met in private houses, and the census of 1851 reveals they were then using the old Poor House with an average attendance of about 150. They soon decided to build their own chapel. The selected piece of land stood alongside the new railway line which had dramatically severed Twerton High Street from the main road between Bath and Bristol of which it had formed a part. In 1852 the land with two tenanted cottages was acquired for the Wesleyan Reformers by James Britton, a Bath upholsterer. Zion chapel was built and the cottages were demolished; the whole was conveyed to the Trustees in April 1853; eight came from Bath, one from Weston and the remaining seven were clothworkers from Twerton, Mr Bromley lent them the £150 involved at 4½% interest. As Chapter 8 revealed, he had received 100 guineas the previous year from his supporters "to place him above pecuniary want".

The extract from the first entries in the baptismal register of 1853 shows the signature of James Bromley and of lay preachers who performed the ceremonies.

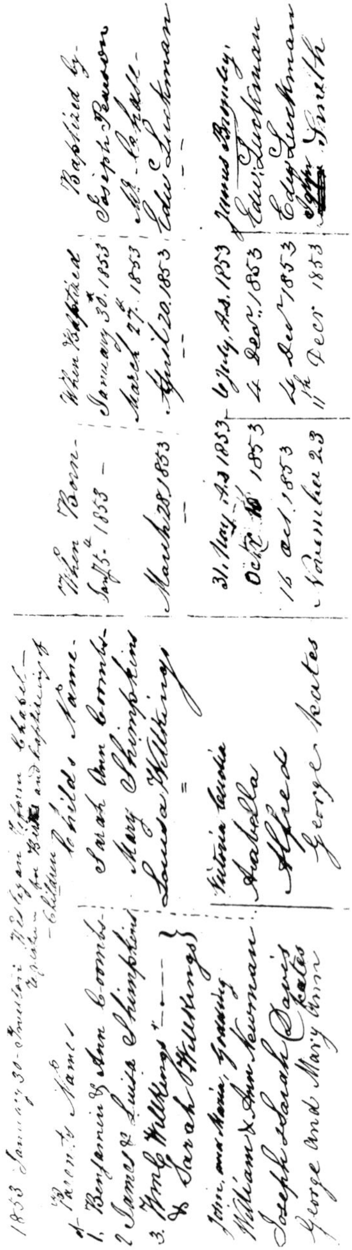

Extract from first page of Twerton "Reform Chapel" Register of Baptisms, 1853.

When the Rev. James Bromley died in 1869, his estate was left to his son Frederick Bromley, surgeon of Oldham, and his son-in-law Thomas Bell, professor of music of Bath. The mortgage, being still outstanding, was taken over by Isaac Carr & Co. This debt was finally cleared by the church in 1906. As the extract from the church accounts reveals there was a need in 1878 to substitute weekly for quarterly collections "in hopes to improve our Phinanchle Condision".

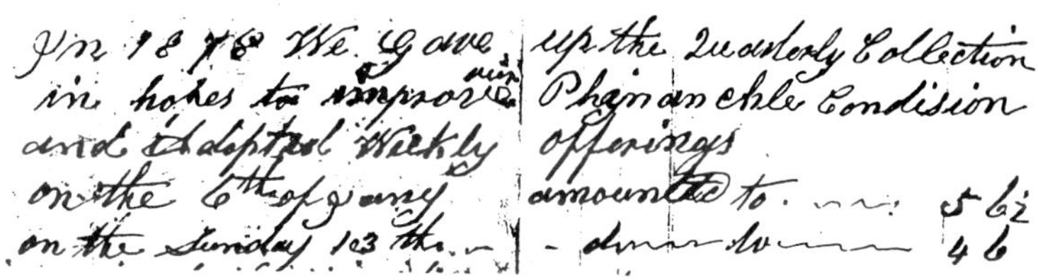
In 1878 We Gave up the Quarterly Collection
in hopes to improve our Phinanchle Condision
and Adopted Weekly offerings
on the 6th of Jany amounted to 5 6½
on the Sunday 13th - ditto ditto 4 6

Extract from Twerton Society Accounts, 1878, indicating a change of policy.

Until premises for a Sunday School could be erected, temporary accommodation was used at "School House, Shophouse Lane" (now Shophouse Road). It was sold in 1891. Premises at 8 Shophouse Lane were also used for several years. By 1886 the process of building a school was started. After negotiating with the Great Western Railway for a piece of their land, and with Mr Newman (of Newman's Buildings) for some of his, the Trustees designed the building themselves. The cost was £243. Fosters of Bath were the Contractors. The stone-laying took place on 12th December 1891, and was performed by Mr H. Shellard. It had been hoped that Mr T. Carr or a member of the family would have done this.

When the school opened, 63 scholars and 20 teachers moved in. Boys and girls were taught separately and classified according to ability in Select (later Senior), First, Second, Third and Fourth classes. Annual outings went to Dundas (by barge in 1909 at 7d each), Box Hill, Frenchay, Castle Combe, Rush Hill, Kingsdown (by brake in 1916 at 6d each), Bathampton (by tram at 4d each), Penn Hill Farm and of course Weston-super-Mare by rail. In 1919 the Superintendent asked the Great Western Railway whether Twerton station might be opened for the occasion, but without success. It had been closed down two years earlier.

This minute of 1910 describes the Sunday procedure: "Open school at 1.55 pm. Give out reward tickets until 2 pm. Sing a hymn, have prayer, call register. After second hymn go to classes. Scholars in before first hymn receive both ticket and mark; all those arriving after 2pm only to have a mark. Ninety marks must be made for a prize. Scholars not attending who have fever in the house shall receive a mark." They reported one death from diphtheria in 1915, and one of lockjaw in 1920.

Teenage trouble was not unknown in those days. In 1913 it was recorded: "Most of the lads connected with the Bible Class stayed outside and would not come in". A Boys' Gymnasium was established in 1919 with parallel and horizontal bars costing £1 15s 0d. A Girls' Gymnasium followed in 1920 for which the equipment cost a more generous £8! Several events were inaugurated around this time which have continued to the present, like the joint harvest festival services with the West Twerton Baptists and the Easter egg services. By 1920 there were 180 in the school. Dedicated Superintendents throughout the period include Herbert Carey, Hubert Selby, Desmond Tanner and Judith Harvey.

A Bombing Tragedy

The main bombing of Bath occured in April 1942. Twerton was unfortunate in being the victim of an earlier, minor raid in which all the fatal casualties were associated with Zion Chapel. This occurred on the night of 16th January 1941. The Trust Secretary, Mr Herbert Carey, and the Church Secretary, Mr Fred Hudd both recorded graphic written accounts of what happened. Seemingly a bomb fell on No 18 High Street where Mrs Pease, a member of the congregation, lived. Two girls, ironically evacuees to escape the bombing in London, were killed along with their brother. Another brother, and Mrs Pease's son were seriously injured. All the children attended the Sunday School. In the street not 20 yards from the chapel a respected church member was killed. He was Mr Alec Phillips, aged 33, a Trustee who had just been elected Assistant Sunday School Superintendent. Another Trustee's house was struck killing Mr William Rogers, the brother of the leader of the Beginner's Dept. The destruction of the Pease's house, and of the adjoining cottages belonging to the chapel, probably protected the chapel itself from serious structural demage, though it was quite unusable. Temporary accommodation was offered by the Baptists and Anglicans. Both were accepted for a few months until the chapel was patched up.

It was not until May 1948 that proper restoration was completed and celebrated with great joy. Another happy occasion was the centenary service on 30th April 1953 when the guest speaker was Dr Eric Baker, Secretary of the Methodist Conference.

The interior of the church and the adjoining rooms have been brought up to modern standards in very recent years so this Grade II listed building provides adequate and comfortable conditions for its growing congregation whilst retaining its historic exterior (see photograph).

Zion Chapel, Twerton, in 1989.

24

Walcot

The Building of the Chapel

THE VERY FIRST mention of Walcot for Methodist witness is in an early account book in which we read:
"2 July 1793 Licence for Walcott Preaching House 2s 6d"
There is no documentary evidence to tell us where this was.

During the early part of the 19th century the pressure on space at New King Street had become unbearable and a second large chapel to serve the city was essential. A suitable site was discovered on the London Road opposite Walcot Parade on which there were six old houses and a three-quarter acre site falling away to the bank of the river Avon. On 16th January 1815, the owner, John Hooper, conveyed the land for a yearly rent of £110; this was on the understanding that no less than £3000 would be spent on building. The ministers involved were the Revs. Samuel Taylor — then the only minister in the Bath circuit — Thomas Roberts and Henry Roberts. The laymen included John Shum and Joseph Pearson; both men were destined to play vital roles in Walcot's history.

The chosen architect was William Jenkins from London, a seemingly unusual choice since there was so much local talent. However he had designed Methodist chapels at Sheffield and Trowbridge; he may have had family connections with Bath. He was certainly sympathetic to the cause for he deducted 25% from his fee "in consideration of its being a Methodist chapel".

There is no doubt that the trustees opted for a prestigious building which must have been quite a landmark at the time, even in such an architect's paradise as Bath was in those days, and indeed still is. According to Walter Ison, the author of *The*

Georgian Buildings of Bath, "the facade is an arresting composition in spite of certain oddities in detail". There is a mixture of Doric and Corinthian columns and pilasters. The interior measures 71 feet by 52 feet and contains a three-sided horseshoe gallery, a high curved rostrum "behind which is a room for Communion Service". The estimated cost was £5500. The chapel bears the familiar superscription "DEO SACRUM". One small boy was heard to translate this as "Daddy Shum's Chapel"!

The foundation stone, covering a small collection of English coins, and bearing the words "The Lord will provide" was laid on 31st March 1815, and appropriate addresses were given by the Revs. Samuel Taylor and Thomas Roberts. With typical speed and thoroughness the edifice was erected to enable the opening celebrations to take place on Thursday, 30th May 1816 when three famous preachers attracted large congregations to three services.

The respected Joseph Benson preached in the morning. Wesley had appointed him Headmaster of Kingswood, then, on his personal recommendation, Principal of the College at Trevecca in Breconshire, which had been founded by the Countess of Huntingdon. Also, as a Methodist minister he became on two occasions President of the Wesleyan Conference. The afternoon preacher was Robert Newton, then early in his career during which he would become one of Methodism's most sought-after preachers. His presence and preaching ability were such that he is said to have got away with preaching a small number of sermons hundreds of times each! He was destined eventually to become President of Conference on four occasions.

The evening preacher was a man who became one of the most dominant personalities in the Methodist Church, and whose sheer ability and obstinacy would subsequently spark off jealous separations within Methodism. That man, Jabez Bunting, was eventually to find himself occupying the President's chair on no less than four occasions — interestingly each time exactly four years before Robert Newton. No other man occupied the President's chair as many times as these two.

The collections that day were respectively £100, £73 and

£96, truly stupendous sums. An item under "Bad money" came to 1/11d! Gifts produced a further £1500; the rest of the capital was raised by virtue of investments totalling £5000 which were said to pay an annual interest rate of five per cent.

There was no organ to begin with. A fascinating entry records: "Violin etc. £3 14s 4d" which shows how they managed initially. Just three years later an organ costing £168 was installed. This was a remarkable achievement at a time when organs were considered to be of doubtful virtue in Methodist buildings. Indeed the Conference of 1820 ruled that in the larger chapels organs could be installed only with specific Conference approval. At Walcot the organ blower was paid 1/- a week.

The engraving reproduced shows the chapel in 1818.

Walcot Chapel in 1818 showing adjacent cottages and no chapel house.

Life at Walcot

Collections were not taken every week. Aside from the monthly Sacramental services, collections for chapel and other funds were taken monthly. Some of these were allocated to local charities such as the General Hospital and the City Infirmary, while others went to Kingswood and Woodhouse

Grove Methodist Schools. Special collections were taken at the door rather than in the pews. Some unique appeals stand out:

		£	s	d
1840	Ashantee Mission	20	1	6
1843	West Indies Earthquake	14	16	3
1843	For warming chapel	10	11	8
1844	Free Scotch church	17	0	0
1847	Starving Irish & Scotch	45	14	0
1847	Local Preachers Horse Hire	3	14	1½

Anniversary collections were always high. Ladies were employed to take these!

Expenditure figures are sometimes revealing, at other times mysterious:

	£	s	d
Supper on rearing of the Roof	7	1	1½
Turnpike man		2	6
Crooks and extinguishers		4	9
Snuffers, fireirons & tinder box	1	0	10
Wine and spirits for Walcot chapel	1	7	6
Brandy for Walcot vestry		7	0
Mrs Worth's confinement (minister's wife)	3	10	0
Grinding 3 doz. knives		3	6

Trustees were faced with all manner of interesting problems which on the whole they tacked in a very business-like way:

1824: Graves "under the vestry" to cost 30 guineas each. Head stones to be charged one guinea, head and foot 1½ guineas. Standard sizes and materials were specified. All funerals to be performed by travelling preachers "except under extreme necessity".

1826: Trustees at liberty to have a "tablett" placed in the chapel to their memory free of expense.

1833: Vote of thanks to Mr Field the organist for years of gratuitous service. Organ to be discontinued and seven persons appointed to "superintend management of singing". Mr

Bell to be principal of choir, helped by Mr Phipps. Following a three month's trial of these new arrangements it was decided that the organ should be repaired and brought back into service.

1837: Complaint to be made about the inefficiency of the gas. Chapel debt was £3750. Trustees to be given preference of lending money on the chapel which was to be registered for the celebration of marriages.

1838: Annual income of Trust:

	£	s	d
House rent	30	0	0
Day Schools rent	20	0	0
Sunday Schools rent	30	0	0
Pew rents	147	17	0
Quarterly collection	22	5	11½
Burial Ground	173	1	8
Anniversary	55	0	0

(This statement is interesting in showing the main sources of income 150 year ago)

It was decided to charge Wesleyan Literary Institution 2s 6d for gas on lecture nights. All tea meetings were to pay 4s for gas and 4s for coals. The sexton was instructed to collect arrears of seat rents.

1842: "It is highly desirable to warm the chapel." To be investigated. (This implies that no heating had been provided for 26 years). Any trustees absent from quarterly meetings will be fined. Pulpit to be lowered one step.

1843: Total collected for warming and altering chapel: £50 0s 6d. The chapel-keeper was told to devote all his time to the premises and burial ground, for which he was paid 12s per week plus rent and coals. Any persons occupying sittings without paying to be "induced" to become renters.

1844: The "Organ Committee", consisting of 27 persons (no less!), recommended £160 be spent on the organ.

1845: Back rails to be put to forms of free sittings. Entrance to chapel to be at side door "after the 2nd singing" (ie for latecomers arriving after the second hymn).

1846: No standing head or foot stones to be allowed in future. All the present ones to be laid flat. A "neat toilet" was fitted up adjoining the preacher's vestry.

1847: To make enquiries about providing a suitable place for funerals "to obviate the necessity of taking the corpse into the church". The charge for interring an adult reduced from 15s to 12s, a child from 12s 6d to 10s 6d.

Some of the graves reveal the tragic infant mortality figures of the 19th century. For instance the children of John and Harriet Slip are recorded as follows:

Name	Died	Age
John	20th Sept. 1828	1 year 9 months
Charity	4th Nov. 1831	1 year 6 months
Matilda	21st Nov. 1831	3 year 6 months
Charles	13th Jan. 1837	5 years
Virtue	29th May. 1863	17 years
Elijah	10th Jan. 1865	16 years

However, the mother died in 1879 at 73, and the father in 1893 at an incredible 93.

1849: Agreed to purchase "adjoining property" from Mr Skeate for £150. Miss Granger, 1 Grosvenor Place, gave an entire silver Communion service. The church leaders allocated money "to the poor on account of cholera."

The Schools

Beneath the chapel was a large hall said to be able to accommodate 800. To this room Joseph Pearson transferred the Sunday School which he had founded in a "newly erected room situate in Parsonage Lane" in 1810. Mr Pearson was born in 1774 near Nottingham. As a youth he had been influenced by John Wesley's preaching. His calling was to deal with the ignorance of poor children in matters of religion. No doubt aware of the work of Robert Raikes of Gloucester, he found on setting up a shop in Bath in 1803 that there was already one Sunday School here — in Rev. William Jay's church in Argyle Street — but scope for more. Many of the children came from the slums of Bath which then and throughout the 19th century were an utter disgrace. Indeed a 20th century social historian, Kellow Chesney, has described Bath's slums as among the most revolting in Europe. Joseph Pearson eventually took a prominent part in setting up the Bath Sunday School Union in 1813.

We are told that by 1817 there were 414 scholars and 82 teachers at Walcot. Many teachers could attend only on alternate Sundays. They also served in the villages. The only register to survive from these early days concerns the girls. They were taught not only "Testament" but also spelling, writing, reading, "easy lesson" and ABC. Ages in any one class could vary from four to 16. Some of the frank comments against the names of individual girls provide a telling commentary on the social conditions of the day:

Marie Cook, left Jan 1818 aged 10. A very bad scholar and cannot be found.

Ann Wotton, entered Nov 1818 aged 1, died Sept 1819, buried in the Methodist Burial Ground.

Sarah Neal, entered Dec 1819, left Feb 1828 to be teacher in Baptist School.

Susannah Hicks, entered Dec 1821 aged 10. Father died nine weeks ago leaving ? children and his wife in the family way. All they have is 4s per week from the Parish.

Hannah Paulding, entered March 1823 aged six, left Dec 1831 to be an assistant in this school. A good girl and better teacher than many of the old teachers and doubt not but will continue to be so.

Eliza Money (orphan), entered May 1824 aged six, left Jan 1826, gone to service.

Elizabeth Compton, entered May 1827 aged 15, discharged 1828 for bad conduct in morning service in chapel, taken into school again June 1828 and became a teacher before she left in Jan 1830 aged 18.

The school was financially independent and paid an annual rental for the use of the premises. No doubt much of this came from the Sunday School anniversary collections. Joseph Pearson was much involved in the work of the S.S. Union in the villages, an early ecumenical effort. He died in 1844 at the age of 70. His splendid memorial tablet once displayed in the church now languishes in the crypt. His cousin William Pearson succeeded him as Superintendent.

In 1835 a Day School was opened at Walcot; the two entrances with "Boys" and "Girls" carved in stone (see the sketch) are still in use today. There were to be no more than 100 children of each sex. Information about what went on is scanty. The heads were Mr and Mrs Gaites and they adopted the "monitorial" system introduced by Joseph Lancaster. Children of all denominations were accepted. Each day began with hymn and prayer. The Gaites were succeeded by Mr Richard Stow, who also ran the Sunday School. In his day there was a gallery in the school-room.

Walcot After the Bromley Affair

The early 1850s proved to be a particularly traumatic time for Walcot, as their own minister (Rev. James Bromley) played a prominent role in what was to become known as the 'Agitations' (see Chapter 8). After he was forced to leave the Wesleyans he led an independent denomination in the city and the Walcot membership figures fell dramatically. From a total of 304 in 1849 they dropped to 132 by 1857; then things gradually improved so that by 1880 membership had risen to 255. The next 50 years saw various fluctuations, and in 1935 Walcot entered the amalgamated circuit with 183 members. The 1950s showed an upsurge, so that in 1955 when Walcot became the Superintendent's church it had a total of 256 members.

Such a large Chapel and premises obviously needed vigilant Trustees to maintain the fabric of the church they loved. Over the years they included among their ranks people from all walks of life. For instance in 1906 we find: two drapers, three schoolmasters, two carpenters, two clerks, one school attendance officer, two nurserymen, one hotel keeper, one sanitary inspector and one postal overseer.

The entrance to Walcot Schoolrooms still carries the carved inscription separating the sexes. Line drawing by Stan Roe.

This gathering in the schoolroom at Walcot during the ministry of Rev A Hanley Smith, 1925–31, centred round the presentation of a canteen of cutlery.

The first female Trustee seems to have been appointed in 1917. She was Nurse Clara Perman who died aged 85 in 1944. She is remembered by a memorial window bearing the inscription "following in the steps of her Master, she went about doing good in this neighbourhood". (She may be seen on the extreme right of the group probably photographed in the late 1920s). Further ladies joined the Trust in 1934.

Money was sent in 1857 to the Indian Relief Fund and in 1862 for the relief of Lancastrian weavers. Financial problems inevitably occupied most of the Trustees' time; in 1874 they were forced to obtain a loan of £700 from the Wesleyan Chapel Fund with a further £800 to be raised locally. A Trust deficit persisted for years, and matters were in a very serious state by

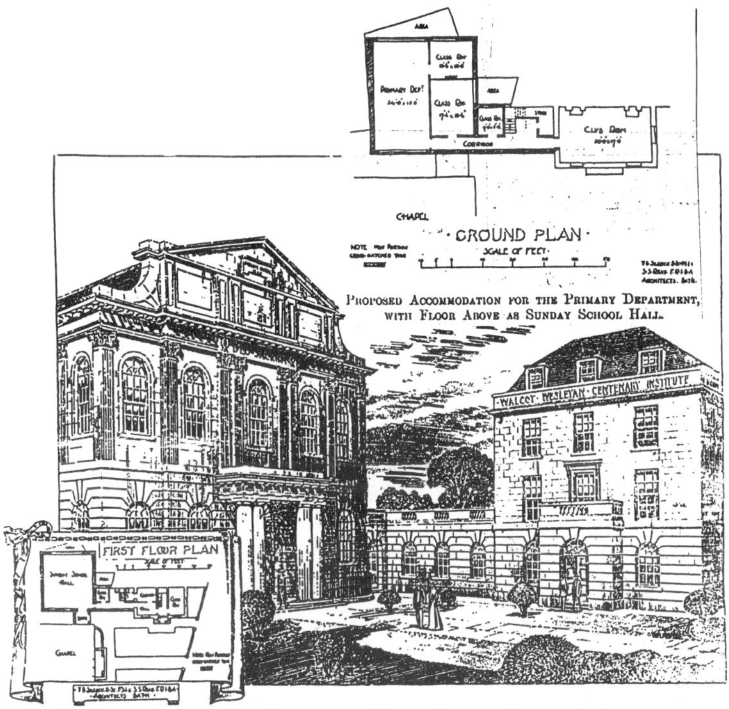

THE NEW BUILDING CANNOT BE FULLY SHOWN, AS IT IS LARGELY BELOW THE LEVEL OF THE CHAPEL YARD, BEING ON THE EXTREME LEFT OF THE CORRIDOR WHICH CONNECTS THE TWO PRESENT BUILDINGS.

This architect's sketch of the extension proposed in 1911 shows the chapel house connected to a new two storey building which is virtually out of sight below the corridor wall.

Walcot Centenary 1916. From left to right: Revs F Luke Wiseman with the local ministers, Francis B James, George Charter and W Harold Beales.

1906. At this time a special Society Meeting decided to set aside the collections on 12 Sundays a year for Trust funds, and to invite big names to preach and attract crowds. In 1907 when the T.U.C. held their 40th Conference in Bath, an attempt to secure the services of Arthur Henderson, M.P. failed. He chose to go to Manvers Street Baptist Church instead.

However, despite financial worries, the Trustees were soon to embark on the most ambitious scheme since the building of the chapel in 1815. The School had been growing in a steady and satisfactory manner. By 1900 there were 280 scholars and 43 teachers. From 1909 the introduction of "the Graded School principle" increased the demand for space. The Sunday School Centenary in 1911 sparked off the idea for a grandiose scheme, which was to be linked with the Chapel Centenary in 1915/16. At least £1,000 was to be raised to clear off all the existing debts, and erect a building on the site of the old Infants' School, for the growing Primary Dept. By November 1911 an even larger scheme was mooted (see reproduction), which was to include a lecture hall, and the cost had now risen to £1,500.

Some Trustees were not at all in favour for they recalled that Walcot had struggled with debt for over 20 years and claimed that ministers in the past had said over and over how much this had hindered the work of the church. They did not want therefore to put another millstone round its neck by providing an Institute and "a smoking room for the Brotherhood". So it was agreed in 1913, when the costs had already risen again, that the time was not ripe for further building operations. This was an almost inevitable decision as annual expenses were still not being met. Eventually only a minor renovation scheme was carried out and completed in November 1915. The guest speaker at the 1916 Centenary Meetings was the Rev. F. Luke Wiseman, ex-President of the Wesleyan Conference who may be seen in the photograph. The theme was: "At the portals of a second century of usefulness."

In 1874 Mr Batchelor (a Trustee) had conveyed the Infants School, its playground and 2 Nelson Cottages on liberal terms to the Trust. The cottage was sold in 1929 and the old Infants School is now used by T. R. Hayes & Co. for furniture storage. What was obviously the playground now serves as a small garden. The Chapel House was altered in 1927 to provide a new meeting room, and in 1941 the living accommodation of 6 rooms was divided into 2 flats.

The Graveyard

A hole in the burial ground wall was repaired in 1922 as goats and fowls were feeding there and it was said to be "in a deplorable state". In fact the graveyard had always been an embarrassing problem and its recent demise will have been a relief in many ways. As we have seen, prices for interment had been reduced, but this had caused the burial ground to become too popular. If "graves are the footprints of angels" as one Victorian lady claimed, there were too many for the Trustees of 1858 to handle! So they decided to "raise the burial fees in order that the Ground might not be unduly filled with low priced graves".

The new rates were: children 12s, adults 18s, 26s and 31s.6d. This enabled the rich and poor to be separated in death as well as in life. No doubt the cheaper plots were near the river and would therefore be subject to flooding. The three class system was widespread, and was maintained in Bath City Council Cemeteries until as recently as 1974. Interments virtually ceased by 1904, at which time records suggest that burials totalled 5927.

During the year of 1936 a scheme was discussed for installing "Memorial Windows". These greatly enhance the appearance of the chapel, and the last ones were installed after World War II. There are 8 downstairs and 6 in the gallery.

Youth Matters

The Leaders' Meeting reported in 1935 that there was an "improvement in reverence". This could well have been connected with the departure of the Kingswood boys! Since 1851/2 when Kingswood School moved to Lansdown from Kingswood, Bristol, it had been the practice for the Junior boys to attend Sunday worship at Walcot. These boys were a constant source of trouble to the "Apparitors" — as sidesmen were called. Everything conceivable was done to try to control them. The year 1924 found them being transferred from the gallery to the body of the Church, but even there the pews were being disfigured. Some said this was not the sort of behaviour one would expect from future Presidents of Conference! The initials of such may well be found carved into the woodwork amongst the many which can be seen in the gallery today. However, once the War Memorial Kingswood Chapel was used by the boys for Sunday worship, we hear no more of this particular problem at Walcot.

The Sunday School celebrated its centenary in 1911, when there were 200 pupils, with a whole series of special meetings, and a souvenir booklet outlining its history was produced. A portrait of Joseph Pearson, the Sunday School founder, was retrieved from the storeroom of the Bath Art Gallery by the Pearson family. After undergoing restoration it was presented to Walcot during the centenary celebrations. The 1911 School staff numbered 37, including 30 ladies, not one of whom was married (see photograph).

A Sunday School Bible found recently in the old Infants' Dept. contains the following inscription, revealing schoolboy theology and spelling, probably from the 1920s:

> Do not steel this book
> If you do, when you die, the Lord will say:
> "Where is that book you took away?"
> If you say you do not no,
> The Lord will say: "Go down belowe!"

The leaders sent parcels at Christmas in 1932 to Sunday School children whose parents were unemployed. After the war they distributed leaflets welcoming the tenants to their new homes when the Snow Hill scheme was completed, and discussed how to make the local West Indian community more welcome.

From Whit Sunday 1960 onwards the school transferred to Sunday mornings. During 1966, when the pupils numbered 84 (the average attendance was 54) it was re-named Walcot Methodist Junior Church.

Mention has been made of "The Brotherhood", which may sound to some a sinister name for a church meeting. Although the organisation was in no way unique to Walcot (and still

The Walcot Sunday School staff of 1911 pose on the church steps.

exists nationally), the minister in 1924 is recorded as being puzzled about them, for he asked the Trustees for information regarding this very independent body. He eventually arranged to meet them. In fact "the Brotherhood" at Walcot had originated from the time when the "Graded School" principle was introduced into the Sunday School around 1909. The three upper classes on the boys' side were formed into a Bible Class under the leadership of Mr Fred Riddle. It shortly developed into a "Brotherhood" and held services in the chapel every Sunday afternoon.

The first general meeting was held in 1910, under the Rev. Edwin Owen, a committee was formed, and a set of rules was drawn up. These stated that the society was to be unsectarian, and that its object was to promote Christian brotherhood and citizenship. Any man over 17 years of age was eligible for membership but would have to be introduced by an existing member. Attendance cards were issued bearing the motto "All ye are Brethren". Any unexplained absence of three months would lead to loss of membership. A "Sick and Dividing" benefit fund was set up together with a "Trip and Bank Club". They joined the Bristol and District Federation of Brotherhoods in 1911 at which time the photograph was taken.

Two Wars

There were 100 members in 1914 with an average attendance of 50–60. By 1915, no less than 35 members were serving their country. A set form of service included four hyms and two solos. All music had to be sacred, and 'gospel singers' were favoured. The organisation continued long enough to celebrate its Golden Jubilee in 1958, but death and the Snow Hill clearance scheme were accounting for falling attendances. The young men of 1910 had long become senior citizens when it finally closed down in 1967. However the Brotherhood, with its simple reverent services, had served the church well for nearly sixty years. Latterly it embraced a Sisterhood too. Mr Ben Nation is particularly remembered as organist over a long span of years and the Blackman family were strong supporters from 1939 onward.

In 1911, 50 members of the Walcot Brotherhood are photographed outside the church.

Of the 8 men Walcot lost in the 1914–18 war, one was the organist, Mr W. A. Membery. One of the 3 who did not return from the World War of 1939–45 was Mr Denis Frazer who was killed in France whilst caring for the wounded with the Friends Ambulance Unit. His parents had served for many years, and continued to do so, in the Sunday School, as class leaders and Trustees.

There was a large influx of Admiralty personnel from 1939 onwards, and they helped to maintain church activities despite the national situation. The Knitting Circle produced 3,242 garments for the Services. The premises were patrolled at night by fire watchers recruited from the congregation — a rota of 28 were required. The Annual Society Meeting of February 1941 was "adjourned with prayer owing to air activity in the vicinity". The schoolroom was used as a refuge centre during the main bombing of Bath in April 1942. The Editor of this book was on duty there at the time and has vivid memories of watching German bombers flying overhead and of casualties being brought in.

By the end of the war in 1945 the Trust Funds showed a credit balance of £281, and it was agreed that it was some years since the finances were in such a good condition. The post-war years 1947–8 saw repairs to the war damaged roof being carried out. The railings and gates, which had been removed for scrap, were also eventually replaced.

Some Famous Names

Amongst the Trustees during the second half of the 19th century were Samuel Evans, Thomas Owen and Edward Reed. Their families and fortunes were interwoven, and the names are still widely known today.

Samuel Evans (1816–1885), the son of a Wesleyan minister in Wales, the Rev. William Evans, came to Bath in 1846 and opened a drapery business in Bartlett Street. In 1863 he took into partnership his sister's step-son Thomas Owen, then aged 23. The firm of Evans & Owen prospered and to produce their own wrapping paper they purchased the Bathford Paper Mill.

Thomas Own (1840–1898), the partner, who was also a Circuit Steward in Bath, went on to become a newspaper proprietor and later Liberal M.P. for Launceston in 1892. When he died accidentally at his home in Wales, Rev. W. Perkins, Chairman of the Bath & Bristol Wesleyan District conducted his funeral.

Owen Owen (1847–1910), his half-brother, came to Bath when 13, as an apprentice at Evans & Owen, and whilst there also attended at Walcot. He left at the age of 20 for Liverpool to found the chain of shops which still bear his name. In 1892 he sent 40 guineas towards the renovations at Walcot.

Edward Reed and his wife Eliza were lifelong Wesleyans, his own grandparents Edward and Mary Rowe having been local preachers and friends of the Wesleys. An excise officer, he seems to have settled in Bath in the 1860s and became a trustee at Walcot. He lived at "Gays Cottage", Camden Place. His son, Albert Edward Reed (1846–1920) was made manager of the Bathford Paper Mill by Messrs. Evans & Owen, and then of their larger mill at Cardiff. When he subsequently started his own company he laid the foundation of what is today the giant Reed International, one of Britain's largest companies. Nicknamed the 'Wizard of the South' for his business skill and acumen, he nevertheless laboured in Walcot Sunday School as joint Superintendent with Mr Alfred Neate during the four years (up to 1878) he was in Bath, along with his younger brother and two sisters, Helena and Bertha. He married Emma Victory at New King St. on 9th October 1875.

William Henry Reed (born 1850) also became successful in the paper industry and was in Bath much longer than his brother, possibly for 20 years. He was particularly associated with Walcot Sunday School, as scholar, secretary, teacher, Bible class leader, and as a young inexperienced organist, appointed in 1870 (see photograph).

Mr W H Reed.

Modern Times

Walcot celebrated 150 years of witness in 1965 but it was also a year of decisions. With Anglican-Methodist conversations taking place, Walcot voted overwhelmingly for proposals favouring union. On a more personal level it was also decided by the Circuit that to meet the influx of students on the founding of Bath University, Walcot should become the Methodist University Church. The Leaders' Meeting said it was 'a duty and privilege to serve this way' and Methsoc became a vital part of Walcot's life. The minister also became a University Chaplain and Chapel House became accommodation for students.

Despite prolonged and frustrating delays the old Burial Ground is being developed so that accommodation for the elderly may be built on the land. Walcot is catering for the housing needs of both young and old, and for the spiritual needs of all ages. The chapel and schoolrooms are in excellent order, with an attractive foyer, good kitchen and comfortable lounge. The cleaning of the exterior stonework has done wonders for the appearance of this Grade II listed building.

The influence of such saints as humble Nurse Perman, who "went about doing good in this neighbourhood", still persists and motivates today.

For the future the importance is being emphasized of the church's pastoral responsibility towards those living in its near vicinity, as well as to visitors to Bath. Further improvements and renovations to the premises are being planned and funded. These will include easier access for the handicapped and elderly.

25

Weston

Cottage Worship

LIKE MOST of the rural societies, the earliest Methodists in the village of Weston met in the home of one of their members. In this case it was the "dwelling house of Joseph Loscomb". Unfortunately we do not know exactly where he lived, only that like many of his contemporaries in the village, he was a labourer. From the Churchwarden's Accounts we find that his widow, Hannah, received 2s Poor Relief from 1833 onwards, so we can assume that Mr Loscomb (or perhaps Loscombe) was regularly employed until he died in 1830 aged 54. His house would have been no more than a two- or three-roomed hovel, to which a handful of friends would be invited to meet for worship, Bible study and fellowship, all of which were much needed in those days of considerable hardship.

In accordance with the Act of Parliament requiring all Dissenters' meeting places to be registered with the local Bishop, the Loscomb's home, somewhere near Brass Mills, was duly licensed on 30th July, 1812. These early class meetings were led by Jasper Jones, who was also class leader for the Twerton Society, for that was where he lived and was married on 4th December, 1820, to Mary Gardner. His signature appears on the application for the licence of 1812.

This is the first record of Methodist activity in Weston. John Wesley when visiting Bath would no doubt have passed along what is now Newbridge Road on his way from Bristol (or along Newbridge Hill on his way from Kingswood). His journal records some 100 visits to Bath so his horses would have been familiar with these roads near the village. In those days the population of Weston was only 300. By 1821 it had risen to 2,000.

What records there are indicate that certainly two Methodist Societies existed at the same time within the extensive parish of Weston. The 1814 register of members of the Bath Society of Methodists, lists the following names at Brass Mills in the Weston parish:

Leader — Jasper Jones, Members: William Gane, Jos(eph) Loscombe, James Broad, John Watt, John Hopkins, Mary Gane, Hannah Loscombe, Phiby Broad, Sarah Hopkins, Hannah Peacock, Elizabeth Peacock and Sarah Hannam. The following were listed as meeting at "Weston":-

Leader — J. Rossiter, Members: Marthy Taylor, Amelia Biggs, Elvira Smith, Ann Reeves, Ann Longdon, Rebecca Scudamore, Jane Bartlet and Thomas Reeves.

In 1816 meetings were taking place in the home of Martha Allen, a widow.

Scattered Groups

Much of the story of the Methodists in Weston until the 1880s is wrapped in mystery because records are so sparse and the only real evidence lies in tiny references in the minute books of preachers' meetings etc. Thus the following is recorded:

November 1823. Payment to Rev. Reece for law expenses for prosecuting riot at Weston, £1.2s.6d.

April 1826. Primrose Hill services stopped due to non-attendance of inhabitants.

September 1830. Due to bad attendance, decided to hold prayer meetings instead of preaching once a month at Brass Mills.

1836. Propose to "try" Primrose Hill. (One wonders whether these were open-air services).

1839. Discontinue services at Brass Mills. Hold services at Bristol Road instead at 3 and 6pm.

It is possible, but by no means certain, that four or even five separate congregations were meeting in Weston during the first part of the 19th century, these of course included Primrose Hill, Brass Mills and Bristol Road. Of the size of these congregations little is known — the earliest Circuit Schedules which mention Weston, show 12 members "in society", a figure which varied very little until the early 1890s. From 1852 to 1856 services at Weston had dropped to one or two per month and finally stopped altogether. The opening of the Countess of Huntingdon Chapel in Trafalgar Road, Weston in 1856 may have had some influence here. Again some may have joined the Bromleyites across the river at Twerton.

The Society Stewards received little mention in the circuit records despite the amount of work they must surely have undertaken in those days. However, we do know that Mr Fisher served as steward until his death in 1840, and for some years afterwards a Mr Pollinger took over the job. The Parish Registers give us no information about them.

A Central Chapel

From 1857 onwards the Upper Bristol Road appears to have been the centre of Wesleyan influence in Weston, and weekly services were held there until the 1880s when, for a time, they too were stopped. By 1879 the membership of the society had dropped to five. So it comes as somewhat of a surprise that the Circuit Quarterly Meeting minutes of 25th June 1888, record:

"Reference was made to the growing neighbourhood of Lower Weston and the need of a place of worship there. Rev. R. Jenkin stated to the meeting that Mr Owen had already purchased a piece of land and was willing to transfer to the Circuit, provided a chapel was built thereon". (This is a reference to Mr Thomas Owen about whom more information appears towards the end of Chapter 24).

Inevitably a committee was set up to examine the problem. It consisted initially of Messrs Tabb, Fox-Andrews, Hancock, Pornforth and Southwell and Circuit Ministers. This committee was extended at the September meeting to include Rev. G. Bowden, Rev. Robinson, Messrs Bladwell, Jefferson and Short. Discussion centred around the extent to which the necessary money could be raised in the neighbourhood. Mr Owen generously gave £500 as well as the land. Eventually the bold decision was taken and Mr R. Curwen of London was engaged as the architect and Messrs. J. Long & Sons as the builders of a new church.

By 1890 the building was under way. On Monday, 29th September, a ceremony was held to lay a number of memorial stones, the donors of which gave amounts varying between £3 and £25. On 2nd June of the following year the new chapel was finally opened. The Trustees were: Messrs T. Owen, S. Fox-Andrews, W. Tonkin, W. C. Harding, S. Griffin, S. J. Shutter, T. W. B. Cox, J. Clark, G. Hancock, W. H. Langford, W. Walker, R. Goldsworthy, J. Kerry, G. B. Caple, J. L. Hancock, T. Southwell (Secretary), and D. Caple (Treasurer).

The chapel was designed to accommodate as many as 400 people and cost £2,350. It had a gallery where an American organ lent by Mr A. J. Hammond was installed as a temporary expedient. Beneath the chapel was a substantial schoolroom. Fortunately the plot was large enough for future expansion, and the foresight of those early pioneers in that direction is now being utilised.

The Rev. G. Fletcher, Chairman of the Bristol District was the preacher at the opening service. After tea a further meeting was addressed by no less than four named ministers and 13 named laymen "and others" if the account in the *Bath Chronicle* is to be believed! By the end of the day only £530 was needed to clear all debts.

Early Expansion

With the rapid expansion of housing in Lower Weston at the end of the 19th century came an improvement in the fortune of Methodism there. Things happened quickly once the new chapel was built. Within a year membership rose from 11 to 40. Much of the credit for this must be lie with the stewards, Mr Hinchliffe (Chapel Steward) and Mr Laytham (Society Steward and Sunday School superintendent). No minister had been appointed to Weston at the time. The first was the Rev. Alfred Garland who moved from Handsworth College. He was "on supply" ie not Conference appointed. His responsibility covered both Oldfield Park and Weston chapels, the former having been built a year later than Weston.

There are few records of those early years, the Sunday School accounts being the only ones going back that far. They show a balance carried forward on the 6th January, 1892, of ½d! Like the rest of the church the Sunday school grew rapidly so that ten years later the sum of £3.15s.5d. was spent on hymn books and prizes for the scholars. Sunday School treats were on a grand scale, some £8.11s.5d being spent in 1908 to take the scholars by train to Weston-super-Mare. This growth continued and by 1910 the facilities for the scholars were found to be inadequate. The Trustees meeting on 15th March set up a sub-committee to look into proposals concerning the infants' class room.

Music became an important part of Weston's heritage. The chapel continued to use the "temporary" American Organ situated in the gallery above the entrance until 1910 when the opportunity to buy a second-hand pipe organ occurred. Towards this the Sunday School offered £5, and astutely £5 for the old one. The new(er) organ was soon installed but 20 years later was proving unreliable. It was replaced by the present organ which was dedicated on the 4th January, 1935. This particular instrument had been the private property of the (then) organist of Bath Abbey; it is still going fairly well over 50 years later.

Pews and Other Comforts

The need for creature comforts gave rise to complaints about poor ventilation in 1912. However, other things were felt to be more important and it took two years for the needed improvements to be made. The luxury of a toilet for the Minster's vestry, then downstairs, was also seen to be justified. The chapel had originally been furnished with chairs. During the First World War it had been hoped to replace them with pitch-pine pews, but action was deferred until after the hostilities. It was not until 1923 that the pews were finally installed and the chairs sold. This development was of course contrary to modern trends. Indeed, amidst a little controversy, some front pews have in recent years given way to chairs again. The space released became a resource for a variety of worship activities.

Pew rents provided the church with an important source of income until the end of the Second World War. From 1914 the rents ranged from 9d to 2s.6d per seat per quarter. By 1944 only five people still availed themselves of this privilege, by which time the rent had risen to 5s. In 1945 the system was allowed to lapse. The only remaining evidence is the numbers and empty name-plates on the backs of the pews (numbers seven to 45 being the more expensive pews).

The enthusiasm for chapel anniversary teas seems to have waned during the Great War years, *The Myrtle* for June 1916 contains the following lament:

"Tea was provided in the schoolroom on Monday at 6pm, at which we had the company of the Rev. W. H. and Mrs Beales. One cannot help thinking that the day for chapel anniversary teas is over, if one is to judge by the support given to these functions at Weston. One visitor expected to see the schoolroom crowded — Alas!"

The author of this report went on to warn his readers of the dangers of "being members of a dead church". From this, one could be excused for imagining a despairing church at Weston, yet the report continues by referring to a social evening organised by the Guild for soldiers billeted in the area prior to posting to France. Also mentioned is a concert for which the Guild Secretary, Miss R. C. Parker, is singled out for praise for her "untiring energy". The money raised at these events was shared between the Guild, the Trust Fund and "the War Hospital", the latter being the forerunner to the Royal United Hospital at Weston. The children of the Sunday School were also "anxious to do their bit" for the hospital, raising £5.0s.5d between March and November 1916, the money buying "luxuries for the wounded soldiers there".

Between the two World Wars Weston grew in size as a village and this was reflected in the life of the church. The various youth activities were soon overflowing the available space. This was overcome to some extent by the purchase of a large hut in 1925 for the Sunday School and the Youth Club. By 1929 the minister, the Rev. E. Ralph Bates, was able to report to the Annual Church Meeting on "the good spiritual condition of the church and the possibility of increasing the membership. The reports from the Guild, Sunday School and Men's Bible Class are also considered encouraging." The Men's Bible Class met on Sunday afternoons in the aforementioned new hut. According to the few records available, it would appear that the good folk of Weston were so deeply engrossed in what they were doing at the time that the excitement of Methodist Union in 1932 passed them by. The only mention of it comes a year later when it was pointed out at the September Leaders' Meeting that the notice board outside the church had not been altered! No doubt they joined in the Circuit celebration in October along with everyone else. A programme for the weekend in question shows the Sunday School taking part along with nine others from the new circuit.

Wartime Episodes

As the storm clouds gathered over Europe the situation at Weston was hopeful. Membership was just under 100 and the minister, Rev. W. G. Harris, at the 1937 Annual Church meeting spoke of "the joy and pleasure and rich harmony that exists at Weston". Even the harsh years of wartime could not dampen people's spirits. The minutes of the Leaders' Meeting in January 1940 open with a delightful and generous tribute to the ladies of the church for preparing the meeting room.

The usual Air Raid Precautions were carried out — blackouts, light locks, etc. In spite of fuel shortages and the rationing of food, the social life of the church carried on as well as could be expected. In winter the church was poorly heated and refreshments were hard to come by for socials, etc. It was a problem with the heating that led to one sad casualty of the war — the caretaker. Mr Hawkins was unfortunately knocked down and killed one night in the blackout, having left home to stoke up the boiler. His widow carried on church cleaning for some time until she had to give up due to ill health.

Myrtle Meredith recalls an evening service: "the preacher was a 'local', Miss Marjorie Miller. She stood firm in the pulpit notwithstanding the continuous sound of anti-aircraft gun-fire a few miles away. The congregation also stayed put and the last hymn was: *There's a light upon the mountains*. When we got outside we saw a crimson glow in the west where countless incendiary bombs had set Bristol well alight. . ."

During the war youngsters were strongly encouraged to join some form of youth organisation. Weston responded by starting a company of the Girls' Life Brigade in 1940 and two years later a troop of Boy Scouts. The girls were later disbanded but have reformed in more recent years as the Girls' Brigade at the Moravian Church at the bottom of Lansdown Lane. The ladies also began regular meetings around this time. The current Women's Fellowship was inaugurated on the 6th May, 1947, and was originally known as the "Women's Bright Hour".

Post-War Progress

Luckily the church was not badly damaged during the war, but shortages meant that it was not until 1950 that all the necessary repairs were finished. Since the war there have been many changes at Weston and several improvements to the facilities.

The year 1955 saw a kitchen built downstairs. The vestry was extended in 1962 and an amplification system was installed in the following year. While Britain revelled in the "swinging sixties", Weston was enjoying a period of considerable growth. The year 1962 was described at the Leaders' Meeting as "a year of definite progress". By 1966 membership had risen to 158. All areas of youth work showed improvements. Some of the teenagers formed a preaching group which was welcomed everywhere in the circuit. Some of them have since become Local Preachers. Girl Guide and Brownie companies were started in 1963 and Family Services in 1967.

The 1970s saw some decline at Weston. The Guild was disbanded in 1970 and membership has fluctuated. As jobs have brought people into Weston and also taken others away, so the fortune of the church has varied. Leaders of the various groups have moved on, causing temporary crises but the work has gone on.

The virtual restructuring of the inside of the building took place between 1970 and 1972, which altered it to the present state. The church was re-opened on Saturday 18th November 1972. Subsequent redecoration was carried through by a young team under the administration of the Manpower Services Commission.

There are reasons for optimism for the future: the choir is probably as strong as it has ever been. The Sunday School in recent years has been the largest in the Circuit, the Women's Fellowship and the "Monday Circle" and House Groups still flourish, as do the uniformed organisations. The folk of Weston Methodist Church are involved in just about every aspect of the work of the Bath Circuit and are making a positive response to the problems and challenges of today. The need to extend the premises at the rear for youth work is currently under consideration, and fund raising has started.

The photograph shows the church today standing on its prominent corner position. It has the advantage of being the sole representative in the vicinity of non-conformist churches, of being close to a large and expanding hospital and in the midst of an area where residential care is given to the elderly. Stratton House, a Methodist Home for the Aged (see photograph), is not far away.

Weston Methodist Church in 1989.

Stratton House, Park Lane, Bath, a Methodist Home for the Aged.

26

Ministers Appointed to the Bath Circuit

THIS LIST has been compiled from various sources, but cannot claim to be complete or necessarily accurate in every detail owing to gaps in the relevant source documents. Supernumary ministers have not knowingly been included. The Wesleyan records are the most reliable; those of the independent branches least so.

Authorities which have been consulted include: *Hall's Alphabetical Arrangement, Hill's Arrangement, Garlick's Register,* Minutes of Conferences, Circuit Minute Books, Preaching Plans and Bath City Directories.

It may be useful to record here the dates of the historical (i.e. over 50 years old) preaching plans which are held in the Bath City Archives or known to be elsewhere as stated. Several of these cover only a part of the years in question:

Wesleyan
1825 (at Drew University USA)
1829
1835
1839–1840
1844
1852–1859
1877 (at Methodist Archive Centre)
1884–1903
1909–1927
1932 onward

Primitive

1857–1858 (at Methodist Archive Centre)
1874 do
1876 do
1904

United

1888 (at Methodist Archive Centre)
1903–1912

Wesleyan Ministers

1746– ?	Joseph Cownley
1749–1753	John Jones
1753–1755	John Haime, Paul Greenwood
1753–1758	William Hitchens
1755–1758	Peter Jaco, Richard Lucas, John Furz
1765–1766	John Helton*, John Gibbs
1766–1767	Richard Henderson, John Nelson
1767–1768	John Murlin*, Peter Price
1768–1769	John Whitehead, William Whitwell
1769–1770	John Helton*, Barnabas Thomas, Samuel Wells
1770–1771	Alexander Mather, Thomas Janes
1771–1772	John Murlin*
1771–1773	John Pawson*
1772–1773	George Hudson
1773–1774	John Allen, Francis Wolfe, John Bradford
1774–1775	James Cotty
1774–1777	Hugh Saunderson, John Murlin*
1775–1776	William Severn, William Ashman
1776–1777	John Floyd, John Helton
1777–1778	Thomas Carlill, John Pritchard*
1777–1779	John Goodwin
1778–1779	James Wood
1778–1780	John Valton*
1779–1780	Alexander M'Nab, John Bristol
1780–1781	Thomas Tennant*
1780–1782	John Pawson
1780–1783	Thomas Rankin
1781–1782	John Murlin*, William Moore

* Indicates that a minister's name appears again at a later date.

1782–1783	Charles Boon, Thomas Payne
1783–1784	George Shadford, John Hampson, William Green
1784–1785	Thomas Lee, James Hall
1784–1786	Samuel Bradburn*
1785–1786	John Murlin
1785–1787	Jeremiah Brettell*
1786–1787	John Pritchard, John Valton, Christopher Watkins
1786–1789	Thomas Tennant*
1787–1788	Benjamin Rhodes
1787–1789	John Broadbent*
1788–1789	Thomas Warwick
1789–1790	Adam Clarke, George Wadsworth, Samuel Hodgson
1790–1792	Thomas Roberts*
1790–1793	Henry Moore*
1791–1792	Alexander Suter, James Hall, George Button, John Broadbent, Thomas Tennant
1791–1793	Thomas Rutherford
1792–1793	Lawrence Kane, Joseph Sutcliffe*
1793–1794	Jonathan Barker
1794–1795	Richard Elliott
1794–1796	Samuel Bradburn*
1795–1796	John Grant
1796–1797	Richard Gower
1797–1798	Henry Moore*, Thomas Simmonite
1798–1799	William Palmer
1799–1800	Thomas Roberts*
1799–1801	Charles Greenley
1799–1802	Walter Griffith*
1801–1802	Samuel Bardsley
1802–1803	William Henshaw
1802–1804	Jonathan Parkin
1803–1805	Thomas Rogers*
1804–1806	Thomas Roberts, James Buckley
1805–1806	Booth Newton
1806–1807	James M'Bryan, Jonas Jagger
1806–1808	George Highfield
1807–1808	James Denton
1808–1809	Samuel Bradburn
1808–1810	Jeremiah Brettell
1810–1811	Henry Moore

Ministers Appointed To The Bath Circuit

1810–1812	William Myles
1812–1813	Thomas Taylor, Robert Johnson
1813–1814	Miles Martindale, William E. Miller
1814–1816	Samuel Taylor
1816–1819	Theophilus Lessey Jnr
1819–1820	Walter Griffith, William Worth*
1820–1822	Henry S. Hopwood
1821–1824	Richard Reece
1822–1824	William North
1823–1824	John Watson Jnr
1824–1827	Jonathan Edmondson, Edward Batty, John Lomas
1827–1829	Joseph Sutcliffe, John Lancaster
1829–1831	Joseph Entwisle Snr, George H. Rowe, Joseph Entwisle Jnr
1831–1833	Jacob Stanley Snr
1831–1835	John Bustard
1831–1836	Thomas Rogers
1833–1836	William Atherton
1835–1837	Robert L. Lusher
1836–1837	Joseph Jennings
1836–1838	Thomas Martin
1837–1838	Robert Sherwell
1838–1841	John Brown Snr, William L. Thornton
1841–1844	Daniel Walton, Samuel D. Waddy
1843–1844	Thomas Ashton
1844–1847	Richard Waddy, James Carr
1846–1849	William Davison
1847–1850	John Rigg, James Bromley
1850–1851	J. V. B. Shrewsbury
1850–1853	Peter Duncan, William Willan
1853–1856	Robert Newstead, William Davenport
1856–1858	Edward Walker
1856–1859	George T. Perks
1858–1861	Isaac Keeling
1859–1861	William R. Williams, George R. Osborn
1861–1862	John Tindall
1861–1864	John Bond
1862–1865	Thomas B. Goodwin
1864–1866	Edward J. Robinson
1865–1868	Thomas Brookes
1866–1869	John Bonser BA
1868–1871	Richard Jenkin*

1869–1872	Matthew T. Male
1871–1872	Matthew Gallienne
1872–1875	George Blanchflower, Charles H. Floyd
1875–1876	Owen Watkins
1875–1878	William Ford
1876–1879	Ralph M. Spoor
1878–1881	William Andrews
1879–1882	Alfred Llewellyn
1880–1881	Thomas E. Ham
1881–1884	W. Davies Williams
1882–1885	J. Reeves Brown
1884–1886	Thomas Haslam
1885–1888	Richard Jenkin
1886–1887	Amos Cleaver
1887–1890	R. Wentworth Little BA
1888–1891	William Burchell
1890–1893	John Grimshaw
1891–1894	J. Richard Hargreaves
1892–1894	Charles A. Duthie
1893–1896	John Dymond
1894–1896	George MacNeill
1894–1897	John Holmes
1896–1899	William A. Labrum, J. Sidmouth Cooper
1897–1900	Thomas Featherstonehaugh
1899–1901	John Henry Sanders
1899–1902	Arthur Hoyle
1900–1903	William Brookes
1901–1903	George W. Thorn
1902–1905	William Hindes
1903–1905	Percy B. Jenkinson
1903–1906	Conrad S. Sargisson
1905–1906	Llewellyn N. Tyack
1905–1908	Edward Blair-Allen
1906–1909	Thomas F. Lockyer BA
1907–1910	J. Ebenezer Howard
1908–1911	Edwin Owen
1909–1912	Stephen Burrow
1910–1913	Arthur E. Shooter
1911–1914	J. Marwood Sanderson
1912–1915	G. Neal Willis
1914–1918	Francis B. James, W. Harold Beales
1915–1918	George Charter
1918–1921	Albert G. Tuck, Vincent Taylor BD

1918–1924	J. Walthew Simister
1921–1922	W. Turnbull Balmer MA BD
1921–1924	W. James Beckett
1922–1925	R. Coburn Kellie
1924–1928	Francis G. Gatehouse, Herbert Phelps
1925–1931	A. Hanley Smith
1928–1929	Irvonwy Morgan
1928–1931	James Goudie, E. Ralph Bates
1929–1931	Arthur H. Jerx
1931–1935	E. Revers Jones
1931–1936	Edwin A. Spear, Albion J. Trebilco
1935–1939	Thomas Oakley BA
1936–1938	Andrew R. Bates BA

Primitive Methodist Ministers

1828– ?	W. Towler
1833– ?	E. Foizey
1837–1839	Henry Pope
1839–1840	Edward Bishop
1841–1844	John Owen
1845–1848	Robert Tuffin*
1848–1853	Thomas Hobson
1853–1854	Moses Breach
1853–1855	Charles T. Harris
1854–1857	Moses Harvey
1855–1857	Robert Tuffin
1857–1859	Joseph Best
1859–1862	John P. Bellingham
1862–1863	W. M. Beswetherick
1862–1868	William J. Mottram
1863–1865	James Hawkins
1865–1866	Joseph Harding
1866–1868	Samuel J. Southwood
1867–1872	Thomas S. Shields
1868–1869	S. Griffiths
1869–1871	John Gibson
1870–1871	Samuel Johnson
1870–1875	George Mitchell
1871–1873	John Fleming
1873–1875	John Lane
1875–1877	Arthur Beavan
1875–1879	Murray Wilson

1877–1880	James Whittock
1878–1880	William Taylor
1879–1882	John Mitchell
1880–1881	C. W. Cliffe
1880–1882	R. Jackson
1882–1884	T. S. Brown, Thomas Humphries
1884–1887	Jeremiah Pickles
1884–1889	T. Meakin
1887–1892	Joseph H. Daish
1889–1893	James Blayney
1892–1894	A. H. Smith
1893–1896	Samuel Bryant
1894–1896	Benjamin Senior
1896–1898	John Hawkey
1896–1899	James Richards
1898–1900	Castle Ross
1899–1901	Edgar Ball
1900–1901	George Cooke, Charles H. Spivey
1900–1903	Edward MacLellan
1901–1904	Thomas Storr
1903–1906	Thomas H. Bryant
1904–1906	Walter Scott Bosence
1905–1907	W. H. Whiting
1906–1909	Thomas Humphries
1907–1910	Joseph Harding, Tyler Tyers
1909–1911	Harold H. Woodward
1911–1913	Samuel Walpole
1912–1915	J. E. Malone
1912–1916	William T. Healey*
1916–1917	William Brass
1916–1919	Charles Crabtree
1918–1922	William Woodley
1919–1922	George E. Lloyd
1922–1925	Oswald E. Brown
1925–1928	Walter W. Price
1928–1932	Thomas Brand
1932–1934	William G. Rutherford
1934–1936	Albert Williamson
1934–1940	William T. Healey

Independent Methodist Ministers

1841–1851?	Ira G. A. Miller	WMA
1850–1869	James Bromley	WR

Ministers Appointed To The Bath Circuit

1851–1857?	Richard Miller	WMA
1857–1861	Samuel Newton	UMFC
1861–1863	Edwin Bailey	UMFC
1863–1865	Thomas C. Pearson	UMFC
1863–1865?	Henry Downes	NC
1866–1865?	Thomas Anthony	NC
1868–1869	do	NC
1869–1874	do	IND NC
1865–1866	Nathaniel L. Fysh	UMFC
1865–1866	Joseph Pott	NC
1866–1869	Richard E. Abercrombie	UMFC
1869–1870	Enoch Grattan	NC
1869–1871	John Rogers	UMFC
1870–1871	Abraham Leach	NC
1871–1872	Elisha Holyoake	NC
1871–1873	Joseph Colman	UMFC
1872–1873	Parkinson T. Gilton	NC
1873–1875	J. Lee Fox	NC
1873–1875	George Whaite	UMFC
1875–1876	W. Hookins	NC
1875–1877	Thomas Bailey	UMFC
1876–1877	J. Hammett (ill)	NC
1876–1877	Rev. Wright	NC
1877–1879	William Dunstan	UMFC
1877–1879	Thomas G. Seymour	NC
1879–1881	Thomas Smith	NC
1879–1881	John Tremain	UMFC
1879–1881	John H. Carr	UMFC
1881–1885	C. H. Poppleton	UMFC
1885–1888	J. Foulger	UMFC
1888–1889	J. B. Booth	UMFC
1889–1891	Francis Dutton	UMFC
1891–1895	J. T. Hodge	UMFC
1895–1897	W. H. S. Snow	UMFC
1897–1898	W. Dawson	UMFC
1898–1901	J. Edwards	UMFC
1901–1903	A. Barlow	UMFC
1903–1910	H. Walker Blott	UMFC
1910–1914	John M. Ward	UMC
1914–1920	Richard E. Wilton	UMC
1920–1927	Philip W. Madge	UMC
1927–1932	William S. Green	UMC
1932–1934	Harold H. Wilson	UMC

Abbreviations:-	WMA	Wesleyan Methodist Association
	WR	Wesleyan Reformer
	UMFC	United Methodist Free Church
	NC	New Connexion
	IND NC	Independent New Connexion
	UMC	United Methodist Church

Ministers of the Methodist Church

1936–1944	Norman Page
1936–1937	R. J. Richards
1936–1938	Thomas H. Howitt
1938–1941	T. D. Cross
1938–1942	Maurice H. Benson
1939–1945	George H. Wayne BA
1940–1944	F. Arthur Ashton
1942–1946	L. Scading Cheshire
1944–1950	Douglas W. Lowis DD
1944–1948	Ernest G. Marley
1945–1948	E. Harold Hardy
1946–1950	Percival W. Luxton
1948–1953	Alan T. Dale BD
1948–1954	Charles A. Clark BD
1950–1953	D. Howard Smith BA BD
1950–1957	Lionel Brayton
1953–1956	C. Horace F. Cory, Stuart S. Luckcock
1954–1958	T. Brian Coleman BA
1956–1959	Keith M. Beck MA
1956–1961	Andrew Crawford
1956–1963	O. Trevor Dyer
1958–1963	Cyril Mitchell
1960–1963	T. Robert Lovell
1961–1966	F. Mervyn Wright
1963–1966	Douglas C. Williamson, Gordon F. Simmons BA BD
1963–1968	Arthur Tuley
1966–1971	Peter B. Philipson, Reginald J. Mitchell
1967–1974	J. Neville Ward MA BD
1968–1974	Alan O. Barber
1971–1977	Peter W. Trembath
1971–1979	William J. Andrews BA
1974–1979	J. Kenneth Meir BA PhD
1974–1985	R. Martin Broadbent BD
1977–1983	Peter J. Perowne BD

Ministers Appointed To The Bath Circuit

1979–1985	David S. Owens
1979–	Ian G. Cramb
1984–1989	Patrick L. Crow
1985–1986	Virginia Kingsolver (USA)
1985–	Frederick G. Manuell BA
1986–1989	H. Edward Lacy BA
1989–	P. W. Hodgson
1989–	M. John Swarbrick

BIBLIOGRAPHY

Works consulted in the compilation of this volume include:

Journal of John Wesley Standard Edition, Ed N Curnock, 1909
Letters of John Wesley Standard Edition, Ed J Telford, 1931
Wesley's Veterans, Lives of Early Methodist Preachers, Ed J Telford
The Memoirs of the Rev Samuel Bradburn
Life of Rev C Wesley, Rev T Jackson, Vol I, 1841
Minutes of Conference 1765 onwards
Letters from Bath 1766–1767 Rev John Penrose
Arminian Magazine 1778–1797
Methodist Magazine 1798–1835
Wesleyan Methodist Magazine 1836 onward
Proceedings of the Wesley Historical Association 1896 onwards
(Articles by Rev E Ralph Bates concerning Bath are in Vol xliii Pt 2 and Vol xliv Pt 2)
Hall's Circuits and Ministers 1765–1912 (also notes for 1749–1765)
Registers of Ministers' appointments listed in Chapter 26
Chronological History of the People Called Methodists, Myles, 1813
Methodist Recorder in particular 15th November 1904, and winter editions 1894 and 1906
Wesleyan Methodism in Frome, Stephen Tuck, 1814
Rise and Progress of the Society in Bath, Rigg, 1848
Life and Times of John Wesley, L Tyerman
John Wesley and the Advance of Methodism, J S Simon
John Wesley the Master Builder, J S Simon
The Early Methodist People, L F Church
More about the Early Methodist People, L F Church
The Life of John Wesley, Robert Southey
Charles Wesley as Revealed by his Letters, Frank Baker (WHS)
Charles Wesley: Journal and Poetry, Thomas Jackson, 1849
Captain Thomas Webb, E Ralph Bates, 1975
Stories of Methodist Music, Lightwood
Christianity in Somerset, Robert Dunning (Ed)
Georgian Buildings of Bath, Walter Ison, 1948
Owen Owen, Victorian Draper, David Wyn Davies
Perspective, Journal for Reed International Executives, March 1984
Just Nothing, Memories of Caroline M Wiseman Anna Hellier
Primitive Methodist Magazine
The Myrtle
The Bath and Wilts Evening Chronicle, various reports

Local Church Histories:

Walcot Methodist Church and Early Methodism F S Cook
It All Began with John Wesley (Batheaston), Eve Parfitt
The Cliff Dwellers' Church (Beechen Cliff), Bruce Crofts
Box Methodist Church, Bill Drinkwater
The History of Claremont, William E Eyles
Methodism in Weston, Ian Duffy

Circuit Schedules
Circuit and Church Account and Minute Books
Registers of Births, Baptisms, Weddings and Funerals
Privately owned documents loaned by individuals
Methodist documents stored in City Archives, Guildhall, Bath

Chronological Sequence

Date	
1739	John Wesley's first visit to Bath
	Encounter with Richard (Beau) Nash
1741	Charles Wesley's first visit to Bath
1757	Death of Mary Naylor
	Bath transferred to "Wiltshire" Circuit
1759	First preaching house built in Bath
1761	Bath returned to Bristol Circuit
1765	Countess of Huntingdon Chapel in Bath opened
	Captain Thomas Webb made his mark
1774	Arrival in England of John Shum
1779	New King Street chapel opened
	Methodists meeting in Twerton
1790	John Wesley's last visit to Bath
	Stranger's Friend Society started in Bath
1791	Death of John Wesley
1793	Methodists meeting in Walcot
1797	Methodists meeting in Batheaston
1806	Roade chapel opened
1810	Pearson's Sunday School founded
1812	Methodists meeting in Weston
1816	Walcot chapel opened
	Twerton chapel built
1820	Methodists meeting at Box
1828	Primitives appoint minister to Bath
1832	Death of John Shum
1834	Wesleyans at Widcombe chapel
	Box (Ebenezer) opened
1835	Day school opened at Walcot
1837	Wesleyan Methodist Association in Bath
1840	Railway reaches Bath
	Methodists meeting at Bathampton
1844	Milk Street Mission established
1845	Westgate Buildings chapel opened
1846	Twerton Primitive chapel erected
1847	New King Street new chapel opened
1850	Wesleyan Reformers established in Broad Street
	Twerton Bromleyites established
	Construction of Kingswood School, Bath
1851	Great Ecclesiastical Census
1853	Twerton (Zion) chapel opened

Chronological Sequence

1855	Methodist New Connexion in Bath
1859	United Methodists at York Street
1865	Fairfield Park chapel rented
1866	United Methodists transfer to Hope chapel
	Westgate Buildings enlarged
1867	Box Hill chapel opened
1869	Wesleyan Reformers united with UMFC at Hope chapel
	Kingsdown chapel opened
1872	Death of Michael Shum
1876	Batheaston new chapel opened
1881	New Connexion ceased to meet
	Bath Census of church attendance
1882	Twerton Primitives ceased to meet
	Claremont Chapel opened
1890	Methodists meeting at Oldfield Park
1891	Weston Wesleyan chapel opened
1892	Twerton (Zion) school-room constructed
	Oldfield Park Wesleyan chapel opened
1897	Box new chapel opened
1902	Circuit Magazine *The Myrtle* launched
1903	Oldfield Park tabernacle erected
1907	Beechen Cliff chapel opened
	Box schoolrooms opened
1910	Walcot Brotherhood founded
1913	Hope chapel closed
1921	First moves towards union
	Batheaston extension built
1926	Twerton Wesleyans ceased to meet
1929	Bathampton site acquired
1930	Combined meeting at Pump Room
1932	Legal union celebrated
1935	Amalgamated circuit established
1938	Southdown site acquired
1941	Bombing tragedy at Twerton
1942	New King Street chapel bombed
1951	Southdown rooms opened
1959	Southdown chapel opened
1964	Westgate Buildings closed
1972	Bathampton new chapel opened
1987	Wesley chalices stolen

Subject Index